The Women Who Made Modern Economics

Also by Rachel Reeves

Alice in Westminster: The Political Life of Alice Bacon
Women of Westminster: The MPs Who Changed Politics

The Women Who Made Modern Economics

RACHEL REEVES

LONDON

First published in Great Britain in 2023 by Basic Books UK
An imprint of John Murray Press

1

Copyright © Rachel Reeves 2023

The right of Rachel Reeves to be identified as the Author
of the Work has been asserted by her in accordance with the
Copyright, Designs and Patents Act 1988.

A CIP catalogue record for this title is available
from the British Library

Hardback ISBN 9781399807449
Trade Paperback ISBN 9781399807456
ebook ISBN 9781399807470

Typeset in Janson by Hewer Text, UK Ltd, Edinburgh
Printed and bound in Great Britain by Clays Ltd, Elcograf S.p.A.

John Murray policy is to use papers that are natural, renewable
and recyclable products and made from wood grown in sustainable
forests. The logging and manufacturing processes are expected to
conform to the environmental regulations of the country of origin.

Carmelite House
50 Victoria Embankment
London EC4Y 0DZ

www.basicbooks.uk

John Murray Press, part of Hodder & Stoughton Limited
An Hachette UK company

To Nick, Anna and Harry

Contents

Contents

Introduction

Where Are All the Women?

Part I

When Milton Friedman won the Nobel Prize for Economics in 1976, someone was missing from both the prize fund and the accolade itself: the co-author of his most famous work, *A Monetary History of the United States* – Anna Schwartz. So while Schwartz's work was awarded a Nobel Prize, she was not. And while her work and her co-author are today known around the world, she is not. Friedman later described their partnership in a revealing quote: 'Anna did all of the work, and I got most of the recognition.'

Too many women have been overlooked despite the role they have played in shaping modern economic thought and policy, as men dominated the field and conventional economic wisdom was driven by their insights and shared experiences. But as Harriet Martineau, one of the economists we will meet later, argued, no one better represents your interests than yourself. As long as only men were economists and had all the economic power, the interests and insights of women were neglected.

Yet there have been extraordinary women who refused to conform to what was expected. Their intellect, curiosity and often their passion for social justice were undimmed as they sought to better understand the economy and society. In this book I aim to write some of these remarkable women back into our economic history and shine a light on their contributions to a field that touches every part of our lives.

I wrote this book to reshape the narrative of our economic history, so that we might inspire a new generation of economic thinkers and policymakers who will not view our economy with mostly male eyes. I explain how these brilliant but often overlooked women have influenced my own thinking as I set out Labour's economic plans for government.

But first, let me tell you a story of a conversation that had a big impact on me and sums up what's wrong with our economy today. Last year I met a family in Worthing, on the south coast of England. A mum and dad who work five jobs between them. They find themselves engaged in a permanent juggling act of work and bringing up their young family. As they try to make ends meet, they are left with only half a day a week together as a family. Something as basic as family time has, for them, become a scarce luxury. The mum said something to me that day that has stayed with me since: 'You just wonder if you are doing something wrong.' She wasn't. And nor are so many working parents like her across the country. But despite being enterprising, hard-working, good parents, life is still a struggle for too many working people. It is profoundly wrong that our economy allows that to happen, and it is a damning indictment of the last thirteen years of Conservative government. The most ordinary of aspirations – owning your own home, having time together as a family, being able to put something aside for retirement – have for too many people become impossible dreams.

The economy in Britain today is not working well enough for working people. The link between hard work and fair reward has been eroded, and as a result working people have been hit hard by the worst cost of living crisis in a generation. Wages have stopped increasing while what's left is being eaten away by inflation – in energy bills, the food shop, mortgages, rent and childcare too. We are living in a new age of insecurity. Not only in terms of the finances of families across the country but also when we consider the insecurity of our national economy in the face of new global threats – from Russia's illegal invasion of Ukraine to the growing oppression of China at home and its assertiveness overseas. At the same time, the climate change crisis and the growing power of Artificial Intelligence look set to change our world in ways we can barely imagine. In this new era we must think again about the role of the state and markets. The state has an important part to play in securing our economy and strategic interests, and ensuring that there are opportunities for good jobs, and markets are a vehicle to drive wealth and prosperity, but those need the proceeds of growth to be more equally distributed. Hard-working families deserve to feel more secure. In this age of insecurity, our top priority must be reconstituting the link between hard work and fair reward, securing the resilience and strength of our national economy to do so.

This new age of insecurity demands innovative policy. The work of the women economists in this book has helped me answer some of the complex questions about how we will secure the finances of families across the country and make our national economy stronger. Their ideas and insights have helped me form the policy that a Labour government will use to make our economy better able to respond to global threats while making the most of new opportunities for inclusive growth. It is an approach that I call 'securonomics', and it addresses the cares and concerns of families like the one I met in Worthing.

It is stories like these that bring economic theories to life. Many of the women in this book have focused on practical economics that impact our day-to-day lives – like Elinor Ostrom, who explained how communities can manage shared resources such as water or green spaces, or Joan Robinson, who explained why workers are so often underpaid for what they do.

My children have lived their whole lives under a Conservative government. I also lived my entire childhood with the Conservatives in power, which is why I am so determined that my children will see a Labour government before they enter adulthood. I experienced the impact of the Conservative agenda in the 1980s and early 1990s at first hand. At my school in South East London we had great teachers, but as those eighteen years of Conservative government wore on, the disastrous effects of underfunding schools for a whole generation became more and more obvious. Our sixth form consisted of two prefab huts in the playground. Our school library disappeared and became an extra classroom as there were more children than space. And textbooks were always in short supply. When I was growing up I had the very strong feeling that the government simply didn't care about schools like mine. It's these experiences that politicised me. I joined the Labour Party to fight for the changes I wanted to see, not only in communities like the one in which I grew up, but across the whole country. I worked hard at school and wanted to prove that whatever your start in life, you could be just as good as anyone else. When I got a place at Oxford University, I was only the third student from my school ever to manage this. I studied Politics, Philosophy and Economics there, but it was the 'E' in PPE that I then wanted to pursue.

For a decade before being elected, I worked as an economist in banking and financial services. In 2010, I entered parliament as the MP for Leeds West. The House of Commons felt positively diverse compared to the profession I had left behind. I had become so accustomed to being the only woman in the room in banking and financial services that being part of the 22 per cent of women MPs elected in 2010 seemed pretty good. It wasn't and it isn't.

Today I serve as Shadow Chancellor of the Exchequer. Apart from the 'Shadow' in the job title, this is my dream job. But there has never, in the eight hundred years that the role of Chancellor of the Exchequer has existed, been a woman in the role. It is worth repeating that: in eight hundred years, Britain has never had a woman in charge of the Treasury. If Labour wins the next election, I would be Britain's first ever female chancellor.

In my twenty-five years studying and working in economics, I've analysed the works of some of the greatest economists, met central bankers, chancellors, and lots of brilliant economists working in academic and practical economics. But not nearly enough of them have been women, and not nearly enough economics considers the economic position of women. As Caroline Criado Perez points out in her book *Invisible Women*, policies and products have too often been designed by men for men. As the saying goes, if you're not at the table, then you're on the menu, and we've seen that proven true in economic policy – especially during my time as an MP. Women were disproportionately hit by the years of austerity. Being on average poorer, more likely to be carers, and therefore more likely to rely on the welfare state, the cuts to benefits hit women harder than men. Women were more likely to work in the public sector too, where a barrage of pay freezes and job losses also took their toll. Again, in the Covid years, the challenge of home-schooling disproportionately fell on women, taking many out of the workforce, and all while the dominance of women in the care economy meant women had a higher risk of catching the virus.

If I become Chancellor of the Exchequer, one of my driving missions will be to end the male bias in policymaking and focus on what I call the everyday economy of work, place and family. I want to rebalance the economy to consider those jobs that are often underappreciated, undervalued and in many cases done by women – from care, to retail, to hospitality. I want to open up more of our economy to women by providing more mentoring; more affordable childcare; and better care for older people and the disabled. We need to support more women so that they can reach the top, smash the remaining glass ceilings and go wherever their talents take them.

In my final year at Oxford, my macroeconomics tutor described the Bank of England as the 'finishing school' for economists. I applied for a job both there and with the investment bank Goldman Sachs. It was a choice between two jobs, with salaries multiples apart. I chose the Bank of England, which also funded me to study for a master's degree in economics at the London School of Economics. Under the governorships of Eddie George and then Mervyn King, I worked first in the international division, focusing on Japan, China, and then the US, and later looking at UK productivity and investment performance. I wrote papers on everything from Japan's zero interest rate policy to the link between R&D and productivity, and even on the effectiveness of Bank of England communications. I loved my work and loved being at the centre of a proud economic institution that had been given new life by central bank independence two years earlier. While it might not be at the top of most people's list of New Labour achievements, granting operational independence to the Bank was a powerful and enduring contribution to the economic stability of a country finding its way out of a period of consecutive crises. We had experienced the dire consequences of the political short-termism labelled 'stop-go economics', and the Labour government was determined to safeguard our economic interests. I still believe that independent central banks are the best way of providing stability with monetary policy, rather than politicising the monthly choice to raise or lower our interest rates.

As exciting a place as the Bank of England was to work, it was incredibly male dominated. Only six of the thirty-six people in my graduate intake were women, and I was the only one of us remaining by the time I left the Bank in 2006.

In 2002, I was seconded to the British Embassy in Washington. It was just after 9/11 and the US economy had plunged into recession. Planes were grounded, and confidence was on the floor. Sir Christopher Meyer was the Ambassador, and I reported back to the British Treasury. As well as meeting with Treasury officials, I regularly met with the World Bank and the IMF, where I met Nick, my future husband – he had been Gordon Brown's speech writer at the Treasury, and was at this point part of the UK delegation to the IMF. We were so well suited that, instead of going for a romantic meal out, one Valentine's Day we decided to spend the evening watching a *Newsnight* special on lessons from the Swedish banking crisis!

After the Bank and Washington, I moved to the private sector, working for Halifax Bank of Scotland (HBOS) for three years in retail banking in the lead-up to, and eventually through, the financial crisis. It was a terrible time and, globally, confidence was hit, jobs lost and recession returned after more than a decade of growth and prosperity. The causes were multiple but, as with all the banks that collapsed in the UK – Northern Rock, Bradford & Bingley, the Royal Bank of Scotland – the Chair and CEO were men. More diversity at the top of banks, politics and economics wouldn't just be good for equality, it would be good for decision making too. All the evidence shows that diverse groups make better decisions. Talent is widely distributed, but still most top jobs go to a similar type of candidate. As Christine Lagarde, the President of the European Central Bank, quipped, perhaps if the bank had been called 'Lehman Sisters', things may have been very different in 2008.

As Northern Rock and then Bradford & Bingley failed, we saw savers queue up on street corners to withdraw their money in scenes reminiscent of the bank run in *Mary Poppins*. At HBOS we knew we could be next. The share price tumbled as the consequences of poor lending decisions and a collapse in confidence took their toll. For the people who worked there, and for the places where they worked, like Halifax in West Yorkshire where I was based, it was catastrophic. Today, Halifax is known for a slew of fantastic TV series, from *Happy Valley* to *Gentleman Jack* to *Last Tango in Halifax*, but in 2008 it was gripped by a very different drama as the run on the bank and its inevitable collapse unfolded. Thousands of people in the local community worked at the Bank – often whole families were employed there – and local shops, cafes, marketing businesses and consultancies all relied on the town's big employer for business. Lay-offs and cutbacks began and the shares that employees owned through share-save schemes collapsed in value, wiping out people's life savings. Working at HBOS during this period convinced me of a number of things: the need for more mixed economies that are less reliant on a small number of sectors; the importance of strong regulation of retail banks to protect both savers and tax payers; and the value of diverse leadership teams.

We've had three women prime ministers. But never a woman Governor of the Bank of England. We've never had a woman as Chancellor of the Exchequer, nor as the Permanent Secretary at the British Treasury.

We suffer from a massive deficit of women in economics, and economics suffers because of this deficit. The UK is not unique in its lack of women in top economic jobs, but we are close to the bottom of the pack. The US has a woman serving as Treasury Secretary, Janet Yellen, who previously served as the Head of the Federal Reserve Bank, the US equivalent to the Bank of England. Yellen is an inspiration – not just as a woman in economic policy-making, but as a serious economic thinker. Her vision of a 'modern supply-side economics' is shaping economic policymaking in a more inclusive and dynamic direction around the world. The IMF is head-ed by Kristalina Georgieva, and her deputy is a woman too: Gita Gopinath. Before Georgieva, at the helm of the IMF was former French finance minister Christine Lagarde, who now heads up the European Central Bank.

When I studied economics at Oxford and then later at the London School of Economics, I was never taught by a woman. I only remem-ber one textbook being co-written by a woman – Wendy Carlin's *Macroeconomics and the Wage Bargain*. The economists we studied were invariably men, too. If you are an economist, you have to define yourself by a dead man – are you a demand-management Keynesian, an Adam Smith free-marketeer or a monetarist Hayekian?

In this book, I uncover the stories of the women who have pushed against those remaining glass ceilings, and smashed others in their own right. You might not have heard of all of them, and I definitely don't agree with them all, but by the end I hope you'll agree that against the odds, they and their ideas have shaped economics in more ways than is recognised. My ambition is that by writing the women back into our economic story they will inspire students and the young women setting out in careers at central banks, Treasury departments, investment banks, politics, development organisations and many other areas of economics, to continue on the journey towards equality for women in the field. And finally, I hope that these women and their stories act as role models so that the outlook of the next generation of economists may be more diverse – and more female – than mine.

I

Harriet Martineau and Popularising Economic Theory

Harriet Martineau was one of the few women able to
support herself as a highly successful author, writing
on a wide range of topics including economics.

Some of my earliest political memories are of the major economic
announcements that would come to define the 1980s and 1990s: the
brutal crushing of the trade unions, the privatisation of nationalised
industries, the deregulation of financial services in the 'Big Bang',
the closure of steel works and coal mines, high unemployment and
rising inequality. Although I was only young – born in 1979, the same
year Thatcher became prime minister – the incessant repetition of

the 'free market' as a cure-all by successive Conservative governments is seared in my memory of that time.

In many ways, my generation of politicians are Thatcher's children, growing up in the era of radical economic and political thinking. Some would come to want to emulate Thatcher, others to reject what she stood for and the damage she caused. Although I disagreed with so much of what she did, Thatcher politicised me. But she did something else too. She showed that the top job in politics did not have to be done by a man. She smashed glass ceilings and even if I did not like how she wielded her power, I never doubted that a woman could take charge and lead. Although Thatcher herself promoted so few women, in her own way she inspired future generations of women to get involved in politics. Today, around 220 or just over one-third of MPs are women; when Thatcher became prime minister it was just nineteen.

When we associate this concept of the 'free market' espoused by Thatcher with economists, we think of Adam Smith, David Ricardo, Friedrich Hayek and Milton Friedman. But what about Harriet Martineau? She should be on that list too. The politics of Thatcher followed closely the early economic and political writings of the first woman economist, who was born over a century before Britain's first female prime minister.

As a political economist who popularised the classical liberal economic theories of the era, Harriet Martineau empowered working people to understand the economy and economic theory. Martineau allowed normal working people to understand, for the first time, the theories that dictated decisions being made in Westminster and Whitehall about their money and businesses, and for that reason, she too should be remembered as a hero of classical liberal economics.

The author of the best-selling *Illustrations of Political Economy* and *History of the Thirty Years' Peace*, Martineau used her writing to espouse the free trade and free-market economic philosophy of the era. Her stance as a liberal economist earned Martineau the nickname 'Adam Smith's daughter'. An advocate of unfettered free trade, an opponent of factory regulation, a minimum wage or a ban on child labour, Martineau was a radical free-market liberal. But towards the end of her career, and her exposure to conditions in the cotton mills of Lancashire and the sugar plantations of the West Indies, Martineau began to call into question her once certain views. Still a liberal, Martineau was increasingly questioning whether an economy with no constraints on action could deliver the freedom she desired for all citizens.

While she is regarded today as the most prominent female political economist of the Victorian period, Harriet Martineau's early life did not suggest this would be her calling. Born in Norfolk in the East of England in 1802, and brought up in an unaffectionate household, neglected by her parents, Martineau suffered numerous health problems. Among them, the gradual loss of her hearing, starting at the age of twelve, rendered Harriet increasingly isolated. However, in her autobiography, she described deafness as 'the best thing that ever happened to me', serving as 'the grandest impulse to self-mastery'.

Along with her deafness, the collapse of the Norwich manufacturing business of her family might have been another blessing in disguise. Once a renowned cultural centre and manufacturing town, Norwich missed out to the burgeoning towns and cities of the North and Midlands, better connected by rail and canals: 'Railways, free trade, and cheap publications have much to do with the extinction of the celebrity of ancient Norwich, in regard to both its material and intellectual productions,' wrote the young Martineau in one of her essays. Even at a young age, she had a love for writing. Her early published writings were for the *Monthly Repository*, a Unitarian periodical, and her first article was published in 1821, when she was just eighteen years old. Harriet's father, Thomas Martineau, was a leading member of the Unitarian movement of the time, which strongly advocated for social and political reform and greater educational opportunities for the poor. Her father's status as a leader in this, at the time, radical movement perhaps explains why this publication was the home of the young writer's earliest works.

Harriet Martineau's young life was not without tragedy. After the death of her father in 1826 on the back of the collapse of the family business, her fiancé John Worthington died from a long illness in 1827. Although her father left her a small sum of money in his will, it was not enough to sustain Martineau. So, in 1829, aged twenty-seven, she was faced with what at the time was considered a most unladylike challenge: earning her own living. Given her hearing loss, she was unable to become a governess – the most common full-time job for middle-class women fallen on hard times – and, convinced that her calling was to 'be useful in' her 'day and generation', she moved to London and tried to support herself through writing. Initially intimidated by the world of publishing in London, she maintained a strong love of writing, describing how nothing else could offer her so much satisfaction: 'How I once marvelled at the manufacture of a volume! Now I wonder that those who once write do not always write.' Martineau resolved that her 'chief subordinate object in life shall be the cultivation' of her 'intellectual powers, with a view to the instruction of others' by her writings. But despite her enthusiasm, the lack of recognition and, more importantly, the lack of financial reward forced her to return home at her mother's insistence, and there she took up sewing to earn a living, only being able to write at night.

Harriet's new archetypally female occupation helped her supplement her small inheritance, but she disliked being remanded in this 'position of helpless dependence, when a career of action and independence was opening up before me'. Refusing to abandon her dream, she kept in touch with literary society in London and convinced her mother to let her go back to the city for three months every year. In time her family grew more supportive of her literary efforts, and, after reading one of her articles, her brother Thomas was so impressed that he immediately told Harriet to pursue a career in writing: 'My dear, leave it to other women to make shirts and darn stockings, and do give yourself to [writing].'

Martineau's Illustrations

By 1831 the *Monthly Repository* had lost most of its religious affili-
ations and became more associated with radical views on war and
slavery, and was increasingly a vehicle for liberal thought. Martineau
was a regular and leading contributor, and her thinking was rapidly
developing on liberal economics in the age of huge industrial change
in England. Her interest in the relationship between society and
the economy grew, as did her reputation as a journalist and com-
mentator. However, although respect for her writing and thought
grew greatly, this work did not leave Martineau free from financial
worries. In 1832 she completed what was to be her most famous
work, *Illustrations of Political Economy*. After being unable to find a
publisher to purchase it as a single volume, Martineau took advantage of the reputation she had gained as a journalist to publish it as
a subscription, sending an advertisement to every MP and receiving
rave reviews in the press of the time. By the second instalment, she
was financially supported totally by her writing.

Martineau's self-declared purpose in life, as stated in her autobiography, was to 'become a forcible and elegant writer ... so as to be
useful to refined as well as unenlightened minds'. On economics,
Martineau believed the public had a lot to learn. Her target audience
for her journalism and the *Illustrations* was 'the mass of the people',
meaning all classes:

> If it concerns rulers that their measures should be wise, if it con-
> cerns the wealthy that their property should be secure, the mid-
> dling classes that their industry should be rewarded, the poor
> that their hardships should be redressed, it concerns all that
> Political Economy should be understood.

Committed to the instruction of her 'great pupil, the public', Martineau
popularised Adam Smith's fundamental ideas through an innovative

and instructive approach which involved presenting economic principles through fictional tales. Having shown her liberal credentials in her earlier writing for the *Monthly Repository*, it is no surprise that it was Smith, considered the father of classical liberal economics, whose gospel Martineau wished to spread. Smith's works had been earlier popularised to a broader audience by British writer Jane Marcet in the United States in an accessible format. The key difference between Marcet's *Conversations on Political Economy* and Martineau's *Illustrations* is that Martineau did not limit her target audience to schoolchildren and instead sought to explain Smith, and the economic conversation that surrounds his thought, to the general population irrespective of age. The impact of these volumes cannot be overstated: by 1834 more than ten thousand copies were being sold each month. By comparison, only three thousand copies of John Stuart Mill's *Principles of Political Economy* (1848) were sold over the span of four years. Martineau derived considerable satisfaction from the sense that her book educated and entertained the public while popularising new ideas. As Martineau reflected in her autobiography: '[Political Economy] was never heard of outside of the Political Economy Club, except among the students of Adam Smith; but the series made it popular, aided as it was by the needs and events of the time.'

Martineau's *Illustrations* included cautionary tales on risk in markets; critiques of slavery; and the standard of living of the industrial poor. But at this stage there was little of the 'moral sentiment' that Smith wrote of. Martineau was a very traditional, liberal, classical economist – in favour of a free market and against regulation. In the story *Berkeley the Banker*, a parable on the theme of the morality of the market, her characters' experiences reflected the insufficient information possessed by people about money and banking. A Mr Berkeley wants to open a bank in a small town and remarks that opening a local bank would imply 'little risk and even less labour'. Mr Berkeley's son expresses his enthusiasm for the idea, contending that 'you can scarcely lose anything, however little you may gain'. They come to find out how wrong they are when the Cavendish family moves into their town and decides to open a rival bank. Mr Cavendish does not intend to make an honest investment like Mr Berkeley – instead he comes up with a pyramid scheme that would help him to enjoy an extravagant lifestyle. In addition to his pyramid scheme, he circulates forged bank notes and their large-scale distribution ultimately brings about the bankruptcy of both banks. Perhaps to ensure that readers were clear as to where the moral of the story lay, Martineau ended her story on a happy note by which the creditors forgive Mr Berkeley's debts while Mr Cavendish languishes in the debtors' prison.

As well as more conventional moral tales such as that of Mr Berkeley, some of Martineau's stories ignited a great deal of controversy, touching upon such taboo subjects as birth control and slavery. In her short story *Demerara*, Martineau presented the story of the son of a plantation owner in the West Indies who, having encountered abolitionist arguments on a trip back to England, returns home newly aware of both the immoral nature of slavery and its negative impact on productivity. Trying to explain the meaning of property rights to his family, he argues that 'man has no right to hold man in property'. The son even sets up an experiment to demonstrate the superiority of wage labour over slave labour, which confirms the increase in productivity triggered by paying wages, rather than using bonded labour.

The aim of the short story was not a critique of the total immorality of slavery but to convey Martineau's criticism of the British mercantilist trade policy, which made the importation of sugar from any other place except the West Indies illegal. She argued, along with David Ricardo, that a shift to free trade would render slavery unprofitable and lower the price of sugar for the British consumer. Martineau strongly condemned the government for its misunderstanding of economic principles: 'Since the slave system is only supported by legislative protection, the legislature is responsible for the misery caused by direct infliction, and for the injury indirectly occasioned by the waste of labour and capital.'

Despite the intense criticism she received for daring to address contentious issues – especially as a woman – the *Illustrations* were undoubtedly an immense success. Writing in the *Edinburgh Review*, William Empson disparaged Martineau for having the audacity to 'legislate for mankind anew on its most complicated institutions'. However, somewhat grudgingly, he acknowledged that she was the sole reason why they 'have [recently] heard more political economy' than they 'believe was ever before heard outside the Political Economy Club'.

In one of her most acclaimed stories, *A Manchester Strike*, Martineau addressed the vital, yet seldom discussed topic in nineteenth-century England: the standard of living of the working poor. The story of William Allen, a working man in the factories and a labour organiser, and two factory owners, Mr Wentworth and Mr Elliott, vividly tells of the conditions in England's factories and the evil of child labour – but its conclusions were more liberal economic than reforming. The story itself is the progression of a strike for the equalisation of wages – from its inception to its brutal, unsuccessful finish. The main protagonist of the story, William Allen, a factory worker, is persuaded to spearhead the strike, despite his initial reticence. Two of the four masters of the factory show the range of responses from employers in the face of strike – Mr Wentworth is empathetic and somewhat supportive, as he himself once faced bankruptcy, while Mr Elliott violently punishes the workers for daring to question the class system by whipping them.

Martineau also presents the struggle of the working class through the eyes of Martha Allen, William's daughter, who is working at the same factory as her father, and in Hannah Bray, a homeless street performer, Martineau shows the unbearable suffering child workers experienced. Ultimately, William Allen shares the same fate as Hannah Bray's father, who gets fired because of his involvement in a strike, condemning his family to greater poverty and misery.

Martineau framed her story as a cautionary tale, illustrating the supposed futility of strikes and the dangers associated with them.

While acknowledging the need for change, her conclusion was not for fairer wages, an end to child labour or regulation of factory conditions, but that workers should have fewer children.

Using government reports, she described in *A Manchester Strike* the 'awful interior history of the time', while most writers were preoccupied with the glamorous lifestyle of the upper classes. But unlike the later industrial novels of Elizabeth Gaskell, Charles Dickens, or even the future Tory prime minister Benjamin Disraeli, Martineau's story depicted the free market as the solution to, not the underlying cause of, the inhumane working conditions in England.

Despite her sympathy for the poor, Martineau fundamentally rejected government regulation in the labour market. She was categorically opposed to the principle of factory regulation, even for women and children. Speaking as an unapologetic free-marketeer, she was not willing to accept even the slightest interference with the workers' unique possession – their labour: 'Legislation cannot interfere effectually between parents and children in the present state of the labour market.' Contrary to today's conventional wisdom, and that of increasing numbers of people even in the 1830s, she adopted this position with children's interests in mind, arguing that regulating the labour of children would have devastating effects on their quality of life: 'Any law which should deprive them of the free disposal of their own labour would steal from them their only possession, and be in fact a more flagrant oppression than any law had inflicted on their order for centuries.'

Additionally, she was one of the most prominent critics of the subsistence wage, which she believed would increase, rather than diminish, poverty rates: 'if the men themselves could not manage to escape [suffering], nobody could help them to do so.' Bringing forward classic liberal arguments, she associated the introduction of a minimum wage with higher birth rates and lower productivity. Martineau genuinely thought that this reform would make the working class worse off: 'It is rather hard on the poor ... that we should complain of their improvidence when we bribe them to it by promising subsistence at all events. Paupers will spend and marry faster than their betters as long as the system lasts.'

At the core of her beliefs stood the 'identity of interests' principle, according to which: 'Every man knows his interests best, and as the interest of the public is that of congregated individuals the part of justice and benevolence is to interfere with none in the direction of their own concerns.' In other words, Martineau agreed with Adam Smith that a country could only prosper if every individual seeks their own best interests, and therefore championed people's right to dispose of their labour and anything else they owned, while opposing any infringement on this right. She perceived competition as a vital driver for innovation and rejected any form of regulation.

For Martineau, equality meant an open field, where everyone was allowed to play according to a pre-established set of rules, advocating for the 'sacrifice [of] short-term humanitarianism in favour of the long-term benefits of political economy.'

Martineau came under attack, not so much for her views, which were shared by much of the liberal ruling classes, but because she was a woman. As a woman, she was expected to show empathy and care, rather than engage in rational argument and debate. As a result her economic position was perceived to be inconsistent with these feminine attributes and she received numerous negative reviews from outraged conservatives, denouncing her liberal ideology: 'An unmarried woman who declaims against marriage! A young woman who deprecates charity and a provision for the poor!!!' one reviewer mocked.

Despite her anti-state, pro-market views, and again aligning with Smith, Martineau believed that social inequality hindered the prosperous development of any society, and recognised that there were several areas where governmental intervention was indispensable, particularly in education and justice. In fact, she was convinced that 'the universality of education is inseparably connected with a lofty idea of liberty'. As a supporter of Jeremy Bentham's utilitarian principle that the goal of policy should be the greatest happiness to the greatest number, she argued that social improvement through radical reform was not only necessary, but also unavoidable. She agreed with Bentham that 'it is the greatest happiness of the greatest number that is the measure of right and wrong'. Furthermore, she viewed educational advances and knowledge as the primary drivers of economic progress, rejecting the Luddite claims regarding the negative repercussions of technologies on the displacement of workers.

Experience in the United States

Following the breakthrough in her literary career, Martineau went on a two-year trip to the United States, where she closely studied American political and social institutions. Her visit to the New World served as inspiration for two books, one of which is a thorough sociological analysis of the country, published in 1837 in three volumes as *Society in America*. As a political economist, she expressed her admiration for American capitalism, which she viewed as a living example of the laissez-faire theory: 'In a country where the whole course is open to every one; where, in theory, everything may be obtained by merit, men have the strongest stimulus to exert their powers, and try what they can achieve.'

While recognising all the benefits of economic individualism illustrated by the American experiment, she openly criticised two key phenomena incompatible with democracy and republicanism – slavery and the exclusion of women from the political and economic scene. She asserted that 'the personal oppression of negroes is the grossest vice which strikes a stranger in the country', and added that slavery in the Southern states undermined their capacity for self-government, alienating and demoralising the labouring population. Drawing similarities between the class system in the UK and slavery, she argued that the latter was an immoral institution, which still pervaded American society only because of the disproportionate influence of Southern slave-holding states in Congress.

William Lloyd Garrison, one of the founders of the American

Anti-Slavery Society, was advocating for the immediate and uncompensated emancipation of slaves in the United States. Martineau was not afraid to express her sympathy for the Garrisonian ideological platform, even if aware of the risks associated with openly endorsing abolition. Even after returning to the UK, Martineau continued fighting for this cause. During the Civil War (1861–5), she made sure the British public was constantly reminded of the growing discontent about slavery. Her work had a considerable impact on public opinion in Britain, with the UK remaining committed to abolition, despite the temptation to support the South, given the British dependence on Southern cotton and the North's protectionist tariffs. Even if Martineau disapproved of the North's scepticism towards free trade, she commended its ethical commitment to the eradication of slavery.

Martineau also denounced women's exclusion from participation in the democratic process. What she viewed as a violation of their personal independence, Thomas Jefferson described as a measure 'to prevent depravation of morals, and ambiguity of issue'. Casting doubt on the sincerity of this justification, she blamed women's disenfranchisement on the same material liabilities that prohibited slaves' involvement in public life – their 'deprivation of property, including property in their own productive capacities' which are 'presumed necessary for citizenship'.

She was outraged by the limited employment opportunities for women in the US. In a country 'where it is a boast that women do not labour [and] the encouragement and rewards of labour are not provided,' she wrote, it 'is difficult, where it is not impossible, for women to earn their bread' – rather generously attributing it to Americans' 'chivalrous taste and temper'. Martineau also decried the portrayal of women as too fragile for the professional world. Noting the similarities in terms of gender discrimination between the UK and the US, Martineau emphasised that these restrictions were detrimental not just to women, but to the entire national economy. In line with her belief in the right of individuals to identify their own best interests and pursue them, she condemned men defining women's place in society, instead of giving them the freedom to decide their own roles.

On Women's Rights

It is perhaps not surprising, given her own abilities and gender, and the limiting of expectations and opportunities in Victorian England, that Martineau was a passionate advocate for girls' education and for women's participation in the professions and in politics.

In an influential article 'On Female Education', published when she was barely twenty in the *Monthly Repository*, she vehemently criticised sex-role differentiation and called for a more inclusive educational system that would encourage the development of all students' accomplishments, regardless of gender. She found the lack of educational opportunities for girls worrying: 'If the soul be early contracted by too great attention to trifles, if it be taught that ignorance is to be its portion, no later endeavours will be of any avail to ennoble it.' Quite paradoxically from today's perspective, especially given her own desire to escape a life of sewing in the family home, Martineau never questioned the validity of other prescribed gender roles. So while supporting stronger educational opportunities for women, she also emphasised the importance of traditional women's housekeeping duties and did not seem to find a contradiction between them. Instead, she passionately argued that education would not interfere with women's 'natural' responsibilities – the housewifely chores:

> Men do not attend the less of their professional business, their counting-house or their shop, for having their minds enlarged and enriched, and their faculties strengthened by sound and various knowledge; nor do women on that account neglect the work-basket, the market, the dairy and the kitchen.

In many ways Martineau's writing on female education echoes much of the work of the British writer and early feminist philosopher Mary Wollstonecraft, at the end of the eighteenth century. Wollstonecraft, today considered by many the 'mother of modern feminism', argued in *A Vindication of the Rights of Woman* that both men and women should be educated together under the same model. Similarly to Martineau, Wollstonecraft contended that a woman's relationship to her husband was that of a 'companion' rather than simply a wife, and that to her children she was an educator as well as a mother. In her view, the woman herself should be granted an education befitting the importance of these roles.

Martineau was also firmly convinced that the inclusion of women in the productive economy was just as important as the diversification of educational opportunities. In 1859, she vindicated British women's right to work in the article 'On Female Industry', published in the *Edinburgh Review*. Martineau demanded equality of employment opportunities, equal pay for women, and their inclusion in those professional fields which had been previously open only to men. She presented these requests from the perspective of a political economist, explaining that it was finally 'time for the principle of free trade to be applied to the labour market'. On a typically optimistic note, Martineau declared that industrialisation would eventually lead to the elimination of double standards and to women's complete emancipation. Her confidence grew as she noticed the encouraging developments from the last decades: by 1851, 16 per cent of British women were earning their own living, and another 50 per cent had at least some sort of job.

Although Martineau disregarded the topic of women's voting rights in her *History of the Peace*, throughout her career she repeatedly expressed her utter discontent with women's disenfranchisement. At the time, a popular alternative to women's full political representation was James Mill's notion of the household franchise, that would see the vote exercised by husbands or fathers, but whose opinions would and should be indirectly influenced by their wives or daughters. In *Society in America*, Martineau was adamant that women should be allowed to vote and straightforwardly repudiated Mill's proposal, saying that women could not possibly be represented by their spouses or fathers, for 'no person's interests can be, or can be ascertained to be, identical with those of another person': probably the most important maxim for Martineau's economic and political thought.

The History of the Thirty Years' Peace, AD 1816–46

Martineau was a prolific and wide-ranging author, successfully trying her hand at novels, books for children and travel guides, as well as her work on political economy. With her work's success described by Scottish philosopher and historian Thomas Carlyle as 'a sign of this country and time', Martineau was commissioned in 1849 by the publisher Charles Knight to chronicle the last thirty years of peace in England (1816–46), following a decade marred by war with both France and the United States. She gladly accepted the challenge of recounting British contemporary history, acknowledging that it would spark controversy and that the final product would be far from perfect: 'But who would ever stir a finger, if only on condition of being guaranteed against oversights, mis-information, mistakes, ignorance, loss, and danger?'

Addressing the nation's economic progress, the period studied in the *History of the Peace* was a celebration of the free-market ideals Martineau believed in, concluding that 'men were going unconsciously into the great change which the next twenty years were to accomplish'. In her book she examined the two issues that dominated mid-nineteenth-century British politics and economics: the implementation of legislative proposals to either liberalise or regulate, and the liberalisation of old commercial monopolies. Martineau recognised the importance of the progress made in the direction of democratisation and liberalisation, but she believed these processes were still at an incipient stage. Unlike Whig historians such as Thomas Babington Macaulay, she did not perceive mid-nineteenth-century England as heaven on earth. Drawing attention to the suffering of the working class and other pressing social issues (namely the Irish protests), she argued that the extension of economic or democratic reform was imperative.

Additionally, she thought the democratic reform from 1832 marked the beginning rather than the end of the necessary changes. At the time, the UK had a representative government only on paper, with parliament still dominated by the aristocracy while the working class (and women) had no voice in the political decision-making processes. Martineau was heavily critical, stating that a 'vast proportion of the people – the very part of the nation whose representation was most important to the welfare of the state – were not represented at all'. With all the changes to the electoral system, the right to vote remained a privilege awarded only to landowning men, a situation that, in Martineau's view, was unsustainable.

Free Trade

Martineau's political views and preferences were mainly determined by candidates' and parties' stances on trade – the issue she cared most deeply about. She actively advocated for the repeal of the Corn Laws – the statutes imposing tariffs and trade restrictions on imported grain since 1815. They were introduced to protect domestic producers by keeping corn prices high, and thus encouraging the export of corn and limiting its import. In other words, the Corn Laws maximised the profits of landowners. Meanwhile, food prices skyrocketed, which in turn made the cost of living unbearable for a growing number of people who could not afford enough food to eat, leading to widespread hunger and malnutrition. The Corn Laws impeded growth and had a negative impact on the living standards of British working people.

Going further than David Ricardo, the economist at the fore-front of the attack on protectionist tariffs (known today for the 'Ricardian model' of trade), Martineau believed that the Corn Laws negatively affected everybody, including landlords. That is why she became an ardent supporter of Sir Robert Peel, who adopt-ed anti-protectionist principles despite his political affiliation as a Conservative. Martineau had no doubt that the transition towards free trade, and particularly Peel's decision to annul the Corn Laws, triggered the economic growth that was experienced from the 1860s. The increased prosperity that ensued confirmed Martineau in her belief in the interdependence of all segments of society, namely the 'unity of interests between the agricultural and the manufacturing populations', which were reaping the rewards of the liberalisation of trade.

Another crucial political debate concerned the legitimacy of governmental regulation of labour. In her youth, when she wrote *Illustrations*, she did not see any merit in paternalistic policies. A few decades later she was still talking about the right of workers to dis-pose of their own labour: 'Nothing must be done to impair any one's right ... under the constitution which presumes every man's condi-tion and interests to be in his own hands.' Nonetheless, her views and economic analysis evolved with time. She began to agree that the poor, being unrepresented in parliament, deserve special protec-tion: 'It is impossible under the far higher constitution of humanity, to refuse attention to the case of the depressed, ignorant, and suffer-ing, of our people,' she wrote. 'Having permitted a special misery, we must meet it with a special solace and aid.'

The trip to the United States might have been the turning point – the experience that ultimately altered her political and economic views. While initially in awe of the American capitalist spirit, she soon became aware of the other side of the coin: the atomising nature of economic individualism. Examining the lifestyle of workers and mer-chants in the US, she sorrowfully concluded that capitalism thwarted individuals' happiness – a sentiment heavily in tension with her other views as a free-marketeer. Surprisingly amending her unqualified criticism of socialism, at the end of her book *Society in America* she significantly conceded that 'there is no way of securing perfect social liberty on democratic principles but by community of property'.

Some historians, such as Valerie Pichanick, who authored a wide-ranging review of Martineau's life and writings, argued that at least part of the inconsistencies in Martineau's philosophical, political and economic stances were anchored in her 'sympathy for the less fortunate members of society'. It is clear that the Lancashire cotton famine (1861–5) had a significant impact on her. Brought about by overproduction, the depression in the textile industry of North West England affected thousands of factory owners and workers. Witnessing first-hand the challenges faced by them, Martineau herself helped organise relief for the unemployed. She labelled the 'suffering operatives' as a 'national charge', supporting the provision of clothes and soup kitchens. Nonetheless, instead of offering free food as charity, she suggested that the unemployed could earn the donations through work. In this manner, society would preserve 'the honest pride of good working men' and 'keep off the encroachment of the idle and the debased', adding that, 'Every man must owe his true welfare to himself,' and that 'all dependence on Government for any of the essentials of private life is a delusion as enslaving to the spirit of man as disappointing to his hope'.

Originally, Martineau's commitment to the principle of laissez-faire was anchored in her 'faith in the ultimate fair-mindedness and benevolence of middle-class employers'. She believed that the condition of the working class was bound to ameliorate, specifically due to the altruistic and compassionate spirit of employers, with whom she identified, as a daughter of a middle-class textile manufacturer. However, she increasingly came to question that assumption, endorsing more and more exceptions to her initial categorical free-market theory. By the 1850s, she was arguing for increased governmental intervention in several fields, advocating for public health and political, legal and prison reform.

Why Martineau Matters Today

For liberals, there will always be a tension between 'freedom to' and 'freedom from', and for Harriet Martineau these tensions grew over time. The freedom to run your business how you please, and pay the market rate for goods and services, or to 'dispose' freely of your labour, came increasingly into conflict with the right to freedom from the poverty and exploitation which Martineau saw in the Lancashire mill towns and the West Indies sugar plantations.

As a liberal and as an advocate of the free market, Martineau wanted as little regulation and as few controls as possible, whether that was in the workplace or in limiting free trade. But as a liberal and as an economist, Martineau also believed in the liberating capacity of education and the importance of the vote as a vehicle for women and the working classes to express their views and be heard. An ideological fellow of much better-known male economists such as Smith, Ricardo, John Stuart Mill and Bentham, Martineau's *Illustrations* and *History of the Peace* have been largely forgotten. Yet her stories of free trade, slavery and the conditions in the mills of Lancashire brought them to life, popularising economic ideas for a mass audience and making them accessible to all for the very first time.

For me, real freedom means having the opportunities to fulfil your potential. A good education, decent housing, a functioning health service when you need it, fulfilling work that pays a decent wage so you can support a family. I therefore reject much of Martineau's early thinking. But Martineau's own thinking changed. When confronted with slavery or the lack of opportunity for women, she was forced to question how society worked, and her economic writings spoke of these injustices too. Today, slavery looks very different – but it hasn't disappeared. Instead, it takes new forms, such as the gangs that control migrant workers – trafficking them to developed countries from some of the poorest places in the world and exploiting their lack of rights. It's why Home Secretary Suella Braverman's recent immigration legislation is so immoral, as it makes no allowance for modern-day slavery, against which former PM and Home Secretary Theresa May had herself legislated. Similarly, while conditions for working people have changed significantly since Martineau visited the mills in Lancashire, the power of overmighty employers and the weakness of organised labour continue today – something that we will pick up in Chapter 5 on Joan Robinson, who showed how stronger trade unions can help improve the functioning of the labour market when employers get too powerful. Although Martineau was sceptical about trade unions, she was concerned about what happens when work dries up and poverty abounds.

Martineau's own financial situation simultaneously motivated and discouraged her from a career as a writer. Forced to make her own way in the world after her father's death, she had the courage to pursue her flair for writing as a path to financial liberation, despite the expectations of society and her own family that she would earn a living through more conventional, 'womanly' means such as sewing. By managing to support herself solely through her writing, she did what few women of her era were able to do, and managed to combine financial self-sufficiency with intellectual fulfilment. In doing so, Harriet Martineau demonstrated enormous perseverance, vision and tenacity. Nearly two hundred years after her first *Illustrations*, much is dated, but the principles of liberal market economics she explained remain influential today, and her capacity to popularise and communicate new ideas remains inspirational.

The following pages tell the stories of many wonderful women economists, but Harriet Martineau stands out as someone whose impact transcends the economic sphere. While she remains a central figure in the development of thinking on free trade, anti-regulation and economic individualism, she must also be remembered as a fierce anti-slavery advocate and as someone at the forefront of the fight for women's equal right to education. Before they were popular ideas, she understood the importance of votes for women and working people, and was prepared to go against the Church to support Darwin's ideas on evolution. To only describe Harriet Martineau as an economist would be an injustice: she should be celebrated as a passionate champion for those marginalised by the society in which they lived. Add to this that she opened up economic theory to the masses, and you have someone whose position as one of the great economic women of history feels in need of proper and solid recognition.

2

Beatrice Webb, Social Research and the Emergence of Welfare Economics

I joined the Labour Party in 1996, aged seventeen, when Tony Blair was leader. My school, the local comprehensive where I lived in South East London, had for its Sixth Form block two prefab huts – freezing cold in winter and baking hot in summer. Our library was turned into a classroom as there were more students than there was space. And as for textbooks, there were never enough to go round. I felt very strongly that the government of the time was not interested in schools like mine, or indeed communities like mine. I wanted to do something about it, and for me that something was joining the Labour Party. I joined the Fabian Society, a research group closely connected with the Labour Party, shortly afterwards, because I was interested in the specific policy ideas for how we could change the country and make it fairer and more equal, and enact the change we all strived for in the Labour Party. I was active in both, becoming Secretary of the Young Fabians in the early 2000s and writing regularly for their magazine.

Fabianism plays an important role in the history of the Labour Party. In 1900 the Fabians came together with a number of other socialist and left-wing organisations, including the trade unions, to form the Labour Representation Committee, and after winning a number of seats in the 1906 parliamentary elections, it became the Labour Party. The Fabian Society provided much of the intellectual framework for the fledgling party, publishing pamphlets and organising committees to take forward policy ideas. And the Fabians are almost synonymous with two people: Beatrice and Sidney Webb.

When I was secretary of the Society, we used to meet at the Fabian offices, then on Dartmouth Street in Westminster, where the Webbs once gathered with George Bernard Shaw, Bertrand Russell, Margaret and G. D. H. Cole, Edith Nesbit and others. I always felt it was very special to be in that building where so much Labour history had unfolded.

At university I read Carole Seymour-Jones's biography of Beatrice Webb, describing a woman from a privileged background who gave up society life, and an on-off romance with the charismatic but controlling Joseph Chamberlain, to live among the poor in Lancashire and London's East End and then marry 'a Cockney hairdresser's son in a brave act of class rebellion'. I instantly became, and remain to this day, a great admirer of Beatrice Webb's achievements as an economist.

Beatrice Webb was a political campaigner, social reformer and economist. For her, these issues were inextricably linked, and like many of the women in this book she dedicated her life to promoting political and economic change based on her work and her beliefs.

Her brand of socialism was driven by reason and argument, and a conviction that, through persuasion and campaigning in a parliamentary democracy, you can bring people to your cause. Her economic principles were rooted in analysis, based on her first-hand experiences as a social researcher in the slums, and her understanding of the institutions that shaped the lives of the working classes, including trade unions and welfare provision. She argued powerfully, both in public meetings and in pamphlets, that inequality and poverty were the result of an economic and social system that was stacked up against the poor and working classes. She challenged those in power to abolish the workhouse and tackle inequality, unemployment and low pay. While prime ministers Asquith and Lloyd George did not follow her advice, Beatrice Webb built a political and economic movement around the causes she believed in, which she brought with her when she joined the Labour Party.

Although Webb saw two minority Labour governments under Ramsay MacDonald, one in 1924 and one between 1929 and 1931 (in both of which her husband, Sidney, served as a minister), it was not until after she died that there was a majority Labour government. But Labour prime minister Clement Attlee's 1945 government did finally create a welfare state that owed much to Beatrice Webb and the Minority Report on the Poor Law that she had written two decades previously.

Webb's influence in the Labour movement and the country are all around us today – from the world-renowned London School of Economics she founded with her husband and others, and the Fabian Society that she helped to create, to today's welfare state itself, even though the modern welfare state is worlds away from what Webb either envisaged or desired. Webb is one of the most important figures in the history of the Labour movement and one of the most significant women involved in shaping economics in the twentieth century.

Early Life

Martha Beatrice Potter was born in 1858 in Gloucestershire. She was the eighth of nine daughters of businessman Richard Potter and Lawrencina Heyworth. Richard Potter was a successful timber merchant and a director for the Great Western Railway. Lawrencina was the daughter of a Liverpool merchant, Lawrence Heyworth, whose own family had been weavers at Bacup in Lancashire. Beatrice's paternal grandfather was Liberal Party MP Richard Potter, co-founder of the Little Circle group, which was key in bringing in the Reform Act of 1832, extending the voting franchise. From an early age, Webb was largely self-taught by extensive reading and discussions with her father's visitors, including philosopher Herbert Spencer, who was an important influence on her. Richard and Lawrencina's only son died in infancy and Beatrice's relationship with her mother was difficult, with Beatrice describing her childhood as 'creeping up in the shadow of my baby brother's birth and death'.

After her mother's death in 1882, when Beatrice was twenty-four, she acted as her father's companion. 'The death of my mother revolutionised my life,' she later wrote. 'From being a subordinate, carrying out directions, and having to fit into the framework of family circumstance, studies and travels, friendships . . . I became a principal, a person in authority, determining not only my own but other people's conduct.'

Beatrice helped her father with his business interests, and did so with the same skills she subsequently used as a social researcher: 'Apprehending, recollecting, and afterwards recording complicated series of facts, gathered in conversation, is part of the technique of a social investigator; and I owe the skill I had as an interviewer to this preliminary practice with my father.' She also owed her interest in society and its problems to Herbert Spencer, who encouraged her to believe that social ills could be understood through investigation and cured by properly designed reforms.

Social Investigation

Beatrice Webb's first experience of doing the social research that proved so important in shaping her ideas was at the mills in Bacup, where long hours, child labour and dangerous conditions were still rife. Some of Webb's mother's family still worked there and, under an alias, she went to the mills, staying with her Lancashire cousins, learning about working life in the textiles industry, the chapel and cooperatives while recording her impressions in a diary and a series of letters to her father. Her studies led her to conclude that 'destitution is a disease of society itself' – a theme that she would take up a decade later on the commission looking at the Poor Law.

Back in London, after a stint working as a housing manager at Katharine Buildings in Wapping, collecting rent and acting as a custodian of housing built specifically for the poor, Beatrice worked on what was to eventually become Charles Booth's seminal multi-volume work *Life and Labour of the People in London* (1902). Her cousin Mary Macaulay was married to Booth, and aware of Beatrice's interest in social research, she and her husband approached her to help him carry out a survey, looking at the situation of the poor and working classes in London in the mid-1880s. Beatrice was to focus specifically on the lives of dock workers and Jewish residents of London's East End. Booth's survey was a meticulous, data-rich study of working-class London. The amount of work involved required a small army of researchers, of whom Beatrice Webb was one willing recruit.

Another recruit to the Survey of London was Clara Collet. Collet, like Webb, was from an upper-middle-class family. Unlike Webb though, Collet had a more formal education – first at the North London Collegiate School for Girls, and then at University College, London, from where she graduated in 1880, at a time when very few women had a chance to study for degrees. Webb and Collet had a mutual acquaintance, Eleanor Marx, and in 1887, Collet attended the Toynbee Hall conference on women's work and wages, which had also been attended by Booth, who was on the search for more researchers for his ambitious project. Collet was recruited to work alongside Webb and was responsible for the study of women's work in the East End, where, like Webb, she lived and worked for three months. Collet's time in the East End coincided with strikes at Bryant and May, a match factory in Bow, East London.

The women and girls who worked at Bryant and May had to endure fourteen-hour workdays, low pay and severe damage to their health caused by handling white phosphorus without any form of protection. The social activist, Fabian and women's rights campaigner Annie Besant became involved with the women and children working at Bryant and May, publishing an article exposing the appalling conditions at the factory. The management tried to get the workers to contradict Besant's report, but the women refused, and then, when a worker was dismissed, it set off the strike, with approximately 1,400 women and girls refusing to work by the end of the first day. A month later more than 4,000 women and children downed tools, and the whole factory stopped. Collet wrote about the women and their trade union for Booth's survey, describing how 'the prolonged strike in July 1888 resulted in the formation of a union, the largest union composed entirely of women and girls in England'.

Webb and Collet were part of a proud tradition of female social investigators, including the future independent MP Eleanor Rathbone, and her friend and partner Elizabeth Macadam, whom she met while doing similar work in the Liverpool slums, eventually culminating in Rathbone's call for a family allowance to be paid directly to mothers to reflect the work that they did at home.

Another researcher, in Lambeth in South London, was Maud Pember Reeves whose husband was posted in 1896 as the representative of the New Zealand Government within the British Empire to London. The Reeveses became friends with a number of left-wing intellectuals, such as George Bernard Shaw, H. G. Wells (who went on to have an affair with Reeves's daughter), and Sidney and Beatrice Webb. Reeves joined the Fabian Society, where she founded the Fabian Women's Group, which 'intended both to give women more prominence in the Fabian Society' and 'to study women's economic independence in relation to socialism'. Members included Beatrice Webb, Edith Nesbit (author of *The Railway Children*), and future Labour MPs Susan Lawrence, Margaret Bondfield and Marion Phillips.

Initiated by Pember Reeves, the Fabian Women's Group Motherhood Special Fund Committee began a study of the domestic lives of families with new babies living on a subsistence wage of about a pound a week. Forty-two families were selected to have weekly visits, medical examinations from Dr Ethel Bentham (another future Labour MP), and five shillings to be paid to the mother for extra nourishment for three months before the birth of the baby and for one year afterwards. The mothers wrote down their weekly expenditure, and this data was analysed by Pember Reeves.

The conclusions from the project were first published in 1912 as a Fabian pamphlet, and later became Reeves's book, *Round about a Pound a Week*, which was reprinted a century later in 2012 by Persephone Books (a wonderful small publisher focusing on bringing books by women back into print). It was poverty, the book argued – and not maternal ignorance or degeneration as the wealthy elite used to claim – that caused ill health and high mortality. The introduction of policies that alleviated poverty could solve the problem. Had the children of Lambeth been 'well housed, well fed, well clothed and well tended from birth', Reeves argued, who knows what they would have become?

The tradition of women social investigators didn't end with Beatrice Webb and this generation of women, nor was it confined to Britain. In the United States, economist Sadie Tanner Mossell Alexander is known for her work as an economist and investigator studying what became known as the Great Migration – the movement of six million African Americans from the rural Southern states to the urban industrial North in the twentieth century – the subject of Alexander's PhD dissertation.

Born in 1898, Alexander was the first African American woman in the United States to be awarded a PhD in economics. But when, after her graduation, she could not find employment in academia, she went back to university – to law school. Much like Beatrice Webb, Alexander conducted hands-on research, in her case surveying migrant households, asking detailed questions about earning and spending, with the goal of countering the assumption that these migrants would be a drain on the local economy of Philadelphia, where she was studying at the University of Pennsylvania. Visiting migrants' homes, she saw the troubling living conditions many of them suffered, and calculated how much money a family would need to have a 'fair standard of living'. While, in theory, 64 per cent earned above this threshold, the systematic barriers faced by Black families meant their earnings didn't go as far as they needed – they could not access the same rental market as white families, so paid more for poorer housing, and many of the families, often income insecure, could not afford to buy in bulk, and so bought smaller quantities more frequently at higher cost.

Sadie Tanner Mossell Alexander was a tireless campaigner for civil rights, and also the first African American woman to receive a PhD in economics.

The story of Sadie Alexander as an economist was almost lost, perhaps partly because her work as a civil rights activist was better known. In a 1991 article entitled 'Missed Opportunity: Sadie Tanner Mossell Alexander and the Economics Profession', American economist Julianne Malveaux pondered what might have been had Alexander had the opportunity to continue her economic work. Nina Banks, an economics professor at Bucknell University, who rediscovered Alexander's economic thought and published *Democracy, Race and Justice*, a volume of her speeches and writings, took a slightly different approach, arguing that Alexander's writing brilliantly brought together economic and legal analysis in the cause of racial and social justice. Rather than her story being one of missed opportunity, it was Banks's view that it in fact highlighted the need to reframe the history of economics, both in terms of how an economist is defined and what economics is.

As we will see in this book, many women and minorities have made important contributions to economics but have been excluded from its history because they did not take a conventional path as academic or professional economists – often, as in Alexander's case, because they were prevented from doing so on account of their race and/or gender. Part of the purpose of this book is to correct that history. Beatrice Webb, who came from a much more privileged background than Alexander, was not exactly forgotten, but she has primarily been remembered as a social reformer, and an important part of the reframing of economic history is ensuring that we do not discount the contributions she and others made to economics through social investigation and research.

Partnership

While Beatrice started her career as a social investigator, her sisters married, thereby enhancing the family's political and social connections. By the time of their father's death in 1892, Beatrice, at thirty-four, was the only daughter still single – though she had come close to marriage, embarking on a relationship ten years earlier with Joseph Chamberlain, then a cabinet minister in Gladstone's second government. He was twenty-two years older than her, and at various times had been a radical, liberal and influential mayor of Birmingham, and later a Conservative Unionist MP. Beatrice was deeply in love, but Chamberlain could not accept her need for independence, and after four years of 'storm and stress' (as she later described it), their relationship ended. Following her decision not to marry Chamberlain, she noted in her diary in December 1886 that 'my intimacy with the great man brought about a deadly fight between the intellectual and the sensual ... the intellectual has triumphed not by its own strength but by the force of circumstance; it has beaten the sensual and denied to it satisfaction.'

In 1890, four years after the end of her relationship with Joseph Chamberlain, Beatrice was introduced to Sidney Webb by her cousin, Margaret Harkness, a novelist, journalist and political activist. It was Sidney who introduced Beatrice Webb to the Fabian Society. Sidney Webb came from a poor family in central London, a world apart from Beatrice Webb's social milieu, and while for Sidney it was love at first sight, Beatrice was hesitant, telling him that nothing more than friendship and working together was possible. But, in July 1890 they spent an afternoon together in Epping Forest: 'We talked economics, politics, the possibility of inspiring socialism with faith leading to works. He read me poetry as we lay in the Forest – Keats and Rossetti.' By the summer of 1891, they were engaged – in secret, for fear that, during the last months of her father's life, he wouldn't approve of Sidney's lower social status and more left-wing political views.

The power dynamic between them, along with Sidney's attitude towards Beatrice, seems to have been the diametric opposite of that with Chamberlain. As Beatrice reflected on those differences in a diary entry of 20 June 1891:

> On the face of it, it seems an extraordinary end to the once brilliant Beatrice Potter (but it is just because it is not an end that she has gone into it) to marry an ugly little man with no social position and less means, whose only recommendation, so some may say, is a certain pushing ability. And I am not 'in love' with him, not as I was. But I see something else in him (the world would say it was a proof of my love) – a fine intellect and a warm-heartedness, a power of self-subordination and self-devotion for the common good.

Despite her fiancé's 'devotion for the common good', her friends and family did not approve of Sidney. As her cousin's husband, Charles Booth, told her, 'He is not enough of a man. You would grow out of him.' And Beatrice's diary suggests she had her own doubts. When Herbert Spencer heard of Webb's relationship with Sidney, he decided she was no longer fit to be his literary executor. Nor were her sisters and their husbands enthusiastic.

Beatrice Webb's father, Richard Potter, however, died on New Year's Day 1892, leaving Beatrice a substantial private income of £1,000 a year for life with which to support herself and the research projects she pursued. Her father's death not only gave her financial independence, it also removed any obstacle to marriage, and Sidney and Beatrice were married in a civil ceremony in London in July 1892, spending their honeymoon in Dublin researching Irish trade union records. Back in London, they moved into a house in Westminster, where they did most of their writing, working every morning, sitting at opposite ends of the breakfast table, with a researcher to look up references and file away papers. It was a partnership that lasted for over fifty years of marriage.

Trade Unionism

The first fruits of the Webbs' collaborative effort were *The History of Trade Unionism* (1894) and *Industrial Democracy* (1897). In these books the Webbs, in effect, introduced the economists and social historians of Britain to an important, but previously overlooked part of British economic architecture: the trade union movement.

In many ways, these volumes build on the investigative social research that Beatrice Webb first undertook in the mills of Lancashire (where Harriet Martineau also learned about working poverty) and then with Charles Booth in London. Webb understood that in order to find any solution to the problem of poverty, she would have to learn more about the organisations that the working class had created for itself, including the trade unions. As we shall see later, Joan Robinson built on this in her work on 'monopsony' power in the 1930s, where she explains to a sceptical audience how trade unions can be an important corrective to overly powerful firms, and – as Webb believed – at the same time being compatible with democracy, not in conflict with it, as many in Victorian England believed.

The Webbs' second work, *Industrial Democracy*, describes in great detail what unions actually did: providing insurance services for their members, negotiating collective agreements, and pressing for legislative change. It was the Webbs who coined the term 'collective bargaining' for the process by which trade unions negotiate collectively for workers in a firm, rather than everyone individually negotiating their own pay rates, terms and conditions, or firms simply dictating them.

Industrial Democracy also made policy recommendations that would later influence Webb's recommendations for changes to the welfare state. One of them was that government should legislate and enforce 'the minimum conditions under which the community can afford to allow industry to be carried on; and including not merely definite precautions of sanitation and safety, and maximum hours of toil, but also a minimum of weekly earnings'.

Two years after the volume on trade unions, Beatrice Webb, through the Fabian Society, published a pamphlet entitled *Women and the Factory Acts*, which made the case for protective legislation exclusively on behalf of women. Such legislation, Webb argued, should regulate the working hours and conditions of women in factories.

The Webbs were not the only people arguing that the state needed to better regulate industry and that it should play a greater role in tackling the causes of poverty, not just poverty itself. The Labour Party, ever since its first leader, Keir Hardie, had advocated for a minimum wage, but the Webbs were beginning to construct an intellectual and policy framework for these progressive, socialist reforms.

There is a quote from Morgan Phillips, the great general secretary of the Labour Party in the 1950s, that 'the Labour Party owes more to Methodism than it does to Marxism', due in part to Hardie's non-conformist roots in the Methodist Church. That assertion is true: the Labour Party was specifically created to give voice to working people, to shift the balance in politics. But the Labour Party was also root-ed in local communities and sprang from them, through the practice of democratic, parliamentary politics, not from revolutionary action or Marxist thinking, which was often alien to the culture and ethos of the party and the ordinary people they represented. So, while some of the analysis of the problems in society was common between Marxists and the Labour Party, their solutions were different.

It is therefore all the more ironic that a major and indefensible lapse in judgement by the Webbs was over the Soviet Union, fol-lowing a joint visit in 1932, when they were both in their seventies. While Beatrice had originally been critical of both Russian com-munism and Italian fascism, for some reason (she does not record why her views changed and it seems pointless to speculate) she and Sidney became advocates of the Soviet economic experiment when many of their fellow socialists were already expressing grave concerns about Stalin's 'Five-Year Plan' and the establishment of the gulags. In 1935, the Webbs published a massive volume, over 1,000 pages in length, entitled *Soviet Communism: A New Civilisation?*, which extolled Stalin's actions. It was mostly written by Sidney Webb and drew heavily on publications and statistics provided by the Soviet Embassy in London. In the preface to an anthology of Left Book Club publications, the British historian A. J. P. Taylor is quoted as calling this 'the most preposterous book ever written about Russia'.

The Minority Report

While their views on the economy of the Soviet Union were vastly off the mark, it was the Fabians, and particularly the Webbs, who provided the analysis of what was wrong in our economy and the practical ideas to put it right once Labour was in power. They managed to achieve radical change through persuasion and winning at the ballot box in 1945, not through revolution or despotic rule.

But this was some way ahead. Back in 1905, in the dying days of his term of office, the Conservative prime minister, Arthur Balfour, established a Royal Commission on the Poor Laws and Relief of Distress. Beatrice Webb was appointed one of the eighteen commissioners and her conclusions and recommendations are perhaps her most comprehensive and lasting contribution to public policy.

The review was specifically into the 1834 New Poor Law, hated by all those who came into contact with it. The Poor Law stipulated that no relief could be provided outside of the workhouse, condemning those who needed support to the humiliation of institutionalised welfare. It also limited the support available because the system was based on the premise that welfare encouraged 'indolence and vice' if it were seen to reward idleness over work. The socialist historian E. P. Thompson called the Poor Law 'perhaps the most sustained attempt to impose an ideological dogma, in defiance of the evidence of human need, in English history'. It's certainly hard to imagine any policy that would take the poorest and most vulnerable members of society and then institutionalise them within a regime of appalling working conditions. The combination of the humiliation of being institutionalised, and the hostility it generated towards those who found themselves unemployed, is difficult to fathom today.

The commissioners agreed that the Poor Law should not continue in its current form, a consensus at least agreeing that the provision of support should be standardised, with a recognition that at least some of the poverty that existed was caused by structural problems in the economy and society, and not just poor decisions by individuals. They also agreed that the system should be contributory – you paid in when you were able to work and drew down when you couldn't. Ultimately, however, the Commission could not agree on a single report – and so both a Majority and Minority Report were published.

There were significant divisions among the Commission from its outset. Many sought to transfer the responsibilities of provision for the poor to local government (to county and borough councils), and this became the majority view, while Beatrice Webb, representing the minority, took a much more nuanced one. She and her supporters believed that education and health should be part of one universal system, and not segregated by social class – as it was at the time, for example, with separate 'Poor Law hospitals' to treat the poorest in society.

As the principal author of the Minority Report, Webb wrote, with great prescience, that its ambition was 'to secure a national minimum of civilised life': 'open to all alike, of both sexes and all classes, by which we meant sufficient nourishment and training when young, a living wage when able-bodied, treatment when sick, and modest but secure livelihood when disabled or aged'. She was supported on the Commission by three other members, including George Lansbury, at that time the representative of Poplar Borough Council and their local Board of Guardians.

The central disagreement between the supporters of the Majority Report – largely authored by Helen Bosanquet of the Charity Organisation Society (for which Beatrice herself volunteered in the mid-1880s) – and the Minority Report, represented by Webb, is one that continues today. Webb called for government to focus on the *prevention* of poverty, not just its *alleviation*, and remained convinced that poverty was the inevitable outcome of a society and economy that were not functioning effectively. She and the other dissenters also argued that most recipients of welfare relief were not able-bodied men who could, but would not, work, and that an over-emphasis on incentivising people to work tended to result in less support for those who simply couldn't work, due to ill health or disability. On the other side, the majority of the commissioners took a more hard-line approach, fearing that Webb's remedies would undermine individual responsibility to seek out work. Bosanquet and her supporters also argued that charity-led provision was best, and would be undermined if the state took a more active role; Webb countered that collective responsibility to prevent poverty required a much greater public role for the state in guaranteeing a basic minimum for all.

A significant recommendation of the Minority Report was that families should not be in the workhouse but should instead get 'outside relief'. Webb documented in the report the devastating impact of institutionalising children, highlighting that the infant mortality rate in the workhouse was double that even for impoverished children outside the workhouse.

In relation to 'able-bodied men' or the unemployed well enough to work, the original Poor Law sought to use incentives to work. But Webb's Minority Report was much more concerned about chronic unemployment and underemployment than the authors of the Majority Report. Webb described the structural problems that meant men who wanted to work were denied the opportunity, while also highlighting the 'evil of unemployment', a theme of Joan Robinson's essay 'Disguised Unemployment' three decades later. William Beveridge too described 'idleness' (i.e. unemployment or underemployment) as one of the five evils when he wrote his report for government in 1942 drawing on Webb's analysis. The Beveridge Report set the stage for the founding of the NHS and the broader welfare state. Its reforms made Britain a more caring, equal society under the principle of 'social security' and paved our national path to a post-war reconstruction that looked after the working class who had played a crucial role in the war effort. The Beveridge Report and the reforms of that post-war government owed much to Beatrice Webb's minority report of 1906.

Beatrice and Sidney Webb expected the public to embrace the Minority Report and its recommendations. Despite the fact that a majority of the investigators had signed up to the opposing Majority Report, the Webbs believed that the reforms of the Minority Report would strike a chord with a general public that had seen the proportion of people relieved in workhouses double between 1870 and

1910. Their belief was that their report would be a catalyst for a Britain hungry for change, and when that didn't happen straight away they set to campaigning to get their views across. They created a newsletter called *The Crusade* (a forerunner to the *New Statesman*), recruited like-minded supporters including the poet Rupert Brooke and future Labour chancellor Hugh Dalton, and began to tour Britain, building support for the cause. In an exhausting schedule, Beatrice Webb spoke at public meetings and a movement began. They were conducting a 'raging, tearing propaganda', she wrote in her diary on 14 November 1909, 'lecturing or speaking five or six times a week. We had ten days in the North of England and in Scotland – in nearly every place crowded and enthusiastic audiences.' The Webbs' first biographer, the future Labour MP for Blackburn, Mary Agnes Hamilton, described Beatrice speaking at one of these meetings: 'She was magnificent in a great hat with ostrich feathers, and of course swept her audience with her moving picture of the morass of destitution.'

She was not the only person whose admiration Beatrice Webb earned. John Maynard Keynes nominated Beatrice Webb to be the first woman member of the British Academy and the two were apparently once overheard by W. A. Robson at a party before the publication of Keynes's *General Theory*. 'We are all looking forward to your new book on employment,' Beatrice is reported to have said. Keynes allegedly replied, 'Don't worry, Mrs Webb, it's all in the Minority Report.'

Stormy Relations

The disagreements in the Royal Commission on the Poor Law led Sidney Webb to officially sever his involvement with the Liberal Party, which he and Beatrice both felt was much too timid in its approach to the economic and social inequalities rife in Britain at the time. In 1914 they joined the Labour Party and after the First

World War the Webbs started writing policy statements and pamphlets such as *Labour and the New Social Order* (1918). Beatrice campaigned for Sidney's successful election in 1922 to the parliamentary seat of Seaham, a coastal mining community in County Durham.

But despite such successes, the years ahead were not without their challenges, both personal and political. The Great Depression began in 1929, and then the agreement of the Labour prime minister Ramsay MacDonald, just before the October 1931 election, to form and head a National Government alongside the Conservatives and Liberals, split the Labour Party into Labour and MacDonald's National Labour. This severely limited the ability of reformers like Sidney Webb to get significant legislation through parliament. For a couple who had devoted themselves to socialism through parliamentary democracy, it must have felt that progress was very slow.

On the personal front, as we saw above, many admired Beatrice Webb and the way she abandoned a life of easy privilege to pursue the interests of the working poor, establishing herself in the process as one of the most influential women in the history of the Labour movement. But she often clashed with contemporaries and alienated others with her apparent air of self-satisfaction.

H. G. Wells, who was also a Fabian, was not a fan of Sidney or Beatrice Webb, and became critical of their cautious approach: 'They permeate English society with their reputed Socialism about as much as a mouse may be said to permeate a cat.' For her part, Beatrice voiced disapproval of Wells's 'sordid intrigue' with the daughter of a veteran Fabian member. He responded by lampooning the couple in his 1911 novel *The New Machiavelli* as Altiora and Oscar Bailey, a pair of short-sighted, bourgeois manipulators.

There were also clashes with Labour and trade union women. After the First World War, Beatrice Webb decided that the women of the Labour Party should be educated for politics as well as men. She set up the Half Circle Club, for the wives of trade unionists and

Labour MPs 'to be groomed and trained to play their part in public life'. Some of the intended beneficiaries appreciated this more than others – with one group of dissidents going so far as to establish the 'anti-Beatrice Society'.

As for Winston Churchill, when offered a role chairing the Local Government Board in 1908, his response was blunt: 'I refuse to be shut up in a soup kitchen with Mrs Sidney Webb.' But of course, Beatrice Webb gave as good as she got. When she first met Churchill at dinner in the summer of 1903, her first impressions of him were that he was 'egotistical, bumptious, shallow-minded and reactionary (but with a certain personal magnetism, great pluck, and some originality)'.

Later, though, they did work together and she sought to influence Churchill; in March 1908, Churchill had dinner at the Webbs' house, where William Beveridge (working at the time on the Minority Report) was also in attendance. After dinner Beatrice told Churchill, 'If you are going to deal with unemployment you must have the boy Beveridge.'

Another contemporary, the one-time Fabian, *New Statesman* contributor and philosopher Bertrand Russell, once commented: 'If you set down a list of Beatrice's leading characteristics you would say – "What a dreadful woman!" But in fact she was very nice. I had a great liking and respect for her. I was always delighted by a chance of meeting her.'

The Legacy of the Webbs

The joint legacy of the Webbs is, in part, assured because of the institutions that they helped both create and shape. Through the *New Statesman* magazine, the London School of Economics and Political Science, and the Fabian Society, the Webbs live on in our politics today.

The Fabian Society was established in 1884, and although

Beatrice Webb was not there at its inception, she, along with Sidney, playwright George Bernard Shaw, G. D. H. and Margaret Cole, Annie Besant and others, were among its most influential writers and thinkers. While, early on, many Fabians supported and sought to influence the Liberal Party, they soon turned their attention to Labour. The first Labour cabinet, under Prime Minister Ramsay MacDonald, featured five Fabians, including Sidney Webb.

From the Fabian Society also came the London School of Economics, where I studied for my master's degree in economics twenty years ago. A bequest in 1894 of £20,000 left by Derby Fabian member Henry Hutchinson to the Society for 'propaganda and other purposes' was used by the Webbs, Graham Wallas and George Bernard Shaw to found a research institute to take forward

Beatrice Webb and her husband, Sidney, were both passionate social reformers, and together wrote much of their most important work calling for a more equal economy.

Fabian values. In 1895 the LSE took its first students – and from its inception was open to both men and women. The LSE's first director was William Hewins, but in 1919 William Beveridge took up the role, serving until 1937. Between 2016 and 2023, the LSE was headed by the economist Baroness Minouche Shafik, who features in a later chapter.

The *New Statesman* was founded in 1913, as a successor to Beatrice Webb's *Crusade* newsletter, which was established to campaign for the recommendation of the Minority Report to the Poor Law. With the financial support of George Bernard Shaw and other Fabian Society members, the Webbs recruited Clifford Sharp as the founding editor of the magazine. Sharp stayed at the *New Statesman* for fifteen years until he was conscripted to the First World War as an intelligence officer in 1916. Writing in the *Manchester Guardian* about the new magazine, Sidney Webb said: 'Its general attitude will be best designated by the term "Fabian", but it will endeavour to bring to light and to appreciate in a wide catholic spirit all those features in other social projects or movements which can be recognised as making for progress.'

Sidney and Beatrice Webb never had children, and in 1928 they moved to Hampshire, where they lived for the rest of their lives. Beatrice Webb remarked in her diary in 1936:

In old age it is one of the minor satisfactions of life to watch the success of your children, literal children or symbolic. The London School of Economics is undoubtedly our most famous one but the *New Statesman* is also creditable – it is the most successful of the general weeklies, actually making a profit on its 25,000 readers, and has absorbed two of its rivals, *The Nation* and the *Week-End Review*.

Beatrice died in 1943, and four years later Sidney passed away. Although they had agreed that their ashes should be buried at Passfield in Hampshire where they lived and from where Sidney took his title when appointed to the House of Lords in 1929, at the suggestion of George Bernard Shaw they were reburied in Westminster Abbey in December 1947 – the only married couple to be honoured in this way.

Why Beatrice Webb Matters Today

It was not until after Beatrice Webb's death, however, that her true legacy, her vision for a welfare state based on need and dignity, was finally realised. William Beveridge, a friend and protégé of both Sidney and Beatrice and a witness to the Minority Report, published his own report in 1942 – a year before Beatrice Webb's death and three years into the Second World War. It was commissioned by the Labour deputy leader, and minister without portfolio in the Churchill coalition government, Arthur Greenwood, and while officially it was rather unexcitingly titled *Social Insurance and Allied Services*, it was widely known as the Beveridge Report. It identified five giant evils afflicting Britain's poor – squalor, idleness, ignorance, disease and want – and proposed a welfare system that would protect citizens from cradle to grave. Its recommendations, drawing heavily on those of the Minority Report two and a bit decades previously, proved extremely popular with a society upturned by war. A universal system of social insurance financed by the state with contributions from employers and employees became the centrepiece of Labour's election bid in 1945 and as a result Clement Attlee, who had worked with the Webbs, became the first Labour prime minister with a majority government and the power to put into action the values to which the Webbs had dedicated their lives.

Through the enactment of a series of legislation, including the National Insurance Act and the National Health Act in 1946 and the National Assistance Act of 1948, the dreaded Poor Law was finally swept away and a welfare state, as envisaged by Webb, was created in Britain. The Labour government brought in a National Health Service to provide medical treatment free at the point of need, free milk for school children and a system of social security into which you paid while working and drew down on in old age, disability or time of unemployment. It was a system of social welfare 'from the cradle to the grave'. In his memoirs, William Beveridge wrote that his Report 'stemmed from what all of us had imbibed from the Webbs'.

From her years of working with the poor and her social research in the East End, Beatrice Webb had acquired a clear understanding of the shame and poverty that charitable welfare provision pre-1945 created. Her pioneering work was taken on by Beveridge in his 1942 Report, and the central organising principle of the 1945 Labour government – the creation of the welfare state – stemmed from the work of Webb four decades earlier.

Beatrice Webb was not only important in her own right but also as an example to other women who were interested in social issues. Like Webb, Eleanor Rathbone was born into a wealthy family and was left an allowance which enabled her to live the life she chose rather than one dictated by class and convention. She worked as a social investigator, exploring poverty, especially amongst women in her native Liverpool. Rathbone's most enduring cause was set out in her 1924 book *The Disinherited Family*, which argued that women's unpaid work in the home deserved to be recognised with an income. She wanted a family allowance, paid directly to mothers to recognise their contribution to the family and society. It was this work that brought Rathbone into contact with William Beveridge, as she lobbied him to include a family allowance in the recommendations in his Beveridge Report. Success came a year before she died. In 1945 the outgoing coalition government legislated for the first ever family allowances, paid directly to mothers, in recognition of the work they do in the home.

Successive governments have built on this. Attlee's government introduced the modern welfare state with more generous family allowances; when Barbara Castle was Secretary of State for Social Security she introduced child benefit (and more generous pensions for women in their own right not just through their husband); and after 1997, when Tony Blair was prime minister and Gordon Brown chancellor, a system of family tax credits was introduced – paid directly to the main carer (usually, still, the mother). But, with the advent of Universal Credit under David Cameron and George Osborne, all benefits are paid to the main earner, not the main carer, a depressing redistribution from the purse to the wallet. In this act, the Conservative government undid a huge amount of progress for women and for children. Webb and Rathbone wanted to ensure that mothers were rewarded for the work that they do in the home and in terms of childcare. Cameron and Osborne made the change amid reforms that attempted to limit how much households in total could receive in benefits. Osborne's Treasury argued when making the change that it didn't matter who drew the cheque if the money was still paid. I disagree. Caring work is often unpaid, and the family allowance, child benefit and tax credits were all about providing some support for the person primarily doing that work. Who got the money mattered out of principle but also because money can be a form of control, and taking the money from the carer (often a woman) and giving it to the primary earner (often a man) shifts the balance of control in a household. It has left many women poorer and undoes the attempt to provide some recognition for the caring work that happens in the home.

While Beatrice Webb features in these pages as one of the great women economists, she was cynical about the field of economics as a whole. She wrote in her diaries that the whole discipline of economics required a reorientation towards the future – to improve its ability to 'foretell' – and needed to stop simply describing in academic terms what the 'practical man' could clearly see.

Beatrice Webb is right that economics has spent too much time explaining what the working person knows to be true. She is also correct that economists are at our best when we seek to predict and prepare for the future, rather than simply explain the past. The power of 'predict, prepare and protect' in economics was never clearer to me than during Labour's battle for a windfall tax on energy and gas companies. We realised even before Russia's illegal invasion of Ukraine that these companies were making windfall profits as financial speculation was raising prices but not the cost of production, and that, to mitigate against a major cost of living crisis, the government had to act.

The Conservative government in the UK used every argument against it, failing to rise to the challenge. By the time they did heed the inevitable and introduce an 'energy profits levy' they did so with accompanying investment allowances which mean some of the biggest and most profitable companies get subsidised to extract more fossil fuels. All the while, they fail to improve the energy efficiency of British homes with insulation, and investors find it takes ten years to bring onto the grid more renewable energy because of planning and capacity constraints. This is a failure of economic policy.

This failure to use economics to devise policies fit for the future, as Beatrice Webb called for, has meant that energy bills have skyrocketed for families and businesses as the war in Ukraine grinds on. We remain dangerously reliant on imported gas supplies which we have no control over, while energy companies raked in billions in under-taxed windfall profits.

Meanwhile the welfare state which Webb worked so tirelessly for has been steadily and systematically hollowed out. Since the Conservatives took office in 2010, around one million children have fallen, without a murmur of concern from ministers, into poverty. More and more people find their benefits stopped or sanctioned, waiting for months to appeal seemingly unfathomable decisions while facing destitution. My constituency surgeries are full of cases where parents, usually mothers, are struggling to put food on the table; to keep their children warm; and where the loan shark is the only alternative to the welfare payment that doesn't come or doesn't go far enough. The National Health Service is also at breaking point, with millions waiting for treatment and millions more unable to get a doctor's or dentist's appointment. The challenges facing the next Labour government will be different to those Webb researched and wrote about a century ago. But her plea that policymakers recognise that poverty is structural, that welfare should protect people from the worst economic hardship, and that the recipients of welfare should not be humiliated or stigmatised, are surely the right starting points. Dusting off some of those Fabian pamphlets to rebuild a welfare state that treats all people with dignity and respect will be an important priority for the next Labour government.

The address at Westminster Abbey, the Webbs' final resting place, was given by Prime Minister Clement Attlee, who said: 'Millions are living fuller and freer lives today because of the work of Sidney and Beatrice Webb.' He was surely right. Even seventy years later, in economics and politics, the influence of Beatrice Webb endures and the next Labour government will aspire to build a welfare system that Webb and its founders could once again be proud of.

3

Mary Paley Marshall, Industrial Economics and the Benefits of Clusters

I remember seeing the miners' strikes on the news as a young child. In a matter of years, the industries that had powered the nation were decimated and the communities that supported them scarred by a lack of jobs and the total erosion of the identity that shaped their towns. I don't think I or anyone else could have fully comprehended the scale of the long-term devastation caused by Conservative economic and industrial policy. I studied the economics of industry and productivity at university and learned that there was much that the Conservatives had got wrong, but it was only when I moved to Yorkshire to work as an economist for Halifax Bank of Scotland (HBOS) that I got a true sense of the misery and destruction that those policies had caused to industries and communities in the North of England. As productivity tumbles and growth sputters to a halt we have a lot to learn from the theories underpinning the economics of industry as we work to rebuild the North's economy and generate growth all across Britain.

The first book really addressing industrial economics was *The Economics of Industry*, published in 1879, by Mary Paley Marshall and her husband, Alfred Marshall. Their theories on the benefits to productivity of 'proximity' or 'economic clusters', and that pricing is influenced not just by the costs of production but also the level of demand, were groundbreaking. The book also considers the gender pay gap, and the economics and social attitudes that meant women were paid less than men. Paley Marshall's work on clusters and on gender pay disparities remain incredibly relevant to economic policymakers today – and are central to two questions I want to address as chancellor. First, how can government work with business to ensure that business develops in all parts of the country, creating much needed jobs and prosperity? And second, how, more than fifty years on since the Equal Pay Act, can we finally eliminate the gender pay gap which still sees women earn on average 15 per cent less than men? By exploring the life and work of Mary Paley Marshall we can perhaps help answer some of those questions.

Early Life

Mary Paley was born in 1850, in Ufford near Stamford in Lincolnshire. Like so many women of that era, and indeed in this book, Paley's chances of academic success and financial independence depended on a family with some economic means and an unconventionally liberal attitude. Paley's great-grandfather was a theologian and philosopher. Her father was rector of the church in Ufford and a former fellow of St John's College, Cambridge. Paley's brother was sent to boarding school but her own education (and that of her sister) was not neglected. Her father taught the sisters divinity and mathematics while their governess taught them German, French and science. Engaged at eighteen, Paley's life could easily have followed the usual route for a middle-class Victorian young lady: marriage, children and devotion to wifely and charitable duties. But her fiancé was an army officer who departed for India shortly after their engagement was announced and when he returned three years later Paley had mastered the Cambridge entrance exams and gained a scholarship. She called off the engagement and went to Newnham, a women's college recently formed by the suffragist, campaigner and economist Millicent Garrett Fawcett. Paley was one of the first five female students at Cambridge University, beginning her studies there in 1871.

Cambridge

Many years after Mary went up to Cambridge as part of that first cohort of Newnham College women, she reflected that their arrival had been viewed 'in those days an outrageous proceeding'. Even twenty-six years after her arrival, in 1897, a vote which sought to officially recognise the degrees of women at Cambridge failed by a large margin and turned into a riot. Initially Paley had planned to stay for just a year, but after discovering John Stuart Mill's writings she switched from her initial aim of gaining some 'general cultivation' to the 'serious' study of Moral Sciences. She felt a great sense of responsibility, even trepidation, about being one of the first women to take the Moral Sciences Tripos exam at Cambridge. 'We worked very hard, for we were pioneers and we had to do credit to the "Cause",' she recalled, but despite passing her final exams with flying colours and later teaching at the university, Paley was never able to claim a university degree. Shockingly, it was not until 1946 that women were able to graduate from Cambridge, two years after Mary died. A generation of women who graduated from Oxford and Cambridge became known as the 'Steamboat Ladies'. Travelling by steamboat to collect their degrees, they were able to graduate by exploiting a loophole with Trinity College, Dublin. While the Dublin college opted to not even admit women until 1904 – thirty-three years after Mary Paley was admitted to Cambridge – it saw no reason why women could not be awarded a degree. Because of a long-standing arrangement which meant any student could graduate from any of the three universities, many women denied diplomas by Oxford and Cambridge began to travel by steamboat to Dublin to graduate – often staying only one night. Among them were economics graduates – notably Lilian Knowles and Ellen McArthur, both economic historians.

I was born the same year, 1979, that my own Oxford College (New College) started admitting women – and granting them degrees – less than half a century ago. The women's only colleges at Oxford and Cambridge played a hugely important role in opening up opportunities for women but equality was slow to come. Today, 35 per cent of those studying economics at Cambridge are women. Not equality, but a world apart from the lonely path Paley trod.

Alfred Marshall

It was at Cambridge that Paley was taught by the famous economist Alfred Marshall. They married in 1877, when Mary was twenty-six. Reflecting the progressive views they both shared, they agreed that there would be no promise to 'obey' in their marriage vows, although in later years Alfred appeared to reject his earlier support for greater female emancipation. Due to the celibacy rules that then applied in many colleges, Alfred was forced to give up his fellowship at St John's after their marriage and they moved to Bristol, where he was the first principal of what was to become Bristol University and taught economics. But in 1884, on the death of Henry Fawcett, the economist, Liberal MP and husband to Millicent Garrett Fawcett, they returned to Cambridge so that Alfred could take up Fawcett's vacant professorship in political economy, and the Marshalls lived there for the rest of their lives. Mary and Alfred's relationship defined them both emotionally and professionally, and resulted in a partnership that over five decades saw the publication of a number of influential economic books and pamphlets.

For those of us who studied economics at college or university, our first introduction to macroeconomics is likely to have been through 'supply and demand curves'. The 'elasticity of substitution'? 'Marginal utility'? The 'law of diminishing returns'? Much of this theory can be traced back to the work of Alfred Marshall, particularly his *Principles of Economics*, published in 1890, but written over a period of a decade. Marshall illustrated his arguments and theories through the use of graphs and diagrams – some of which are little changed for the modern student today! His aim was to bring some mathematical rigour to the study of economics and make it more scientific without making it too abstract for the general student, which is why he put a lot of the mathematical content into footnotes and appendices.

Marshall was one of the founders of the school of neoclassical economics, which describes production, consumption and pricing as all being driven by supply and demand in the economy. He was also responsible for moving economics away from its classical focus on the market economy and instead popularised the idea that it was also about the study of human behaviour. In particular, Marshall developed the idea that price was not dependent on the cost of production alone, and introduced the idea of the demand curve – which shows that price depends on supply *and* demand. He noted that, in the short run, supply cannot be changed and so market value depends mainly on demand. In the medium term, production can be increased through existing facilities, such as buildings and machinery, but, since these do not require renewal within this period, their costs (called 'fixed' or 'overhead' costs) have little influence on fluctuations in the sale price of the product. It is therefore the variable costs, which constantly recur, that most influence the sale price in the medium term. In the long term, machines and buildings wear out and have to be replaced, so the initial sale price of the product must be high enough to cover the costs of new machinery and equipment. This classification of costs into fixed and variable, and the emphasis given to the element of time, probably represent one of Marshall's chief contributions to economic theory: equilibrium. The formula 'demand equals supply' is only ever partial, and it changes over time as businesses face different costs at different times.

'The Economics of Industry'

In 1879 *The Economics of Industry* was published under the name of both Mary and her husband Alfred, despite the fact that it was largely based on ideas developed in Mary's Newnham College lectures. The book was immediately popular. Its chief contribution was to establish an economic theory for a phenomenon common in late nineteenth-century Britain, in which firms concentrating on the manufacture of certain products were geographically clustered together. Their theory supposed that areas became specialists for firms and their auxiliary industries – so manufacturers that required raw materials would open near where the raw materials were produced, and products were therefore entirely made in one of the 'industrial districts' they described. They predicted that competing manufacturers would open too, making areas hubs for specific industries. These theories are now widely used by economists and economic geographers globally to describe this phenomenon and to understand the benefits in costs, supply and productivity that such clusters can bring to businesses.

The two dominant characteristics of a Marshallian industrial district are what economists call high degrees of vertical and horizontal specialisation. 'Vertical specialisation' is through the supply chain, so, for example, paper factories are found in the same area as where the wood from trees necessary to make paper is harvested and processed. 'Horizontal specialisation' is where, to use the same example, multiple paper factories and tree farms are found in the same area. Silicon Valley can be thought of as an example of horizontal specialisation – where technology firms have all grouped together in one 'industrial district'. In the Marshallian model of industrial districts, firms tend to be small and to focus on a single function in the production chain. They are highly competitive, and in many cases there is little product differentiation. The major advantages of Marshallian industrial districts arise from the simple proximity of firms to each other, which allows easier recruitment of skilled labour and rapid exchanges of commercial and technical information, often through informal, non-market communications outside of official channels (given the workers in these districts live in close proximity). According to Paley Marshall, this illustrates competitive capitalism at its most efficient, with transaction costs reduced to a practical minimum, keeping prices down too.

Today in Britain productivity is falling behind our closest competitors – 10 per cent lower than in Germany, 18 per cent lower than France, and 23 per cent lower than the US. Growth, which averaged 2 per cent a year under the last Labour government between 1997 and 2010, fell to an average of just 1.5 per cent in the decade of Conservative government leading up to the pandemic. On the back of Liz Truss's disastrous 'mini-budget' and thirteen years of Conservative failure, the UK is expected to have one of the slowest growths amongst industrialised countries in 2023 – except sanctions-hit Russia.

Some people say that this state of negligible or no growth simply reflects a stage in our economic development where there is low demand and low investment, but I don't accept that lack of ambition or its inevitability. We have world-leading firms, fantastic universities and researchers, and some of the most highly skilled workers in the world. In professional services, banking and in some parts of life sciences, creative industries and financial technology ('fintech') we lead the world. So what can we learn from Mary Paley Marshall about the role of government in marshalling the drivers of innovation and wealth creation to make our economy more productive and prosperous?

The short answer is: quite a lot. Paley Marshall's insight into and economic analysis of why firms in similar businesses located near to one another not only explain a significant phenomenon in Victorian England, but also one that is still evident today. What Paley Marshall was describing were the clusters of firms and manufacturers specialising in a particular area in the 1800s, like wool in West Yorkshire (where I serve as an MP today), ceramics in Stoke and steel in South Wales. As more firms located in proximity to one another, the abundance of skills increased, as did the infrastructure required to get the goods these firms produced to market – think of the canals in West Yorkshire and around Stoke. In short a whole ecosystem developed, far larger than the investment any one firm could provide, which encouraged industry-wide economies of scale. Clustering reduces the costs of production, and so the costs of the goods (and later services) produced are lower. There is no reason you couldn't have spun wool in Stoke or made plates in Leeds, but it didn't happen because it would cost more to do so and would be economically and practically unviable. In Paley Marshall's time this theory depended on the goods being produced all being very similar. If you could successfully differentiate your product and charge a higher price as a result, then clustering would become less important since price would not be the only factor in marketing your product. But, even when differentiation (or 'heterogeneity' to economists) exists, clusters still form, as skills, finance and infrastructure can be shared or more easily move between one firm and another. Just look at the City of London and financial services, Silicon Valley and tech, or Bangalore and computing.

The argument about the importance of clusters explains why any national industrial strategy must be accompanied by a regional strategy. Sadly, industrial policy seems to have gone out of fashion in the UK as long ago as the 1970s, when the criticism was that 'picking winners' and supporting local industries meant in practice the state subsidising failing firms and costing taxpayers dearly. Labour, however, has been working hard in opposition to develop our own industrial strategy. It is deeply positive and forward looking, embracing industries that include life sciences, fintech and low-carbon innovation. It also recognises the insight of Paley Marshall about clustering. The industrial heritage of the North East of England and East Coast of Scotland make them perfect for developing carbon capture and storage. The West Midlands has been the traditional home of the UK car industry: they need a gigafactory to build batteries and a rethink of the whole supply chain so it is fit for the new era of electric vehicles. The top research universities have excelled during the pandemic, with Oxford University, AstraZeneca (with headquarters in Cambridge), the government and the NHS all joining forces to develop, manufacture and then roll out a vaccine for Covid in just a year. Many other life sciences firms, including Oxford Nanopore, have grown out of Oxford and Cambridge Universities and their world-leading science research.

A contemporary economist who has followed in the footsteps of Mary Paley Marshall in the field of industrial and innovation economics is Mariana Mazzucato. She works primarily on the economics of innovation, and her most famous book, *The Entrepreneurial State: Debunking Public vs. Private Sector Myths*, published in 2013, points to the role government has historically played in investing in, and driving forward, some of the most radical technological innovations in history. Mazzucato has advised governments around the world about innovation – from serving as Italy's representative on the G7 Panel on Economic Resilience, to joining South Africa's Council of Economic Advisors and her membership of the UK Government's Innovation Expert Group. Perhaps most notably, she has been a leading voice in innovation policy in Europe, working with the European Commission to develop policy that works to implement the insights of her research in *The Entrepreneurial State*.

The UK has huge assets as we move into a post-Covid and net-zero economy. But, as the AstraZeneca vaccine shows, it takes a partnership approach between government and business to respond to our most pressing challenges. The long-term research that underpinned the work of the AstraZeneca scientists carried out at the UK's prestigious universities was critical to the successful development of the vaccine. Similarly, the infrastructure that is needed for carbon capture and storage will require government investment to leverage in the private sector investment that is required to reach critical mass. Businesses will tell you that they are willing to invest but need to know that the government will too, especially in skills and infrastructure, both of which then spill over to businesses who are able to benefit. If we think of electric cars: businesses will not invest in electric car technology until the charging infrastructure exists, but, by the same token, cannot invest in charging technology until the cars to use them are on the market. It's situations like these, so crucial to our green transition, where government investment backing private investment becomes so important. This is why Labour's Green Prosperity Plan has the potential to be such a game-changer – a plan to invest throughout this decade in the industries of the future, from tidal power to battery storage and hydrogen power. We could be global leaders in some or all of these industries, and already have the huge advantage of our industrial heritage, geography and world-class universities. But the government has to play its part. With me as chancellor, it will.

So an effective industrial strategy has to be built from the regions up – to kick-start industries like new small modular nuclear reactors, tidal power and hydrogen gas. It has to draw on the unique strengths, the clustering of skills and the infrastructure already built up, and the expertise that nearby universities can spin out into new businesses and new jobs. One hundred and fifty years after *The Economics of Industry* was first published, there is still much that it can teach students of economics, and policymakers, today.

The Gender Pay Gap

As well as outlining the model for industrial districts, there is, unusually for the time, a less well known chapter in *The Economics of Industry* dedicated to the gender pay gap. Clearly a topic close to her heart, Mary Paley Marshall wrote about it subsequently, suggesting that women may be paid less than men for equal work 'not because the value of the work they do is low, but because they and their employers have been in the habit of taking it for granted that the wages of women must be low'. The chapter also advocated reforming women's education in order that women could 'do more difficult work', and so 'making them more ready to demand, and employers more ready to grant them, higher wages for it'.

This analysis was at a time of big differences in wages between men and women, as well as big differences in the work that men and women did. In an article published in 1997, 'An Investigation of the Female–Male Wage Gap during the Industrial Revolution in Britain', Joyce Burnette states that the female–male wage gap generally varied from one-third to two-thirds during the Industrial Revolution. A study based on the reports of wages and salaries paid between 1850 and 1890 prepared by the Board of Trade found that over those forty years, women in British industry earned a little more than 40 per cent of male earnings. The main categories of women's work in the Victorian era were domestic service, industrial work and teaching young children. Census evidence suggests that around 40 per cent of women in Britain were in employment in the latter half of the nineteenth century, roughly twice the rate found for the United States at the same time, and even two decades before this period, Harriet Martineau wrote of her shock and disgust at the lack of employment opportunity for women in the US in comparison to Britain. Despite such low pay, the earnings of women made a significant contribution to the fortunes of many working-class households at the time, and still do.

The fight for women's economic and political equality goes back decades and continues today, as women earn and own less than men and do a disproportionate amount of unpaid work in the home and as carers. Much of the progress for gender equality has come from political movements and activism, most notably the suffragettes and suffragists, including Millicent Fawcett, whom Mary Paley Marshall knew through her Cambridge connections. Although it is not clear whether Paley Marshall and Millicent Fawcett were close, their paths crossed often. Fawcett had founded Newnham College where Paley was one of the first students to study. Henry Fawcett and Alfred Marshall were both Cambridge professors, and as well as her political campaigning, Millicent

Fawcett was also a published economist. Her book *Political Economy for Beginners*, first published in 1870, was hugely successful, and was reprinted multiple times. Fawcett's second book, *Tales in Political Economy*, used stories to illustrate economic arguments. She wrote in the preface:

> It is hoped that these little tales may be of some use to those who are trying to teach Political Economy. I cannot let them go to press without a word of apology to Miss Martineau for my plagiarism of the idea, which she made so popular thirty years ago, of hiding the powder, Political Economy, in the raspberry jam of a story.

The National Union of Women's Suffrage Societies that Fawcett helped establish at the turn of the century was arguably the most important campaigning organisation in history, and one that eventually saw success in 1918 when some, but not all, women won the right to vote, and then in 1928, when equal suffrage with men was achieved. Paley Marshall certainly identified with the 'cause' (her word) of female equality and is one of the first economists to have written about the gender pay gap.

Other economists soon followed in writing about pay and gender, including Fawcett, Beatrice Webb and Eleanor Rathbone. In 1915, Webb signed a 'Women's Appeal to Women' which asked for 'equal conditions and equal wages for the same work'. During the same year, Fawcett argued that due to the substantial increase in women's productivity which the First World War helped to 'discover', women merited equal pay. In 1918, Rathbone led the Family Endowment campaign, which published a pamphlet to argue that the idea of a 'family wage' (a wage on which you can support a family) was not a men-only right, and that women deserved better pay too. In March of that same year, Fawcett argued for her belief in 'equal pay for equal work' in the *Economic Journal*, edited by Keynes.

Millicent Fawcett was a leading suffragette and campaigned
on a wide range of social issues, as well as writing the
bestselling *Political Economy for Beginners*.

The campaign for legislation on equal pay in Britain in more
recent years will forever be associated with the Dagenham women
workers at Ford, and Barbara Castle who as Secretary of State for
Employment took up their cause and legislated for equal pay in
1970. Politically, women in parliament had been campaigning on a
cross-party basis for equal pay since the 1930s, with Labour's Edith
Summerskill and the Conservatives' Thelma Cazalet-Keir leading the charge with their campaign for Equal Compensation for
Women. But the work of such economists as Barbara Petrongolo in
exposing the gender pay gaps that exist in our economy, and Karen
Mumford in exposing how they exist even in our public services,
remains important, in combination with evidence from industry as
we work to close the gender pay gap once and for all. Mary Paley
Marshall's contribution was an early and surprising addition to the

debate, particularly as it was part of a wider study of the economics of industry. Her insight that it was attitudes, not economic value, that often determined the lower pay rates endured by women is important. Still today, with legislation on the statute book in Britain for more than fifty years, and gender pay gap reporting by businesses existing for more than five years, unequal pay still persists. The work women do (women are over-represented in caring roles, for example) is often valued less than similarly skilled work done by men, and even when men and women fill very similar roles, there remains evidence that men are better at demanding higher pay. Frustratingly, the level of pay a person receives does not always reflect the value of the work that they do but instead how much the person who does it is valued by society.

Progress in eliminating the gender pay gap has been so slow that at current rates of change I will be almost eighty before we have stamped out this inequality between men and women.

The Personal and the Professional

Alfred Marshall later dropped the analysis of the gender pay gap from his own work, beyond asserting that employing women was:

> a great gain in so far as it tends to develop their faculties; but an injury in so far as it tempts them to neglect their duty of building up a true home, and of investing their efforts in the personal capital of their children's characters and abilities.

In his later writings, he took the view that economics applied only to men and should be the domain of men, defining the field as 'the study of men as they live and move and think in the ordinary business of life'.

What caused this change of attitude is unclear. It is tempting to speculate that there may have been an element of rivalry or professional jealousy. *The Economics of Industry* was Mary Paley Marshall's most successful book, yet, despite (or perhaps because of) its success and despite being credited as co-author, Alfred Marshall was known to have disliked the book, and later admitted it reflected her ideas more than his. Keynes later said his father, John Neville Keynes, always felt 'there was something ungenerous in Marshall's distaste for this book, which was originally hers, but was allowed to go out of print without a murmur of complaint from her when there was still a strong demand for it'. Mary Paley Marshall's marriage seems to have been both a blessing and curse for her own development as an economist. His co-authorship lent her the credibility that as a woman she would not normally have enjoyed – certainly not in the 1870s. But Alfred Marshall took much of the credit for their joint work and edited out of hers that which he did not like. It is also striking that although his views grew further away from those he had professed when he was younger, and which she still held on the importance of women's education and of women in the workforce, she never publicly disagreed with him.

As Alfred's health deteriorated, however, he came to rely more and more on his wife, and there is reason to believe that many of the seminal texts he authored, such as *The Principles of Economics*, included significant contributions from Mary. In Sir Henry Hardman's contribution to *Economic Careers: Economics and Economists in Britain, 1930–1970*, there is a sad but telling story about Alfred Marshall wanting to take the credit for a lifetime of shared endeavours:

> I can remember a story which interested me very much of the Webbs going to a meal in Cambridge with Mary [Paley] Marshall and Alfred Marshall; and of Beatrice Webb talking about how interesting it was that there were brought together four people working in two couples, in each case both having contributed, and this was during drinks before they went into the lunch. When they were going into the meal, Mary Marshall said to Beatrice

Webb, 'Don't talk about Alfred and I having done this, it upsets him so much.' Marshall was a great economist, I think, but a stinker of a man.

And as Keynes wrote in his biography of Alfred Marshall:

During forty-seven years of married life his dependence upon her devotion was complete. Her life was given to him and to his work with a degree of unselfishness and understanding that makes it difficult for friends and old pupils to think of them separately or to withhold from her shining gifts of character a big share in what his intellect accomplished.

Paley Marshall's Social World

Whatever the tensions within her marriage, Mary Paley Marshall was part of a social milieu that included many remarkable thinkers, reflecting a broad range of social and cultural interests. A beautiful and stylish woman, many of Paley Marshall's clothes reflected her interest in the arts and were influenced by contemporary designers, including the stunning and rather unconventional Pre-Raphaelite prints she became famous for wearing. And while her circle pre-dated the fashionable Bloomsbury Set, many of her contemporaries were women who sought to challenge the social and moral conventions of the day by treading their own paths in pursuit of greater economic and social freedoms. One of Paley Marshall's closest friends was Florence Ada Keynes (mother of John Maynard Keynes), another early graduate of Newnham College, Cambridge, and the two families and their economic thinking were heavily intertwined. Florence was the first female councillor on Cambridge City Council, elected in 1914, and she became Mayor of Cambridge at seventy. She was a committed social reformer, involved in many campaigns, including serving as secretary of the Charity Organisation Society, which provided pensions for the elderly living in poverty, and worked with those who found themselves in the workhouses, helping to resettle them into society.

Florence Keynes encouraged other Cambridge women to get involved in charitable work, including Paley Marshall's friend, Eglantyne Jebb. Jebb's family were wealthy, but with a strong commitment to social reform. Florence Keynes recruited Jebb to the cause of the Charity Organisation Society, and like other social reforming women of the period (including Maud Pember Reeves, Eleanor Rathbone and Beatrice Webb), Jebb carried out extensive research into the lives of the poor, particularly women and children. It was this experience, and the encouragement of her brother-in-law, the Labour MP Charles Roden Buxton, to go to Europe after the First World War, that encouraged Jebb to raise money for the children of Germany and Austria. In 1919 she and her sister Dorothy (Buxton's wife) set up the Fight the Famine campaign, to raise money for starving children in Germany after the First World War. Following the success of their campaign, they founded Save the Children, and Jebb would go on to write the International Declaration on the Rights of the Child, later incorporated into the League of Nations and then the United Nations. Despite Florence Keynes's friendship and encouragement in these efforts, she also caused Jebb huge pain. Jebb fell in love with Keynes's daughter Margaret (John Maynard Keynes's sister) and for several years the two had a loving relationship during which they wrote to each other about how they hoped to be able to live as a couple. But Florence had other plans for her daughter, more befitting the social conventions of the time, and Margaret married the distinguished physiologist Archibald Hill in 1913. Jebb eventually moved to Geneva, where she is now buried. Save the Children today is active in 120 countries around the world and helps around 150 million children.

The above gives some flavour of Mary Paley Marshall's social circle in Cambridge. She was friends with other successful and highly educated women who developed their own careers in local government, academic research, charitable organising and campaigning, but by far the most important friendships and intellectual stimulation for Paley Marshall came from her connection with the Keynes family. Florence Keynes was clearly a close friend and support, but in terms of Mary's own contribution and legacy as an economist, it was her relationship with Florence's son John Maynard Keynes that was to be the most significant.

Keynes's own economic thinking and greatest contributions built on that of the Marshalls, and on a practical level he relied greatly on Marshall's archives and Mary's research. On his death in 1924, Alfred Marshall donated his considerable collection of books, articles, journals and writings to Cambridge University, and Mary became Honorary Librarian of what was to become the Marshall Library of Economics. She worked there as a librarian for twenty years and in that role she worked most closely with John Maynard Keynes. Shortly after Alfred Marshall died, Keynes spent many happy hours with Mary gathering material from her for a biography of her husband, drawing on the list of Alfred Marshall's published writings made by Mary and preserved in the Marshall Library, and from the Marshalls' scrapbook of newspaper cuttings that included copies of most of Alfred's not inconsiderable number of letters to the press. The friendship continued long after the biography of his life and review of his work had been completed and published in *The Economic Journal*, and Keynes would later note that without Mary's 'understanding and devotion', Marshall's work 'would not have fulfilled its fruitfulness', while according to James Cicarelli and Julianne Cicarelli, in *Distinguished Women Economists*, 'Keynes held her in the highest regard and considered her an intellectual and thinker every bit as significant to the historical development of economics as her husband or any of the other economists about whom he wrote.' The close rapport between Mary Paley Marshall and Maynard Keynes lasted for the rest of her life.

Why Mary Paley Marshall Matters Today

Mary Paley never got her university degree, despite passing her exams and then teaching students at Cambridge. The bar on women graduating from Cambridge University outlived her,

Mary Paley Marshall had to wait until 1927, when she was seventy-seven, to receive formal recognition for her huge achievements with an honorary doctorate from Bristol University.

though Bristol University awarded her an honorary degree when she was in her seventies. But there is much the modern student can learn from Paley Marshall, especially on the economics of industry and the clustering of industries in particular localities and why that is good for productivity and the bottom line. Paley Marshall herself benefited, too, from another sort of clustering. In and around

Cambridge were some great minds, including women, who for the first time were setting out and developing causes and careers of their own – such women as Millicent Fawcett, Florence Ada Keynes, and Eglantyne and Dorothy Jebb.

John Maynard Keynes has always been one of my economic heroes – the lodestar for my own thinking about how the economy functions and malfunctions. But for a long time I didn't know much about the economists and thinkers around him. He is of course associated with the so-called Bloomsbury Set of writers, philosophers and artists, but in economics some of his greatest influences were at home in Cambridge, where he grew up and studied. Among those were the Marshalls, whom he got to know through his mother and through his own study of economics. John Maynard Keynes built upon Marshall's insight that price depends on demand as well as supply. One of Keynes's most important contributions was that of demand management, whereby the level of demand can be altered by economic policy – particularly fiscal policy. Government can boost demand in the economy through demand management – either by cutting taxes or (as Keynes argued) even more efficiently by deficit-financed spending. Conversely, when needed, demand can be reduced through tax increases or reductions in spending. Keynes developed his own thinking in response to the Great Depression in the late 1920s and early 1930s, and his thinking then became popular in the post-war period under both Labour and Conservative governments. The post-war (Keynesian) consensus broke down under the weight of stagflation (the combination of low growth and high inflation) in the 1970s. But Keynes's work built on the groundwork of both Alfred Marshall and Mary Paley Marshall, and he made extensive use of the Marshalls' formidable collection of books and articles, catalogued by Mary for Keynes's use.

As we will go on to see, Keynes's own protégée, Joan Robinson, was to take forward her teacher's work to develop theories that helped make the case for a minimum wage and other more interventionist policy from governments which were especially useful for the thinking of New Labour in the 1990s, and indeed was the theory behind Labour's flagship National Minimum Wage policy.

For her own part, Mary Paley Marshall developed practical insights on industrial policy which still explain the behaviour of firms today, and are still shaping Labour's policy on industrial strategy – where we argue for a close partnership between business, government and intermediate institutions like universities and trade bodies – in developing industry clusters in different parts of the country based on the industrial heritage, skills and research base.

Paley Marshall's work on the gender pay gap – her insight that women are paid less because the work women do is valued less – was also the economic underpinning for another proud Labour achievement, the 1970 Equal Pay Act. If I were to become chancellor, my plans would include an active industrial strategy, with government and business acting in partnership to grow the economy and seize the opportunities for investment and jobs in life sciences and, most of all, in the industries of the future. And, as someone who aspires to be the first female chancellor, I would act with the determination Barbara Castle showed in campaigning for and achieving the Equal Pay Act under law, to ensure it becomes a practical reality.

4

Rosa Luxemburg and Revolutionary Economics

At the age of thirteen, between my races at the school swimming gala, I read a copy of Karl Marx's *Communist Manifesto*. I had borrowed it from my dad's bookshelves – although these days I must admit my swimming is better than my knowledge of the intricacies of Marxist dialectic materialism. I was already interested in politics and ideas at this stage, and spotted the book at home and was intrigued. I enjoyed the utopianism and vision of a more equal society, because I saw all around me inequality and poverty which I instinctively knew was wrong. But it was the Labour Party, not the Communist Party that I joined, because I was drawn to the reformism of the Labour Party and Tony Blair's vision for Britain.

A couple of years later, I first became aware of Rosa Luxemburg – I think at an art exhibition of socialist art in central London, which I went to see with my dad. My early impressions were of a romantic figure, full of revolutionary zeal, blazing a trail for her ideals and dying way too young, as most romantic figures do. But less well known is the fact that she also produced one of the early twentieth century's most remarkable economic books.

Luxemburg never fitted in – not in any of the places she lived. In Poland she fought for freedom against the Russians; in Switzerland she was an exile away from the centre of the action; in Germany she was anti-war when the country was at war; and in Russia she was hounded because of her anti-tsarist activities. But she embraced her position as an outsider. In perhaps her best-known quotation, Luxemburg champions the dissenter:

Freedom only for the supporters of the government, only for the members of a party ... is no freedom at all. Freedom is always the freedom of the one who thinks differently. Not because of the fanaticism of 'justice' but rather because all that is instructive, wholesome and purifying in political freedom depends on this essential characteristic, and its effects cease to work when 'freedom' becomes a privilege.

We remember Luxemburg as a symbol of revolution, but she was also an impressive and important economic thinker, the first Polish woman – and indeed one of the first women anywhere in the world – to be awarded a PhD in economics. Her most celebrated economic text, *The Accumulation of Capital*, is still one of the most serious and comprehensive economic texts of all time. Luxemburg's key economic contribution was to challenge, and take forward, Marx's work in *Das Kapital* in trying to explain both the longevity of capitalism, and also why (as Marx predicted) it would inevitably collapse as the worker rebelled against exploitation, tired of the profits created by their labour never reaching their own pockets.

Luxemburg not only made significant contributions to economic thinking and political theory but also engaged in direct political action, and was known for her integrity as well as a passion for advancing socialist economics and opposing imperialism. Her commitment was such that, ultimately, she was willing to die for what she believed in.

Early Life and Education

Rosa Luxemburg was born Rozalia Luksenburg in Zamość, in Russian-occupied Poland in 1870. Her father, Edward, was the eldest of ten children and heir to his father's timber business. They were a wealthy family, successful in commerce and trade and committed to education and learning. Rosa's father and grand-father were leading members of the Reform Jewish community and were proud of their Jewish and Polish heritage, to the extent of being willing to fight for both when they came under attack. When the January Uprising broke out against the Russian tsarist authorities in 1863, Edward delivered weapons to Polish fighters and organised fundraisers for the insurrection. After the failure of the uprising he became a target of the police and was forced into hiding in Warsaw.

As a result of these traumatic events, Rosa's childhood was full of political turmoil, challenging her family's identity and allegiances. Rosa also suffered poor health in her early years, including what was probably rheumatoid arthritis, which left her effectively bed-bound for a year and with a permanent limp from the age of five. Her early education took place at home, where she learned Hebrew, Yiddish and Polish, as well as Russian and German. In 1884, she enrolled at an all-girls school in Warsaw, which she attended until 1887. The school only rarely accepted Polish girls, and the arrival of a Polish Jew was even more exceptional. All lessons were in Russian, but Rosa attended secret circles studying the works of Polish poets and writers, and at sixteen joined the illegal Polish left-wing Proletariat Party. When she graduated she was top of the class, but the medal awarded to the top student was withheld because of her 'opposition-al attitudes'.

By the time she was nineteen, Rosa had to flee Poland. She was already wanted by the tsarist police due to her activity in the Proletariat Party, which had been banned and its leading activists killed. Rosa hid in the countryside to avoid the same fate before arriving as an exile in Switzerland in 1889. There she attended the University of Zurich – one of the few institutions to admit women – and first studied philosophy, then law, politics, economics and math-ematics. Her doctoral dissertation, on 'The Industrial Development of Poland', was completed in the spring of 1897 and she was award-ed a Doctor of Law degree. Luxemburg's dissertation, her first important contribution to economic debate, was first published in German, and then in translation.

Political Career and Campaigns

Once in Switzerland, Luxemburg's own political career began to advance. Along with her fellow student and partner Leo Jogiches, Luxemburg co-founded the Social Democracy of the Kingdom of Poland (SDKP) party, and her thesis on 'Industrial Development' became the party's economic blueprint. Despite living in Germany for most of her adult life, Luxemburg was the intellectual power-house behind the SDKP, later the SDKPiL as it merged with its Lithuanian sister party.

While in Zurich, Luxemburg's hosts were Karl and Olympia Lübeck, German socialists in exile. Zurich was full of political refugees at the time, from Russia, Germany, Poland and elsewhere. It was a welcoming environment for revolutionaries and dissidents, very different from the oppression that Luxemburg and her father and grandfather before her had experienced in Russian-occupied Poland.

But Luxemburg didn't want to be in exile; she wanted to be at the centre of political activity, and that, she felt, meant being in Germany, where socialists and communists were well organised and numerous. But there was a barrier. As a Pole, she could not emigrate to Germany. The Lübecks came up with a solution – Luxemburg married their son, Gustav, and in 1898 she was living as a Prussian citizen in Berlin. The marriage was purely one of convenience; Luxemburg never lived with Gustav, and within five years they were divorced.

Germany, however, at once opened up the new opportunities she had hoped for. Luxemburg was well connected in socialist and social democratic politics in Germany. She met fellow left-activist Clara Zetkin in the Social Democratic Party of Germany's women's section, and they became lifelong friends and political comrades. Zetkin would later join Luxemburg in launching the anti-war Spartacus League, and served as a communist representative in the Reichstag during the Weimar Republic, after Luxemburg's death. Zetkin is also credited with establishing International Women's Day, first proposing the idea at the International Conference of Socialist Women in Copenhagen in 1910, and now celebrated globally on 8 March, the date chosen after demonstrations demanding franchise and trade union rights for women in New York in 1908. In 1917, a demonstration took place in Russia (deliberately on International Women's Day), in which thousands of women from different backgrounds took to the streets demanding bread and increased rations for soldiers' families. This 'bread revolt' would ultimately kick-start the 1917 Russian Revolution. As a consequence of this, in 1922, Lenin designated 8 March 'Women's Day', and in the 'Year of the Woman' in 1975, the United Nations designated it International Women's Day.

Luxemburg's former student, Friedrich Ebert, would also later become the SPD leader and then the Weimar Republic's first president, by which time his and Luxemburg's politics had sharply diverged.

But Luxemburg didn't limit her political campaigning to Germany after emigrating there. In 1905 she was in Russia during the first Russian Revolution, witnessing the killing by tsarist forces of unarmed citizens – including women and children – in St Petersburg. Luxemburg described what she saw in horrific detail:

The officer swung his sword and came down onto the long, scrawny, humbly bent forward neck of [a] stooped old man. The old man swayed and collapsed, covered with blood. His head hit the ground and I saw how his red blood discoloured the white snow. The soldiers . . . began to swing their swords, right and left. The first rows fell, including the woman with the suckling child. The rest, pressed back against the railings, didn't know where to flee in their terrible fear. Many threw themselves into the Moyka [river], and you saw them being smashed to pieces on the ice.

But instead of being crushed and discouraged by the failed revolution, Luxemburg chose to see it as progress – the working class had attempted a mass strike; the proletariat had dared to attempt revolution. More than ever, Luxemburg believed that revolution was possible, and that it would come sooner rather than later, and it would end the rule of the tsars in Russia and the Kaiser in Germany.

After witnessing the horrors in St Petersburg in 1905, Luxemburg knew she couldn't stay in the city, but neither did she want to return to Germany. Russia was now at the forefront of revolutionary activity, and Luxemburg wanted to stay close by. So in 1906 she returned secretly to Poland with her lover, and fellow revolutionary, Leo Jogiches. But the tsarist authorities had planted an agent within her SDKPiL Party, and she was soon arrested and imprisoned. Luxemburg was in and out of prison throughout her life – in Poland, Russia and Germany. It is estimated that she spent a quarter of her adult life incarcerated, including most of the First World War. In Warsaw in 1906, however, Luxemburg continued to write behind prison walls, and her work was smuggled out. Bribes and poor health got her out of prison within four months on this occasion, and Luxemburg fled to Finland (then an autonomous part of the Russian empire) and subsequently back to Germany, where she was free again.

It was in Finland during the summer of 1906 that Luxemburg met leading Russian communists, among them Vladimir Lenin, fresh from the first Russian Revolution the previous year. Lenin was an important influence on Luxemburg, and vice versa, and that summer they discussed issues in Marxist thinking – from imperialism, to international solidarity, to the right to self-determination.

Russia's 1905 revolution was the first time that mass strikes had been successful in crippling the state. According to Yale professor

Katerina Clark, Luxemburg's *The Mass Strike, The Party and the Trade Unions* (1906) was partly composed 'in response to conversations she had with Lenin in Finland about events in Russia'. But the work was far more than an analysis of what had happened in Russia, since the critical point was that 'she found the experience of revolution in Russia in all its specific detail so crucial for a programme for revolution *in Germany*'.

Lenin and Luxemburg were to disagree strongly on important issues in Marxist thinking, however, including the feasibility of achieving socialism at a country level without international change and the manner in which capitalism would collapse. Luxemburg thought that for socialism to be successful it required a wave of change internationally, that an independent Poland could arise and exist only through socialist revolutions in Germany, Austria-Hungary and Russia too. She maintained that the struggle should be against capitalism, not just for political independence. Luxemburg consistently underrated nationalist aspirations and stressed socialist internationalism. This became one of her points of disagreement with Lenin and his theory of national self-determination and the idea of 'socialism in one country' – namely in what would become the USSR. Much of their tension came from Luxemburg's fierce opposition to imperialism and her dislike of Russian oppression, something Lenin could not appreciate on the personal level Luxemburg did.

The other crucial divergence between them was that Luxemburg thought that revolution was inevitable but would be spontaneous and democratic as the economy transitioned from capitalism to socialism. Lenin, on the other hand, believed in a centrally directed transition to socialism, of the kind he and the Bolsheviks were soon to put into practice in Russia.

Luxemburg saw socialism as a movement of the working class, by the working class – not a gift or a service that could be delivered to the proletariat. Lenin, by contrast, saw socialism as a necessity to be achieved by any means possible, even if it had to be, in essence,

Rosa Luxemburg speaking at a socialist conference in
Stuttgart in 1907, where she first met Lenin.

forced upon the people. The Bolshevik dictatorship of the proletariat
was still to a degree within the bourgeois tradition of top-down politics.

Ultimately, though, Luxemburg was held in high regard by Lenin
and Leon Trotsky, who recognised her revolutionary credentials at the
Third International, a Soviet-controlled international organisation
founded in 1919 that advocated world communism, where she was
declared a martyr to the communist cause. After her death, when Paul
Levi was set to republish Rosa Luxemburg's writings, including her
disagreements with Lenin, he asked for Lenin's blessing. The man
she had disagreed with quoted a Russian proverb in her memory,
'Eagles may at times fly lower than hens but hens can never rise to
the height of eagles', adding: 'In spite of her mistakes she was – and
remains for us – an eagle.'

Economic Thinking

Luxemburg was an ardent believer in Marx's vision of a classless society brought about through revolution by a working-class proletariat who would overthrow the system that allowed the capitalist 'bourgeoisie' to profit from their labour. Marx saw capitalism as history's final hierarchical society, and believed that after its collapse the dream of economic equality would at last become a reality. He felt that the extreme exploitation of the worker under capitalism in the name of the accumulation of wealth for the richest in society was wrong, and that it was destined to implode.

Luxemburg's most significant economic publication was *The Accumulation of Capital*, published in 1913. It was written in just four months in a period that Luxemburg described in a letter to her lover Hans Diefenbach in 1917 as belonging 'to the happiest of my life'.

The book that Luxemburg was attempting to write was an introduction to (Marxist) political economy. But in doing so she discovered what she described as a 'theoretical problem related to the second volume of Marx's *Capital*'. The problem that Luxemburg sought to resolve was how capitalism was continuing to survive and thrive despite Marx predicting fifty years previously its 'inevitable collapse'. Luxemburg's answer combines her Marxist and anti-imperialist analysis. According to Luxemburg, capitalists could increase the size of their markets and so increase their profits as well as find cheaper labour to exploit through imperialist expansion into non-capitalist economies, hence the phenomenon of imperialism as capitalist states sought to dominate weaker economies by way of conquest, trade and violence. 'Capital needs other races to exploit territories where the white man cannot work,' Luxemburg argues. 'It must be able to mobilise world labour power without restriction in order to utilise all productive forces of the globe.'

In the end such opportunities would be exhausted and capitalism would collapse as the workers rose up in revolt. Like Marx, Luxemburg believed that 'the capitalist state of society is doubtless a historic necessity, but so also is the revolt of the working class against it – the revolt of its gravediggers.' Luxemburg envisioned the construction of a new democracy, underpinned by common ownership and open debates and elections. Her conclusion that the limits of the capitalist system drive it to imperialism and war led Luxemburg to a lifetime of campaigning against militarism and colonialism.

A Matter of Principle

One year after the publication of *The Accumulation of Capital*, hostilities broke out in Europe. To Luxemburg's great disappointment, the Social Democratic (SPD) party in Germany, led by her former student Friedrich Ebert, supported the military conflict in the First World War. In response Luxemburg and Karl Liebknecht co-founded the anti-war Spartacus League (Spartakusbund), in which Clara Zetkin was also involved, which eventually became the Communist Party of Germany (KPD). Luxemburg also co-founded the newspaper *Die Rote Fahne* ('The Red Flag') to spread the socialist, anti-war message. At the end of the war, with the SPD now in charge under the new chancellor, Friedrich Ebert, the order was given to suppress the left-wing revolution taking place, disowning former friends on the left as he attempted to restore order and peace in Germany. Luxemburg and Liebknecht were captured in Berlin on 15 January 1919 by the Rifle Division of the Cavalry Guards. They were questioned under torture and then the order was given to summarily execute them. Luxemburg was knocked down by a soldier with the butt of his rifle, then shot in the head. Her body was flung into the Berlin Landwehr Canal.

Luxemburg's last known words, written on the evening of her murder, were defiant and even positive about what the future held:

A new leadership can and must be created by the masses and from the masses ... They are the rock on which the ultimate victory of the revolution will be built. That is why future victories will spring from this 'defeat'. 'Order prevails in Berlin!' You foolish lackeys! Your 'order' is built on sand. Tomorrow the revolution will 'rise up again, clashing its weapons', and to your horror it will proclaim with trumpets blazing: I was, I am, I shall be!

The murders of Luxemburg and Liebknecht inspired a new wave of violence across Germany. Thousands of members of the KPD, revolutionaries and civilians were killed. Four months after Luxemburg and Liebknecht's murders, their corpses were found. They were buried at the Friedrichsfelde Central Cemetery in Berlin, where socialists and communists commemorate them annually on the second Sunday of January.

Contribution to Economics

Most economists develop theories of how the economy works; the best challenge contemporary thinking and help move economic analysis on. In this book there are many economists who through their work have improved the lives of people through new ways of economic management or understanding how to tackle unemployment or productivity. Some of the women in this book have helped people in the poorest places in the world by developing real-world solutions to economic problems. But Rosa Luxemburg stands out as someone willing to sacrifice her life for the cause she believed in. Her aim was not just to describe or prescribe a new approach to economics but to enact change in the course of significant world events. As her biographer, Donald Shepardson, put it, 'she was driven always by the noble cause of socialism'. In 1919 she made the ultimate sacrifice and died for that cause.

Marx's *Das Kapital* was published in 1867 and Luxemburg's *The Accumulation of Capital* in 1913. More than 150 years after Marx wrote the former and more than a hundred after Luxemburg wrote the latter, their predictions about the evolution of capitalism have not been realised. While there is much to admire about Luxemburg's commitment to improving the lives of the working classes, I do not think her solutions were either right or realistic. The welfare state and regulation show that a mixed economy can combine the benefits of capitalism with a good society, while the experiments with communism from the Soviet Union to North Korea have utterly failed and inflicted misery on millions. In all of these very different attempts to implement the principles of a communist state, we have ironically seen autocratic governments with little care for the individual worker. In China, the biggest, most powerful and longest-lasting communist state has had to adopt capitalist economic policies in some areas to achieve economic growth, while maintaining a cultural communist ideology. History has shown that despite the best of intentions on the part of those like Rosa Luxemburg, the best option is that proposed by Beatrice Webb, using the democratic system to bring in reforms to make our economy fairer and more equal, without losing the entrepreneurial and competitive advantages of a market economy.

Sisters in Marxism

Rosa Luxemburg was not the only woman taking forward the political and economic work of Karl Marx. Eleanor Marx, Karl Marx's daughter, was born in 1855 in London, where he was living in political exile. Eleanor was nicknamed Tussy by the family, and was raised playing on the floor of her father's study as he wrote *Das Kapital*, and according to her biographer, Rachel Holmes, that childhood experience 'provided her with a thorough grounding in British economic, political and social history. Tussy and *Capital* grew up together.'

This world view would go on to inform her own life and the work she did editing many of her father's works, including the first English edition of *Das Kapital*.

Eleanor Marx seen here with her beloved father Karl,
her elder sisters Jenny and Laura, and their father's
friend and collaborator Friedrich Engels.

Like Luxemburg, and indeed Beatrice Webb and later Joan Robinson, Eleanor Marx believed passionately in the role of trade unions as a way of organising workers and protecting their rights, but also more generally as a means to raise political awareness. She became involved in the Women's Trade Union League after meeting Clementina Black in 1884 and then helped organise the Bryant and May strike of young female matchstick factory workers in 1888 and the London Dock Strike of 1889, speaking at public meetings and to meetings of striking workers. She later helped organise the Gasworkers' Union, the forerunner to today's GMB union, of which I am a member.

Much of her trade union work focused on the unionisation of women and the support of women trade unionists. In the 1890s, for example, Eleanor visited Derry in Ireland where the city's factories were largely staffed by women, to help them organise – a significant political act when you consider that at its peak in the 1920s there were more than forty factories in the city with a workforce of over 18,000 people, the majority of whom were women.

Trade unions were very different then to how they are now. Although there were committed women trade unionists like Eleanor Marx, many trade unions (especially in traditionally male-dominated industries) were chauvinistic, and for all their notional aspirations to equality, the interests of working women were ignored for far too long. A landmark moment in the campaign for greater equality came in 1968 when women machinists at the Ford factory in Dagenham went on strike seeking equal pay with their male colleagues. The union leadership initially resisted their demands and it was only the intervention of the then Secretary of State for Employment and Productivity, Barbara Castle, that led to the strike being resolved with a significant pay increase for the women. For most of the last decade, the Trades Union Congress was led by its first ever female General Secretary, Frances O'Grady until her retirement from the role at the end of 2022. Britain's two biggest trade unions, Unite and Unison are, at the time of writing, also both led by women – Sharon Graham and Christina McAnea respectively. Women like Clementina Black and Eleanor Marx, as well as female politicians like Barbara Castle, helped modernise our trade unions so that they fully represent all workers, not just men.

Like Luxemburg, Eleanor Marx's life was tragically short. She died at the age of forty-three after taking poison when she discovered her partner and fellow socialist Edward Aveling had secretly married a young actress. Also like Rosa Luxemburg, she spent her short life campaigning for socialism and bringing Karl Marx's writings and political philosophy to a wider audience. Practically, through organising, agitating and raising the political conscience of a generation of women workers, her most important contributions were at a grass-roots level in pursuit of greater equality for all, but in particular the rights of women workers.

This cause also links both women with Clara Zetkin, sometimes known as the 'grandmother of communism'. A key figure in the development of communist and socialist ideology, her intervention at the 1898 London conference of the Second International (a gathering of global socialists) on the subjugation of women redefined the intersection of Marxism and feminism. Zetkin argued that the struggle of the working-class woman is closer to the struggle of the proletarian man than that of the bourgeois woman. The bourgeois woman's final aim was 'to break down the barriers that shut her out from free competition' with men, whereas the interests of the proletarian woman were achieved by fighting alongside rather than against the proletarian man. As Zetkin put it, she did not fight for 'the right of free competition with men, but to obtain the political power of the proletariat'.

Zetkin, while a friend of Rosa Luxemburg and the person to whom she sent her last correspondence, is perhaps most closely linked ideologically to Eleanor Marx through their focus on the subjection of women. Eleanor Marx argued for the liberation of the proletariat regardless of gender but noted that women factory workers

> are proletarians and earn a daily wage on which they and their children live in large part; but they are also household slaves, unpaid servants of their husbands, fathers and brothers. Even before going to the factory early in the morning, women have already done so much that if the men had to do it they would consider it a right good piece of work.

These three women are each, in their own right, icons of the socialist movement. Through their collective contribution to the economic and social ideology of Marxism they underscore the fact that an ideology we describe using solely the name of a man could not have survived, or indeed developed to what we understand it as today, without the work of women economists, social activists and trade unionists.

Why Rosa Luxemburg Matters Today

Rosa Luxemburg hardly needs her profile raised. Communists commemorate and celebrate her achievements and for many she remains a martyr to the socialist cause. Luxemburg the economist, however, is not so well understood. If she had only written *The Accumulation of Capital* without putting into practice her revolutionary brand of socialism, she would deserve to be remembered for her contribution to economic thinking about the exploitation inherent in capitalist systems – both of the workers and of less developed countries.

But Luxemburg was an influence not just on Marxist economic thought but also on British social democracy. In 1951 Luxemburg's *The Accumulation of Capital* was published in English. According to Cambridge economist Murray Milgate, the driving force behind the translation was Werner Stark. Stark had fled Prague in 1939 when the Nazis marched in and was sponsored in his move to England by the Society for the Protection of Science and Learning, an organisation largely driven by William Beveridge, researcher to Beatrice Webb and architect of Britain's post-war welfare state. The Society for the Protection of Science and Learning's aim was to help academics fleeing Nazi-occupied Germany – it was later expanded to assist any academics fleeing political persecution – and hundreds of lives were saved through the scheme.

The English translation of Luxemburg's work included an introduction by the Cambridge economist Joan Robinson. The introduction is critical of the assumptions and oversights in Luxemburg's tract, but the last line sums up Robinson's admiration:

'For all its confusions and exaggerations, this book shows more prescience than any orthodox contemporary could claim.'

Robinson focused on two parts of Luxemburg's work in her introduction to the book. First, the propensity of capitalism to suffer from prolonged and deep economic crises – of great interest to Robinson and the 'Cambridge Circus' of Keynesian economists with whom she worked. And second, the theory of economic growth and development, and specifically Luxemburg's insight that capitalist development is a process with its own dynamic. Interestingly, Robinson used the title *The Accumulation of Capital* for her own seminal work on economic growth and modern macroeconomics published in 1956. In doing so, she showed that Keynesian and modern social democratic economics had its roots not just in classical economics but also in socialist democratic economics too.

For me, Luxemburg, like Karl Marx before her, has too simplistic a view of how the economy works: labour versus capital – and no way to move from one category as an individual to the other; no theory of investment or of the dynamism that competition and innovation can bring; little analysis of the role of the state in correcting the excesses of markets. Yet, there is also much to learn from Rosa Luxemburg's analysis today, especially on the damage caused by rentierism in advanced economies, where much of the population earns income through assets like land or stock. Luxemburg is right about the role imperialism played in boosting the profits of domestic firms; she is right about the rents enjoyed by the owners of capital; and she is right about workers not being paid the value of what they produce – and with one in five workers not even paid a living wage this is a pressing policy issue. The share of national income in the UK that goes to capital compared with labour has increased in recent decades; the share of income that goes to the top earners has also been on the rise. These inequalities cannot and should not be casually brushed off as the rewards for success, or the necessary by-product of a thriving market economy. Excessive profits and insufficient wages can be two sides of the same coin, in which case public policy needs to consider its response.

But I would emphasise the importance of the democratic process and observing the rules that govern how economies and societies work rather than the need for revolution or the inevitability of such a revolution. And the experience of revolution, and the dictatorships that follow, have never led to the socialist utopias that were promised; in fact they have often, if not always, led to a decline in the quality of life of ordinary workers. Parliamentary democracy and persuasion are best – and the elections of Joe Biden in the United States, Olaf Scholz in Germany and Anthony Albanese in Australia show that the centre-left can start winning elections again after a period of decline.

We must ensure the tax system is fair, regulation is effective and that the economy supports the public realm. That is why I believe there should be a windfall tax on the excess profits being made by the big oil and gas companies, that we should close the tax loopholes used by private equity fund managers and why the non-domiciled tax status should be scrapped. It's also why I believe the state plays an important role in regulating industry – especially the privatised utilities, the private rented sector and also, for example, cryptocurrencies and other financial products. I am without doubt a Fabian not a Marxist in my sympathies and beliefs, but centre-left parties in power need to tackle the growing inequalities and rising poverty that we see all around us.

5

Joan Robinson and the Global Reach
of Keynesian Economics

When I studied for my master's degree at the London School of Economics I would sometimes wander around Bloomsbury or explore the second-hand bookshops of the Charing Cross Road and imagine what life would have been like seventy-five years previously for the Bloomsbury Group of John Maynard Keynes and his friends, including Virginia and Leonard Woolf, E. M. Forster, Vita Sackville-West and others. I love visiting too the home of Vanessa Bell and Duncan Grant, Charleston House in Sussex, the country retreat of the Bloomsbury Group where legend has it that Keynes once left a Cézanne painting in the woods on his walk from the bus stop to Charleston as it was too heavy to carry. Luckily it was still there when he and Duncan Grant went to collect it the next day.

Joan Robinson was not part of the Bloomsbury Group of thinkers and writers but she was a close associate of Keynes in Cambridge, where the bulk of his economic writing and thinking was done with a small group of economists including Robinson, Richard Kahn, Piero Sraffa and James Meade. Robinson herself was responsible for important economic ideas in the Keynesian tradition, most of all the economic argument for a minimum wage. Labour's implementation of Britain's first national minimum wage in 1999 lifted thousands of working people out of poverty, and gave the dignity of proper reward for work. My predecessor as MP for Leeds West, John Battle, who was a minister in the Department for Trade and Industry when the legislation was taken through parliament, remembers a job description from the local job centre in Leeds before the minimum wage came in: 'Security guard wanted. £1.50 an hour. Bring your own dog.' With the introduction of the minimum wage in 1999, the days of that sort of exploitation were gone. Joan Robinson's economic work thirty years previously made the economic case for the minimum wage.

Early Life

Joan Violet Maurice was born on 31 October 1903, the third child of five siblings to an aristocratic family in Camberley, Surrey. The Maurices, however, were unconventional aristocrats – outspoken and often radical in their views and actions. Her father was a distinguished officer in the army but was sacked from his post in 1918 for writing a letter to *The Times* accusing the government of deceiving the country and parliament about the strength of the British Army going into the First World War. This deception, Maurice argued, had left British soldiers exposed with 'tragic' consequences. Joan Robinson described her upbringing as the 'old liberal tradition, believing in progress and rationality of human behaviour'. She certainly inherited an instinct for controversy, and despite her immense contributions to economic thinking, some of her political views and willingness to speak her mind cost her the Nobel Prize for Economics in 1975. Yet there was also another side to Joan Robinson, shaped by those same family traditions, a humane and caring person who once said that her aim was 'to do a little good here and there to fit in the scales against all the harm'. That was a motto which might have been handed down to her through generations of Maurices, and she did a good job of living up to it.

Coming from a privileged family, Joan attended St Paul's School for Girls in London. While studying, she volunteered at a settlement house for the poor, developing an interest in poverty and its alleviation that lasted a lifetime. From St Paul's, Joan went to Girton College, Cambridge, where she graduated with a degree in economics in 1925. Like Mary Paley Marshall, who had studied at Newnham almost fifty years previously, Joan fell in love with a fellow Cambridge economist, in Joan's case Sir Edward Austin Gossage Robinson, more generally known as Austin Robinson, whom she married in 1926. Unlike Mary's husband Alfred Marshall, Austin Robinson did not seek to hold back his wife's career. Robinson's own words here are revealing: Alfred Marshall, Robinson felt, treated his wife as a 'housekeeper and a secretary'. Austin and Joan Robinson went on to have two daughters but thanks to their relative affluence and her husband's support, domestic responsibilities were never a barrier to Joan's career as an economist or her prolific writing over seven decades.

Shortly after their marriage, the newly-weds moved to Gujurat, India where Austin served as tutor to a young maharajah. For three years Joan Robinson lived a comfortable life in India with staff and many luxuries. But her personal circumstances did not blind her to the poverty that surrounded them. She wrote about this poverty and the economics of development, a field that was less well defined than it is today, and retained a deep interest in it and an affection for India throughout her career, visiting on many occasions after they returned to England.

Back in Cambridge, Austin took up a position as an assistant lecturer, yet despite Joan's own reputation as an economist it took a long time to get the academic recognition and titles that her talents deserved. She taught at Cambridge from 1931 to 1971 but it was not until 1965, aged sixty-two, that she was finally made a professor. She retired in 1971, with honorary positions at Girton and King's College, Cambridge, to follow.

The Cambridge Circus and John Maynard Keynes

The young couple returned to find economics at Cambridge in turmoil. The certainties they had taken for granted as undergraduates, economics according to Alfred Marshall, had been disrupted by a young Italian economist, Piero Sraffa, brought to Cambridge by Keynes to escape Mussolini. Sraffa had shaken the foundations of Marshall's theory of the firm – showing it to be theoretically flawed. Marshall's analysis of the competitive firm relied on the idea of diminishing returns and rising costs limiting the size of the firm. But why do costs rise, asked Sraffa in 1926, when the firm is so small that its growth has no impact on prices, including the price of inputs? 'It is necessary,' Sraffa instead suggested, 'to abandon the path of free competition and turn in the opposite direction, namely, towards monopoly.'

Joan Robinson took up the challenge laid down by Sraffa, and in 1933 published *The Economics of Imperfect Competition*, creating an overnight sensation that made her world famous in the economics profession. Not only did Joan create the new category of 'imperfect competition', but she also created a then entirely novel geometric and mathematical toolkit that is used to this very day.

Joan Robinson's return to England also corresponded with the Western world drifting into a decade-long depression. The depression, the response of Western governments to it and ultimately the work of John Maynard Keynes in describing a better way forward gave purpose to Robinson's career as she helped Keynes develop his thinking and then took his work forward in new and interesting ways.

In 1930, together with her close friend and intellectual companion Richard Kahn, her friend Piero Sraffa, research student James Meade, and her husband Austin Robinson, she formed the famous 'Cambridge Circus' of economists to discuss John Maynard Keynes's recent *Treatise on Money* and his next book, *The General Theory of Employment, Interest and Money*. Kahn and Joan Robinson had become close personally and professionally after the Robinsons returned from India. Kahn was taught by Keynes and followed him as bursar of King's College, Cambridge. His greatest contribution to economics was the 'multiplier theory' – the insight that increases in government spending are multiplied because they ripple through the economy, resulting in even bigger increases in output.

Sraffa himself was a fascinating character. Arriving in England from Italy in 1921, he was already an established economist. Keynes and he became friends, and Sraffa started writing for the *Manchester Guardian* on the recommendation of Keynes. His writing was largely on fiscal and monetary policy in Italy and it caught the attention of Mussolini, who did not like what he read. As a result Sraffa couldn't return to Italy, so Keynes helped him secure a lecturing position and librarian role at Cambridge before he too ended up at Trinity College. Like Keynes, Sraffa was part of the group challenging orthodox Marshallian theories. Sraffa's friends were eclectic and often politically controversial. The philosopher Ludwig Wittgenstein credits Sraffa in his magnum opus *Philosophical Investigations*:

Even more than to this – always powerful and assured – criticism, I am indebted to that which a teacher of this university, Mr P. Sraffa, for many years unceasingly applied to my thoughts. It is to this stimulus that I owe the most fruitful ideas of this book.

Sraffa was also friends with and supportive of the Italian communist Antonio Gramsci, who was imprisoned by Mussolini and died in prison in 1937. While Gramsci was incarcerated, Sraffa sent him writing materials, books and support, and remained connected with the Italian Communist Party for years afterwards.

The five members of the Cambridge Circus met on a weekly basis in the academic year 1930–1 in Richard Kahn's rooms at King's College, Cambridge. They also held regular seminars open to undergraduates. Together they read, discussed and debated Keynes's *Treatise on Money*. All were serious economists who, in many ways, put Keynes's career and ideas before their own. Each week Kahn, as the Circus representative, met with Keynes to provide feedback and a critique. Keynes's subsequent *General Theory of Employment, Interest and Money*, published in 1936, reflects the debates of the Circus. In the introduction, Keynes remarks that 'it is extraordinary what foolish things one can think when one thinks alone' – a reference to the support and guidance that the Cambridge Circus provided him. Robinson was the first to define macroeconomics, which became a separate field of inquiry only with the publication of Keynes's book, as the 'theory of output as a whole'.

Ultimately, Keynes (Marshall's student and protégé) and the Cambridge Circus spearheaded a revolution in economic thinking, challenging the ideas of neoclassical economics that Marshall espoused. Keynes's key argument was that aggregate demand (total spending in the economy) determined the overall level of economic activity, and that inadequate aggregate demand could lead to prolonged periods of high unemployment from which the economy would not automatically rebound. In response to his experience and study of the Great Depression, Keynes advocated the use of fiscal and monetary policies to mitigate the effects of economic recessions and depressions. He argued that although all economics is underpinned by the individual decisions of businesses, workers, consumers and government, it is when it is all put together that you can see the overall health of the economy – the whole being more than the sum of the parts. That was the key insight of Keynes and the Cambridge Circus, who were also interested in the role of government in the macroeconomy in a way that hadn't previously been analysed. John Eatwell, economics professor, former President of Queens' College, Cambridge, and a Labour member of the House of Lords, refers to Kahn and Robinson as 'Keynesian warriors' who took forward Keynes's ideas, especially during the Second World War when Keynes was occupied organising the finances of the war for the British Government.

In an important respect Keynes never quite escaped his Marshallian origins and it was Joan Robinson who in some ways understood the theoretical revolution better than Keynes himself. If a competitive labour market does not clear, she wrote, if labour demand is not equal to labour supply, then it cannot be the case that wages are determined by the balance of Marshallian supply and demand. Joan Robinson would go on to argue that markets also fail to deliver fair wages because the idea that free and competitive markets attain an 'equilibrium' is an illusion in the real world, where perfect competition rarely, if ever, exists.

By the late 1930s, major Western economies like the United States, led by Franklin D. Roosevelt, had begun adopting Keynes's policy recommendations. Almost all capitalist governments had done so by the end of the two decades following Keynes's death in 1946. Crucially, as a leader of the British delegation in the Bretton Woods talks, Keynes participated in the design of the international economic institutions established after the end of the Second World War, negotiated at the Mount Washington Hotel in Bretton Woods, New Hampshire. The outcome of the conference included the creation of the International Monetary Fund, the International Bank for Reconstruction and Development, which is now part of the World Bank, and the system of fixed exchange rates for major trading currencies. The Keynesian consensus guided economic policy right the way until the mid to late 1970s. But following a period of high and persistent inflation, its popularity amongst policymakers declined when, as we will see in the next chapter, Milton Friedman and Anna Schwartz's monetary economics entered the ascendency. In many ways, even today the key economic dividing line is between Friedman's monetarists and demand-side Keynesians. Robinson was certainly clear as to which side she was on, responding to Friedman in a Chicago lecture hall in the 1970s, 'Don't give me that monetarist rubbish!'

China, Mao and the Nobel Prize

Over the ensuing decades Robinson combined her academic work with involvement in policy development. She published *An Essay on Marxian Economics*, and in 1945 was appointed to the Ministry of

Works Advisory Committee on Building Research, the only economist and the only female member of that committee. In 1948, in recognition of her work on monopolies and monopsonies and with Attlee as prime minister and Harold Wilson as the president of the Board of Trade, she was appointed as the first economist member of the Monopolies and Mergers Commission. Her most important work, *The Accumulation of Capital* – its title taken from Rosa Luxemburg's 1913 book – was published in 1956. Meanwhile her interest in politics was increasing, as was her influence, and she made a number of visits to the Soviet Union, China and North Korea, as well as becoming a visiting fellow at the Centre for Development Studies in Thiruvananthapuram, India (the country she had lived in after her undergraduate studies).

In 1969 Robinson wrote a book, *The Cultural Revolution in China*, that damaged her reputation badly. In it she attempted to emphasise the positive aspects of Mao's 'moderate and humane intentions' rather than the 'violence and disorder' that broke out 'from time to time' – occurrences, according to Robinson, that were 'strongly opposed' to Mao's wishes. Mao ranks among the cruellest dictators of the twentieth century; he was responsible for tens of millions of deaths, and for setting China's economic development back by generations. This was an inexcusable position to have taken.

It surely cost her the Nobel Prize, for in 1975 everyone thought Robinson's moment had come. Aged seventy-two and recently retired, she was widely regarded as the most impressive female economist ever to have lived; 1975 had been declared by the United Nations as the Year of the Woman; and articles were being written about Robinson on the assumption that this was her year. But while her colleague and protégé in the Cambridge Circus, James Meade, would receive his own Nobel Prize two years later for his work on international trade and capital flows, and two students who studied under her have won the Nobel Prize for Economics – Amartya Sen and Joseph Stiglitz – Robinson never did. In 1975, the award went to

Leonid Kantorovich and Tjalling Koopmans for their work on the optimum allocation of resources.

The Nobel Prize in Economic Sciences, which was first endowed in 1968, was not awarded to a woman for another thirty-four years: in 2009 it went to Elinor Ostrom who was born in 1933, the year Robinson published *The Economics of Imperfect Competition*, and whose life and work we will come to shortly. Yet while Joan was known after 1975 as the best economist to have never got the Nobel Prize, her reputation as an economic theorist continued to grow after her death in Cambridge in August 1983, and as Robinson's biographer, G. C. Harcourt, observes, she continued the family tradition with distinction, always a rebel with a cause. I think Joan Robinson would have been pleased with that.

Minimum Wages and Monopolies

Joan Robinson's key contribution to Keynesian economics was to challenge the neoclassical economics view that markets tend to a competitive equilibrium – with a large number of buyers and sellers operating. Piero Sraffa wrote about monopolies and their ability to disrupt Marshall's theory and drive up prices and drive down quality and innovation. Robinson argued that the reality was somewhere in between, and that in the real world, markets tended towards imperfect competition, or oligopoly. These theories had huge implications, especially in the theory and practice of labour market economics.

Most people think of monopolies, or indeed imperfect competition as existing in product markets, where there is one seller or producer of electricity, one train company or one water company, for example. These days it is more often one economic search engine or online marketplace. In those markets, economists would argue that such monopoly conditions bid up prices charged to consumers and reduce the quality of the service and the amount of innovation undertaken. The solution is good regulation that requires the producer to do certain things – setting price caps, allowing only a given level of return on investment, setting standards for the quality of the product, and so on. Another key innovation by Joan Robinson was to apply the theory of monopoly and imperfect competition not to the seller of a product or service but to the purchaser – or specifically, a large employer. She termed it 'monopsony'. At its extreme, imagine a town with just one employer. They would be able to set the wage and working conditions. If a worker didn't want to work for that company then there would be no work for that person. It was a world away from Marshallian economics where workers were paid the precise value of what they contributed to production. Robinson argued that workers almost always faced monopsonistic exploitation from employers. And there's a big political and fairness implication here – workers are being underpaid by the market. The labour market is not working and working people are paying the price.

Joan Robinson's theory, set out in her 1933 book *The Economics of Imperfect Competition*, is the strongest economic argument for a minimum wage, a policy that finally came to Britain in 1999 as a key plank of New Labour's 1997 general election campaign. Before then, working people were routinely paid poverty wages, below the value of what they produced, not because their work didn't deserve better pay but because the worker had no power to bargain for it. The monopsony theory is also the best economic case for trade unions. In neoclassical economics, unions are a dangerous disruptor in labour markets because they risk bidding up wages beyond their fair or equilibrium level. The Austrian economist Ludwig von Mises went as far as to argue that the entire function of trade unions was to prevent fair competition for wages by taking action to prevent anyone crossing a picket line. But Joan Robinson turned this on its head. In a world of imperfect competition, where employers have too much power, unions are a good and proper counterbalance helping workers get what they rightfully deserve. Robinson's insights were profound and her approach was controversial and new. According to the economist Duncan Foley, 'she did not just go along', and because of this became 'a rallying point for many people who thought main-stream economics was becoming too apologetic' over inequalities in society and in the economy.

The real-world impact of the practical applications of Robinson's insights have been huge in lifting working people out of poverty. In Britain, according to a 2016 report from the Centre for Public Impact, 'the national minimum wage made a significant impact at the bottom of the income scale – particularly to women, who comprised 70 per cent of the beneficiaries and were not covered by existing collective bargaining agreements before its introduction. There were a million beneficiaries in all.' According to the former chair of the Low Pay Commission, Professor Sir George Bain, the introduction of the national minimum wage heralded 'a fundamental change to the labour market in the UK. There will be a floor to wages for the first time in this country, eradicating the worst cases of exploitation.' The evidence provided by the government also argues that the minimum wage has not only benefited the bottom few per cent of employees, but through an 'upward ripple' effect it has also influenced the pay scales above the minimum, with employees in lower income brackets receiving larger percentage pay increases than those at the middle or top end.

Robinson also used monopsony to describe the wage gap between women and men workers of equal productivity. In *The Economics of Imperfect Competition*, Robinson was the first to apply the economist Arthur Pigou's concept of price discrimination at a product market level to the labour market. She argued that if groups of workers can be distinguished that differ in their labour supply elasticities (that is the extent to which the willingness to work responds to wages), firms will profit from paying different wages to these groups. Women could be seen, according to Robinson, as being less responsive to changes to wages (their labour supply is less 'price elastic', in the economic jargon) due to their domestic duties and needing often to find work that is consistent with these other responsibilities, and they were also, for the same reasons, statistically less likely to be willing to commute than men. Robinson therefore concludes: 'Just as we have price discrimination for a monopolist, so we may have price discrimination for a monopsonist.' Hence, she continued, 'if women's labour supply at the level of the firm is less elastic than men's, women will earn lower wages', especially where men and women are filling different roles, even if at the same skill level and value to the employer. Like Keynes's conclusion at the whole economy level, Robinson's policy observations at the firm level suggested the need for government intervention. Without it, women workers would not be paid fairly, which is why the 1970 legislation on equal pay was so important. But problems in accessing good and affordable childcare and the much greater proportion of women who have caring responsibilities remain part of the reason for the enduring gender pay gap in Britain, and around the world.

Robinson's theory of monopsony continues to be used today – including in the courts. In June 2019, the United States Supreme Court used Robinson's monopsony theory in its decision for Apple v. Pepper. Justice Brett Kavanaugh delivered the majority opinion, stating that Apple can be sued by application developers on the basis of monopsony theory. Increasingly, too, there has been concern that when the big corporate giants set up a warehouse in a deprived area, they can in the end depress wages by driving out the competition and becoming monopsonies. While minimum wages make a difference, we also need to look more closely at the structure of markets, including labour markets. One in five workers in Britain are not paid a proper living wage, even though we have had a statutory minimum wage for twenty-four years.

The share of income that goes to ordinary working people has declined while wages at the top and profits have been on the rise. The beautiful world of symmetries and market equilibria in Marshall's models do not stand up to real-world scrutiny. Ninety years on from the publication of *The Economics of Imperfect Competition*, this is increasingly true.

If I become chancellor, I am determined to ensure that more

people are paid a wage that they can afford to live on. While many businesses have voluntarily signed up to be living wage employers, 4.8 million working people in Britain are still not paid a real living wage. More than two-thirds of children growing up in poverty today are in a household where at least one person works. That's why I will ask the Low Pay Commission, who set the minimum wage, to look at how they can make the minimum wage a real living wage as quickly as possible. As well as being the right thing to do, I was struck by a conversation that I had with an employer in my constituency shortly after I became an MP in 2010. He said to me how pleased he was when the minimum wage came in. He had never been just a minimum wage employer but that choice had meant his costs were higher than his competitors' and that sometimes he didn't win contracts as he was undercut by those who paid poverty wages. The minimum wage, he told me, had provided a 'level playing field', which meant bad employers couldn't undercut good ones. The government has an important role in shaping markets – not just using the tax and benefit system to redistribute, as important as that is.

But there's something else to learn from Joan Robinson here too, and that's on market structures and competition. Robinson is right that markets often tend to imperfect competition, but there is more that government and regulators can do to improve how markets work. Post Brexit, the UK Government has taken on new responsibilities for competition and markets. Those powers must be used to challenge monopolies – whether they are exploiting consumers or workers.

One other observation from Robinson on labour markets is worth noting from her 1936 essay 'Disguised Unemployment' because it is very relevant for today's labour market. Robinson cites an example where demand in the economy weakens and demand for workers falls. But if the welfare state is limited in its support for the unemployed, workers will find an alternative to 'complete idleness', for example 'selling matchboxes in The Strand, cutting brushwood in the jungles, digging potatoes on allotments'. 'A decline in one sort of employment,' she notes, 'leads to an increase of another sort.' But does that mean there is no problem if there is no unemployment as such? Of course there is a problem! Productivity is less, demand in the economy is less, and as wages are less, poverty is greater. It is an example of what Robinson termed 'disguised unemployment'. Too much of our economy today sees workers not afforded the opportunity to use their skills to their full capability, like the matchbox sellers on The Strand. When people with university degrees or who are skilled in a craft are working in call centres or as delivery drivers, they are employed, yes – but fully employed, using all their skills and operating at their productive potential? Surely not. We should be concerned with job quality and productivity, not just the number of jobs.

Economic Growth

While Keynes's work looks at how aggregate demand needs to be influenced by government to achieve full employment, others in the Cambridge Circus, particularly Sraffa and Robinson, were interested in how economies grow and how that could create conditions of equilibria and disequilibria. *The Accumulation of Capital*, probably Robinson's most important work, published in 1956, attempts to answer these questions. The book draws on the contribution of Robinson's four biggest economic influences – Alfred Marshall, the classical economist whose assumptions she challenged; Karl Marx, the socialist economist interested in the labour value of production; John Maynard Keynes, the founder of modern macroeconomics; and Michał Kalecki, a leftist economist from Poland who used mathematical models for economic problems but who had an interest in the social consequences of economic policies.

Robinson's contribution was to argue that economic growth depends on capital accumulation (the use of equipment and machinery) alongside technological progress. Economic growth or progress, Robinson argued, depended on increases in productivity, which come from technical progress, which in turn comes from new types of equipment that firms can get by the accumulation of capital (or the purchase of that new equipment and machinery). When there is a proper balance between capital accumulation, productivity growth and the acquisition of new equipment, then the economy will grow at a steady rate. But there is nothing to determine that economic progress always happens in this way. This has two real-world consequences, the first of which is very important for post-Keynesian economics. If the economy does not grow at a steady rate, then inflation, unemployment and so forth can all occur when the economy grows too quickly or too slowly compared to its average or trend rate. In these circumstances there is a role for government in ensuring that the economy is properly 'managed' to avoid boom and bust. But I think that there is another lesson here too. We need to ensure that technical progress, and the purchase of the new equipment necessary to that progress, happens at an optimal rate, and not assume that the prevailing rate is the only or proper one. Technical progress, and the growth that accompanies it, depends on a high skills economy, with plenty of research and development and the turning of that research into new innovations. Capital is increasingly embodied in labour or people rather than in machinery, or they are complementary – you need the skills to use the technology. Government has a huge role in investing in schools, colleges, universities and lifelong learning, as well as in basic research and infrastructure.

US Treasury Secretary Janet Yellen talks about how modern supply-side economic policies can boost productivity and economic growth. Policies like increasing the number of people available for work (through better childcare and health services) and the skills of the workforce are key. As are policies to increase domestic investment in capital and innovation in the private sector, through for example Labour's proposed Green Prosperity Plan to speed up the transition to a net-zero economy through financing the industries of the future like electric vehicles, carbon capture and storage, and sustainable aviation fuel. Labour's plan will take a strategic approach to the future shape of the economy to set us on a path towards sustainable growth.

Robinson's work as part of the so-called Cambridge Growth Theory group, which she pioneered with economists including Sraffa and Nicholas Kaldor, helped extend Keynesian theory beyond the short and medium run to make it a more comprehensive theory of economic growth and output for the long term, rather than purely focusing on demand management.

Why Joan Robinson Matters Today

Keynesian economics as developed by Robinson is still relevant for policymakers today, and I would argue that the poor performance of the UK economy since 2010 owes a lot to the failure to heed the lessons of Keynesian economics. When David Cameron and George Osborne became prime minister and chancellor respectively in 2010, they embarked on a programme of austerity that went against everything that Keynes (and Robinson) would have advised. As the UK (and global) economies were coming back to life after the Global Financial Crisis, the incoming Conservative government turned off the taps of government spending and investment. Welfare spending was cut, public sector wages frozen, departmental budgets for everything except the NHS cut – in many cases by one-third. Even the NHS suffered the lowest rate of growth in spending since its creation in 1948. The economic recovery which was picking up steam at the end of 2009 and into 2010 was stopped in its tracks. Economic growth stalled and productivity tumbled. Real wages today remain lower than they were in 2010; productivity has fallen behind our major competitors; and business investment, which Keynes described as depending on the 'animal spirits' of business sentiment, is the lowest as a share of the economy of any major industrialised economy. Cameron and Osborne wrongly claimed that the Global Financial Crisis had been caused by excessive government spending. They used this bogus analysis to rein it in for ideological reasons, with disastrous results for defunded public services and economic activity.

Keynes's biographer, Robert Skidelsky, considers why Cameron and Osborne pursued such a response and what was its impact. He believes that the Coalition government justified austerity with two arguments. The first is their claim that the Labour government before had lived 'beyond its means' and left the exchequer with rising debt; from this they argued that an immediate austerity programme was the only way to bring public finances under control. The second argument was that a rigid austerity agenda was the only way to reassure bond markets that Britain would not default on its debts as Greece had. Channelling Keynes, Skidelsky concludes that both arguments were false. Instead he asserts that Osborne had other motives and that the then chancellor seized an opportunity to cut the size of the state:

> The view, long held by the neoliberal right, that state spending stole resources from the productive economy was re-packed for the purposes of austerity as the doctrine that government spending was 'crowding out' more efficient private sector spending, and therefore damaging recovery: a re-statement of the Treasury view of the 1920s which Keynes had exploded with a common-sense argument: in a slump increased government spending does not take resources from the private sector: it brings into use resources which are idle.

The impact of this economic experiment with jobs, wages and productivity was disastrous for the UK economy. In the three years that came after Osborne's 2010 austerity budget designed to cut the deficit, growth stagnated. While the supporters of austerity blamed this stagnation on what they termed 'headwinds' – the

Eurozone crisis, higher oil prices among other global events – the Office for Budget Responsibility (OBR), set up by the Osborne Treasury to monitor its performance, calculated austerity reduced GDP growth by 1 per cent in 2010–11 and another 1 per cent in 2011–12. Skidelsky calculates that extrapolating these OBR figures puts the cumulative cost of austerity since 2010 at 5 per cent of GDP. Some economists, such as Simon Wren-Lewis of Oxford University, go even further and argue that 10–15 per cent is a more realistic figure. As a result of the Osborne austerity agenda between 5 and 15 per cent of British output has been lost permanently. Even at the conservative estimate of 5 per cent, £100 billion has been lost – the equivalent of £1,500 for every citizen.

This disastrous programme of austerity for the UK economy, and its ongoing impact on growth, productivity, poverty, living standards and public services, could, I am certain, have been avoided with a focus on boosting growth and confidence rather than sucking demand out of a fragile economy. In the end you can't get the budget deficit and national debt down without economic growth. And so despite swingeing cuts on public services and falls in incomes and benefits, national debt is twice the level today than when the Conservatives came to power in 2010.

Economics and What We Value

My economic thinking has been heavily influenced by Keynes's macroeconomics; and his thinking was in turn heavily influenced by Joan Robinson. But, as well as her macroeconomic theoretical contributions, Robinson also made an important observation about ideology and economics.

In her 1962 study, *Economic Philosophy*, Robinson argues that economics is not just a technical discipline, outside the realm of normative values. Instead, every economic model or set of assumptions is based on some value set. Robinson urged economists and

Joan Robinson in 1961. The most famous economist not to be awarded the Nobel Prize, she is widely recognised as one of the most influential economists of the twentieth century.

policymakers to be honest about that, so that the value set underpinning the arguments, and not just the conclusions from the models, could be debated. This makes sense to me. Before I started studying economics I had positioned myself on the political centre-left. I have always been much more attracted to the ideas of Keynes over Friedman – and those of Christina Romer over Carmen Reinhart. That reflects my own value set as much as it does the rigour of one economist or another. And I don't think that it undermines the discipline of economics in any way. Economic models and views of human nature and the good society are political, moral and economic questions. Amartya Sen, who wrote his thesis under Robinson's supervision, is probably the economist who best describes this, in his 1987 book *On Ethics and Economics*.

Economics, Sen argues, is not a discipline separate from philosophy or politics but one based on underlying assumptions about the good society. He believed in a humanised economics, looking past the graphs and instead at the people and families behind them, stating: 'Poverty is not just a lack of money; it is not having the capability to realise one's full potential as a human being.' Another insight comes from Robinson's *Economic Philosophy*: that economists tend to ignore that which does not have a monetary value. Care within the family does not have a monetary value, so economists have too often ignored it. As we have seen above, the politician and social reformer Eleanor Rathbone understood this, and sought to address it, for example by campaigning for an income for mothers to recognise their unpaid work in the home – the family allowance. Just because something is not paid, or paid at a low rate, does not make it low value, economically or socially.

In my 2018 pamphlet *The Everyday Economy*, I argue that there is much work that is undervalued and underpaid but essential for a good society and a functioning economy. Sectors such as care, cleaning, food production, distribution, transport and retail are foundational for the whole economy. The most productive city bank, cutting-edge research lab or factory production line can only function if you have transport to get there, cleaners and security to keep it clean and safe, carers to look after the workers' children, elderly parents or other dependants, and people ensuring the lights come on and the taps run. For too long these jobs have been underappreciated, but the pandemic shone a spotlight on these key workers. Mainstream economics does too little to understand these sectors and jobs, and politicians tend to prefer the construction sites or high-tech labs over the retail and care sectors when they are deciding their industrial strategies. These omissions are a mistake, and I think that Joan Robinson understood that. Even if an economic model can explain why a carer is paid £9 an hour and a city-trader £500, or a footballer even more, it doesn't make it right. What we value isn't always reflected in markets. We clapped for carers during the pandemic, not management consultants.

Another area where markets are not good at calculating true value is the environment and climate change. Even when value is assigned, it is almost impossible to know whether it is of the right order of magnitude. Economics might be described by some as a scientific discipline, but questions of values are rightly at the heart of it – whether we like it or not. These issues are considered by economists such as Elinor Ostrom and Kate Raworth, whom I discuss below in Chapter 7.

Like most of the women in this book, Joan Robinson was a trailblazer. Living and working in an era when women in academia – and in particular economics – were even more of a rarity, it is unsurprising that women who would come to define economics as we know it treasured other awe-inspiring female academics and pioneers as confidantes, supporters and friends. Just as Mary Paley Marshall had an ally in Florence Keynes, Robinson had a network of female academics – both in and outside of economics – to whom she could relate.

Robinson spent every Christmas in Kerala in southern India, escaping the English weather and spending time at the home of her close friend Sita Narasimhan, a fellow and lecturer of English at Cambridge and the first woman of colour to be a Senior Member of Newnham College. Such was the admiration she had for Joan Robinson that in 1983 she penned a biographical essay entitled 'Joan Robinson: In the Radical Vein. A Laywoman's Homage' for the *Cambridge Journal of Economics*.

A woman who perhaps appealed to the rebellious instinct alive in the Robinson family was Joan's friend Elizabeth (G. E. M.) Anscombe. Born in Ireland, raised in England and regarded by some as one of the most important philosophers of the twentieth century, Anscombe is known for her translation of Wittgenstein's *Philosophical Investigations*. Anscombe was Chair of Philosophy in Cambridge in 1970, and remained there until her retirement in 1986. Consistently described as 'outspoken', she is credited with prompting *The Chronicles of Narnia* author C. S. Lewis's pivot from theology to children's literature after losing a debate to her at the Oxford Socratic Club. She protested the decision of Oxford University to award an honorary degree to US President Harry S. Truman on the basis that he had murdered the people of Hiroshima and Nagasaki. She refused to take her husband's last name and usually wore tunics and trousers accompanied by a monocle. Once, when entering a smart restaurant in Boston, she was told that ladies were not admitted in trousers, so she took them off there and then!

Perhaps the woman in Robinson's circle with whom she had the most affinity was Ruth Cohen. A fellow economist, Ruth arrived at Newnham College in 1926 and after her degree and a Commonwealth Fund Fellowship in the United States at Stanford and Cornell, she returned to the UK to work for the Agricultural Economic Research Institute in Oxford. She remained in Oxford until 1939, when she returned to her alma mater, Newnham College. However she was almost immediately called away on war service to serve in London as an economist at the Ministry of Food, and later temporarily at the Board of Trade. She returned to Cambridge in 1945 and retired as a Lecturer in Economics in 1972. Cohen was the first Jewish principal of an Oxbridge College – Newnham – from 1954 to 1972. Outside of academia, Cohen was a committed member of the Labour Party, later serving as a Labour councillor.

Robinson was part of a movement of women who were breaking boundaries in the pre- and post-war eras, a network of trailblazing pioneers unafraid of the societal limitations imposed on them because of their gender. It was the esteemed US diplomat Madeleine Albright who said, 'There is a special place in hell for women who don't help other women,' and it is heartening to know that so many of the incredible women in this book had their own female support system on which to rely and, like we are today, be inspired by.

6

Anna Schwartz and the Mixed Blessings
of Monetary Economics

My first job after university was at the Bank of England in 2000. My macroeconomics tutor at university, Chris Allsopp, had told me that the Bank was the finishing school for economists, and I wanted to be an economist so it seemed the obvious next step. I will never forget my first day at the Bank. The doormen who greet you at the entrance on the other side of the great iron doors of the Old Lady of Threadneedle Street wear pink tail coats and top hats, and the great marble stairs, high ceilings and echoing spaces of the public areas are in sharp contrast with the warren of corridors and crowded desks of the back office. As part of the induction programme we were taken deep into the vaults where vast numbers of gold blocks, like bricks, are stored. It is a place steeped in history, but as the age of low interest rates appears to be drawing to a close, the relevance of the Bank for our everyday lives – our mortgage payments, credit card bills and more – is very real.

Part of the reason I applied for a job at the Bank of England rather than going into the City was that I was already fascinated by the challenges of creating economic policy that worked. When Gordon Brown became Chancellor of the Exchequer in 1997 he promised that there would be 'no more boom and bust' – a good description of the economic approach of Tory governments over the previous eighteen years. Despite the financial services boom in the City, unemployment had reached three million on two occasions, and interest rates peaked at 12 per cent when sterling crashed out of the European Exchange Rate Mechanism in 1992. Although I was only thirteen at the time, I remember the 'For Sale' signs and the fear that ordinary people felt watching interest rates climb, wondering if they would be able to make their monthly mortgage payments and sick with worry if they couldn't that their homes would be repossessed. We've seen the Tory pattern of 'boom and bust' economics played out in this century too – with little boom and continued bust. While Liz Truss and Kwasi Kwarteng's 'mini-budget' may not have survived long after its announcement, its effects will be felt by many for years to come as the spike in interest rates they caused sees the Tory mortgage bombshell for first-time buyers and those remortgaging paying the price.

Gordon Brown's first act as chancellor was to grant operational independence to the Bank of England for setting interest rates to meet the inflation target set by parliament. The Bank of England's Monetary Policy Committee (MPC) makes decisions about interest rates. The MPC includes the Bank's governor, three deputy governors and its chief economist. While a representative from the Treasury can attend the eight annual meetings of the MPC throughout the year to keep the committee up to date with government economic policy, they do not vote. When the MPC makes a decision, it is reflective of, and recorded as, the votes of each individual member, rather than prescribing a consensus to the committee, and in a tie the governor has the casting vote. A committee member in the minority when a vote is taken is always asked what policy they would have preferred, and these votes are published. I remember when Gordon Brown enacted these monumental changes to the functioning of our economy. It was exciting, having campaigned for New Labour and then begun working at the Bank, to have been part, in a small way, of both the delivery and aftermath of that new dawn of economic policy.

Inflation targeting, and setting interest rates to achieve it, became popular in economic circles after the failure of monetarism in the early 1980s in Britain and America. Monetarism, as described by Milton Friedman and Anna Schwartz, sets a target for the growth of the money supply (the amount of currency circulating in the economy) to deliver stable prices and economic growth. In both the US and the UK monetarism worsened deep recessions caused by failed conservative economic policies and, in the UK, brought the highest unemployment and destruction of industry ever experienced before or since: a shameful legacy that still scars communities, particularly in the North of England where industry was decimated and working people condemned to the scrapheap with limited alternatives to sustain them. And not only that, but the relationship between money and prices started to break down soon after the money targets were introduced.

Of course money matters, but it's not all about the money supply, the money circulating in the economy. When I was at the Bank of England there were five key divisions who advised the Monetary Policy Committee. Only one of the five divisions had an explicit remit to look at money and markets. Money was *one* of the variables that the MPC looked at, as it is only *one* of the indicators for what will happen to inflation over the two-year forecast horizon. The economists Milton Friedman and Anna Schwartz on the other hand argued that it is *only* money that matters for inflation. If life was as simple as just controlling the amount of money in circulation then you would need an algorithm not a central bank. Inflation targeting is not easy and money is not the only variable that affects inflation, but there is no simple short cut to economic stability, something that Gordon Brown wrestled with in 2007 when the global financial system collapsed.

In today's economic environment with sustained higher inflation and interest rates, some are calling into question the Bank of England's mandate. But I have been clear: the Labour Party will not interfere with the operational independence of the Bank of England, because history teaches us that that will only lead to higher inflation and higher interest rates. Rather than the chaos and short-term fixes on offer from the Conservative Party, Labour's approach will be based on providing certainty and stability, including through supporting operational independence of the Bank of England.

Despite my disagreements with a purely monetarist approach, Anna Schwartz was a remarkable woman who pioneered new methods of data collection and showed how money matters in the economy. When Milton Friedman got the Nobel Prize for Economics it was an injustice that Schwartz didn't get it too. But it would be fair to say that while I am able to admire her achievements and her intellect, Anna Schwartz's monetarism is something that I react against in my economic thinking and policy rather than finding inspiration from it.

Early Life

Anna Jacobson was born in the Bronx area of New York in 1915, the daughter of Eastern European Jewish immigrants in search of a better life. Her father, Hillel Jacobson, was a manager in the kosher meat department of a shop and was also a local rabbi. Her mother, Pauline Shainmark Jacobson, was a housewife looking after Anna and her four siblings.

Anna first became interested in economics in high school, later recalling that 'the questions [they] talked about in the class seemed so vital'. By the time she was just eighteen Anna had graduated in economics from Barnard College – the women's college of Columbia University in New York City – earning a master's degree a year later. By twenty-one she was married, to Isaac Schwartz, an accountant and fellow Columbia University graduate whom she had met at a Hebrew summer camp. They raised four children together.

Reflecting on family life, Schwartz remembered a former boss and Columbia professor, Arthur Burns, advising her to stop at two children. 'Don't have any more children,' he said, 'or you won't have time for anything else.' She was also advised not to take up the

opportunity to work with Milton Friedman because she was preg-
nant and so her 'productivity would be lower'. Combining motherhood and work, Schwartz reflected, meant having boundaries: 'I was
a mother when I was at home, and when I was in the office I was
doing what I wanted to do.' It is worth remembering that women
at senior levels in business, politics and academia in the 1940s and
1950s were still very rare – combining their career with a family even
more so.

Business Cycles and the NBER

Straight out of university, Schwartz went to Washington, on the recommendation of the woman who taught her statistics at Barnard
College, for a brief stint with the US Department of Agriculture.
Decades later Schwartz reflected on how significant the opportunity to leave New York had been, not just to go to Washington
but also to gather data on farming in the Southern states, where
she helped small groups collate data for a broad study. The use of
big data sets and combining different data sources would become
incredibly important for Schwartz in her work on monetary
statistics with Milton Friedman in the 1960s and for the rest of her
career.

After Washington, Schwartz returned to work at the Social Sciences
Research Council back at Columbia. She worked as a professional
economist for seventy years, and after her spell in Washington and at
Columbia University her career was almost entirely at the National
Bureau of Economic Research (NBER) in New York, where she
took a job in 1941.

The NBER was and remains an important think tank and research
organisation, primarily concerned with dating business cycles (the
cycles by which an economy grows and then contracts) and crucially recessions, looking at a range of data including GDP, industrial
production and employment. For a year and a half in the early

2000s, I was seconded from the Bank of England to work at the British Embassy in Washington. It was just after the terrorist attacks of 9/11 and my job was to analyse what was happening in the US economy for the Bank and UK Treasury. The NBER was the go-to place for economic analysis, and analysts like me would wait in anticipation for the NBER's conclusions on whether or not the economy had slipped into recession – and when subsequently it emerged.

Schwartz's first big break came in 1940 with the chance to work with her Columbia professor, Arthur Gayer, and another young researcher, Walt Whitman Rostow. Gayer had previously been at Oxford University, where he studied British unemployment and was particularly interested in business cycles. In a 2004 interview for the journal *Macroeconomic Dynamics*, Schwartz credits Gayer as the person who introduced her to monetary economics. Together they produced the monumental *Growth and Fluctuations in the British Economy, 1790–1850: An Historical, Statistical, and Theoretical Study of Britain's Economic Development*. But although it was completed in the early 1940s, its publication was delayed by the Second World War for a decade, largely because of paper rationing.

Despite her huge contribution and the scale and originality of the work, Schwartz was initially denied the PhD that she had expected because of the project's collaborative nature. Schwartz's own reflections on this are illuminating. In an interview she revealed the difficulties of convincing Columbia's Professor Arthur Burns (the same man who had recommended against Schwartz having a large family, and a future chairman of the US Federal Reserve) that her work merited a doctorate. 'The expectation was that this British study would yield my dissertation,' remembered Schwartz:

> But Arthur Burns who was the business cycle person (and responsible for awarding the PhDs at Columbia) objected to my using a part of the final manuscript of the British study as my dissertation, [saying that] it had to be an independent study . . . I finally

did get a PhD on the basis of the joint work with Friedman [but] even then, Burns said 'Well, are we setting a precedent by permitting someone to offer joint work for a dissertation?' ... I had probably done more work on it than anyone does on a dissertation.

In 1964, aged forty-eight, and twenty years after her study on UK business cycles was completed, Schwartz finally got her PhD.

Collaboration with Friedman

One of Schwartz's first jobs at the NBER was to put together a time series on US money – measuring the money supply at regular intervals with a goal of tracking how it influenced the US economy as a whole. Schwartz got to work, first looking at currency data and then the bank deposit series. It was at this point, in 1950, that the project leader at the NBER asked, 'What would you think if Milton Friedman were to join you on the money project?'

Schwartz recollected in an interview fifty years later that she had met Friedman just once before this proposition was put to her. In the early 1940s Schwartz's son had just grown out of his stroller. The Friedmans needed one for their child but the war meant that they were hard to come by. Through mutual friends the two families were connected and met on Schwartz's doorstep where the stroller was exchanged. It is not clear whether money passed hands.

Milton Friedman and Anna Schwartz embarked on a professional partnership that would span the next half-century, and shake up macroeconomics in a way that only John Maynard Keynes had ever done before. For almost the whole period of their collaboration they were based in different cities: Schwartz in New York and Friedman in Chicago. They communicated by mail, sending data sets and revisions by post. But it was a partnership that worked, matching Friedman's theoretical genius with Schwartz's empirical knowledge and research skills. Schwartz was a master of data before computing and the automation of the twenty-first century's era of 'big data' revolutionised – and, for the economist, simplified – economic research. If their *Monetary History of the United States* were written today, it would be a book with a vastly different research process – and a much easier one at that. During the research, Schwartz was managing an incredible amount of data, long before the dawn of even the Excel spreadsheet. She was at her core data-driven and Friedman simply could not have produced the work he is credited for without Schwartz's grasp of data and her skill in handling and interpreting enormous sets sprawled across pages of paper spreadsheets, tracing rows and columns by hand. While Friedman developed the theory of monetarism and was awarded the Nobel Prize, it was Schwartz who found the data, crunched the numbers and, like so many of the women in this book, went without due recognition.

When Schwartz studied at Columbia she, like all other students of macroeconomics, read Keynes, and his *General Theory* and macroeconomic framework were influential on her when she co-authored the study on British business cycles. By the time it was reprinted in 1975, however, Schwartz had come to repudiate some of the monetary analysis in the book. Her co-author, Walt Rostow, still a committed Keynesian, was less convinced by Schwartz's change of view. But by then Schwartz, along with Friedman, was on a collision course with Keynesianism which, as inflation began to take off in the late 1970s was falling out of favour. Into that space entered monetarism.

In an interview with the Federal Reserve Bank of Minneapolis in 1993, Schwartz looked back on how radical what they were saying was:

> Taking seriously changes in the quantity of money was not a mainstream position. Our emphasis on the quantity of money, not interest rates, as the variable to measure monetary policy

was unusual. Our finding that monetary policy played a central role in US cyclical developments was met with disbelief by many economists.

Even though many still reject the simplicity of the relationship between money and prices, there is no doubt that economics and policymaking have been deeply influenced by some of what Friedman and Schwartz said and did.

Monetarism

Monetarists argue that the money supply is the chief determinant of short-run economic activity and in the longer term the price level. To quote Friedman and Schwartz: 'Inflation is always and everywhere a monetary phenomenon.'

Underlying monetarism is the 'Quantity Theory of Money': $MV=PQ$, where M is the supply of money; V is the velocity of turnover of money (the number of times per year that the average pound in the economy is spent for goods and services); P is the average price level; and Q represents the quantity of goods and services produced. The theory is an 'accounting identity' – that is, the two sides of the equation must always balance. Monetarists believe that monetary policy alone controls the price level.

On the basis of statistical analysis by Schwartz, monetarists argue that the velocity of circulation of money (V) is constant or predictable and that Q is defined by the equilibrium of supply and demand. This then means that an increase in the money supply would be followed by an increase in the price level in the long run. But in the short run, if we increase the total amount of currency in circulation in the economy (M), there will be temporary effects not only on economic output (Q) but also on employment, because wages and prices will take time to adjust. Thus, while businesses will increase their output to meet the increase in demand due to people having more money to spend, prices and wages will catch up, and as Q settles down at the market clearing (or full employment level), businesses will pass on these cost increases to the consumer with higher prices. So although people may earn more when we increase the amount of money in circulation, they will soon be paying more for goods as well.

Most importantly, Friedman and Schwartz contend that to promote economic stability in terms of inflation and growth, the government should control the rate of growth of the money supply. Everything else adjusts as in an automatically functioning mechanism. Control of the money supply could be achieved by following a simple rule where the amount of currency in the economy is increased at a constant annual rate linked to the potential growth of the economy.

One of the problems with this Quantity Theory of Money is that it gained popularity in policy during the government of Margaret Thatcher and Nigel Lawson – at a time when the increasing availability of ATMs and the increasing popularity of credit cards meant that V (the velocity of money's circulation) was not stable in the way Schwartz and Friedman believed. Thatcher's monetarist experiment failed partly because of this failure to marry theory with reality – exposing one of the key problems with monetarism to be its reliance on theory above all else.

Although monetarism gained in importance in the 1970s, it was critiqued by the school of thought that it sought to replace: Keynesianism. Keynesians believe that demand for goods and services is the key to economic output. They argue that monetarism fails as an adequate explanation of the economy because velocity is inherently unstable (as illustrated above) and the level of employment does not automatically adjust to the full employment level, so simply trying to control the money supply is too simplistic. Because the economy is subject to deep swings and periodic instability, it is dangerous to make central banks a slave to a rigid money target – central banks should have some leeway or 'discretion' in conducting policy.

But, by the 1970s, a decade characterised by high and rising inflation and slow economic growth, and a quarter-century domination of Keynesianism after the Second World War, people and policymakers were looking for new insights and answers. Because Keynesianism prioritises demand management as an economic tool, successive governments failed to grip profound weaknesses on the supply side of the British economy. Monetarism's ascendance was brief. In the 1980s and 1990s the velocity of circulation of money became highly unstable with unpredictable periods of growth and decline. The link between the money supply and prices and GDP broke down, and the usefulness of the Quantity Theory of Money came into question.

Although most economists today reject the singular focus on controlling the amount of money in circulation that is at the heart of monetarist analysis, some important tenets of monetarism have

Anna Schwartz collaborated with a number of co-authors, most famously Milton Friedman, and made significant contributions to both economic theory and policy.

found their way into modern economic analysis, muddying the distinction between monetarism and Keynesianism that was most pronounced during the 1980s. Money supply does have an important effect on inflation, and controlling inflation should be the primary responsibility of central banks.

Central bankers will mostly maintain that monetarism as an approach is just impractical; that experience shows monetary targeting is not a panacea – either because we cannot define what the 'quantity of money' we seek to control is or, once we do define it, we cannot control it as we imagined. Central bankers will point to the fallout from direct quantitative monetary targeting in the US and the UK in the late 1970s and early 1980s to illustrate their case. In October 1979, for example, the US Federal Reserve moved to a form of monetary base control. The episode lasted for three years, until September 1982. Former central banker Charles Goodhart points out that in that period the volatility of short-term interest rates increased fourfold. This is where central bankers usually come down on their assessment of monetarism: that with monetary controls in place there is much greater market volatility, without any particular success in achieving a more stable path for economic output or inflation.

The Great Depression

The book that Friedman and Schwartz published in 1963, *A Monetary History of the United States, 1867–1960*, was a history of money and the economy as well as a manifesto of sorts. It included a chapter on the Great Depression of the 1930s, entitled 'The Great Contraction', which was so influential it was later published as a separate book. In it, Friedman and Schwartz argue that poor monetary policy by the US central bank, and specifically a failure by the Federal Reserve to increase the money supply and understand contagion from bank failures, were the primary causes of the Great Depression, and the Federal Reserve's gravest of errors.

First and foremost, Friedman and Schwartz argued that the correct response of the Federal Reserve during the Great Depression should have been to increase the money supply to support the economy and fight deflation. Schwartz argues that the Fed didn't understand the scale of the problem and worried about the wrong things – price inflation and stoking a boom through an expansionary approach – despite the evidence that showed that the biggest risk at that point was deflation and deep recession.

But they also point to failures in how the Fed responded to the banking crisis itself. It took too long for the authorities to see that the bank failures at the end of 1930 were different to those that had gone before, and this led to a collapse in confidence regarding the creditworthiness of the system as a whole that year. They argue that a failure to identify the seriousness of the situation – both in terms of the collapse in demand and the fragility of the financial system – was the reason for the severity of the Great Depression. 'The economy was dying at its feet and the Fed had no clear vision of what it should do,' Schwartz lamented.

NBER economist Hugh Rockoff describes *A Monetary History* as 'surely one of the most important books in economic history, and indeed, in all economics . . . It has had a profound impact on the way economists think.'

Challenging the Fed

Arthur Burns, Schwartz's old boss at the NBER, became Chairman of the Federal Reserve Bank from 1970 and presided over the central bank until 1978, which despite some of his lack of support earlier in her career, gave her a way in. In 1973, Schwartz, along with two other monetarist economists – Allan Meltzer, from the University of Pittsburgh, and Karl Brunner, Economics Professor at the University of Rochester in New York, and previously at Zurich, the LSE and Chicago – founded the Shadow Open Market Committee (SOMC), to make their own recommendations on what actions the Fed should be taking, but from a monetarist perspective. It was Schwartz's first involvement in the field of economic policymaking and it brought her into contact with both policymakers and the press, who Schwartz felt were sceptical about monetarism because they either didn't understand it or thought it would mean higher unemployment – a criticism of monetarism that she disputed, at least in the long run.

It was not until the late 1970s, with inflation in double digits, that monetarism, and Friedman and Schwartz's ideas, started to gain traction, with the SOMC making the argument that the Fed needed to control the growth of the money supply to get a grip on inflation. In 1979, Democrat President Jimmy Carter appointed Paul Volcker, previously economic advisor to Republican President Richard Nixon, as Federal Reserve Bank chairman, to get a grip on inflation, which peaked at 14.8 per cent in March 1980, but fell below 3 per cent by 1983.

The Fed restricted the money supply, in accordance with the Friedman-Schwartz rule, to tame inflation and they succeeded. Inflation subsided, but at the cost of a big recession. When Margaret Thatcher was elected prime minister in Britain in 1979, she implemented monetarism as the weapon against rising prices in the UK too – again, with the result of a recession and cripplingly high levels of unemployment.

Back in the US, the Federal Reserve led by Volcker raised interest rates to a peak of 20 per cent in 1981, which led to recession with unemployment rising to over 10 per cent. Volcker's Federal Reserve board experienced political attacks and protests due to the effects of high interest rates on the construction, farming and industrial sectors, culminating in indebted farmers driving their tractors into Washington and blockading the Fed. This harsh monetary policy stance eased in 1982, helping lead to a resumption of economic growth. Schwartz supported the action taken by Volcker in his first few years, but criticised him for ending the disinflationary policy too early.

Under Volcker's successor, Alan Greenspan, Schwartz was also disappointed, criticising the Fed for focusing too much on changes in the 'real economy, particularly the unemployment rate', as she said in a 1993 interview, rather than on the money supply, which she continued to maintain was the best determinant of economic growth and prices. In the aftermath of the global financial market crash in 2007, Schwartz argued that the Fed had been too sanguine about excessive mortgage lending, a housing bubble and a failure to price risk properly. While hindsight is a wonderful thing, it is interesting that Schwartz heaps so much blame at the door of the Fed rather than the investment banks developing and profiting from strategies built on the dodgy foundations of the subprime mortgages and opaque derivative trading that were responsible for the financial crisis. In the heat of the crisis Schwartz's key policy recommendation was that the banks and other financial firms should not be bailed out. This conclusion also sits oddly with her analysis of the Great Depression, in which she blames the Fed for not understanding the risks of contagion, which were surely as present in 2008 as they were in 1930.

But Schwartz's greatest criticism is reserved for Greenspan's successor, Ben Bernanke, who served as Chairman of the Fed from 2006 to 2014. Bernanke won the Nobel Prize in 2022 for work on the cause of the Great Depression and the role of bank failures in both deepening and prolonging the recession. His studies build on the groundwork laid by Schwartz and Friedman. Bernanke admits himself that his intense interest in the period began after reading *A Monetary History* and, as Fed chairman, mentioned the work of Friedman and Schwartz in his decision to lower interest rates and increase the money supply to stimulate the economy during the global recession that began in 2007 in the United States.

Writing in the *New York Times* in 2009 in an article entitled 'Man Without a Plan', however, Schwartz made two key criticisms of Bernanke's first term as Governor. First, that while it had been right to slash interest rates as the recession took hold at the outset of the financial crisis of 2007–8, they were then too slow to start raising rates as recovery got underway, thus keeping lending cheap, which risked too much credit being taken out, sowing the seeds of the next crisis. The second criticism was of the role of the Fed in causing the financial crisis in the first place – a criticism that could be extended to Bernanke's predecessor, Alan Greenspan. As a regulator, the Fed had taken far too benign a view of mortgage-backed securities, Schwartz argued, providing no guidance or warnings to buyers about their value – which in many cases turned out to be almost zero as borrowers began to default on their subprime mortgages, spinning the global economy on its axis. When the house of cards came tumbling down, Schwartz accused the Fed of having no plan, behaving inconsistently and pursuing the wrong response in trying to boost liquidity when what was needed was a clear plan and certainty about which institutions were solvent and which were not.

Some of the criticism of central bankers as regulators are fair – but as an ardent free-marketeer, Schwartz struggles to make a credible case for further regulation when so much of her own career had been built on policies linked to the opposite.

Even less convincing is her argument that a contractionary monetary policy (to reduce inflation by reducing the money supply) was needed sooner after the financial crisis. Prominent monetarists, including Schwartz, argued that the ongoing monetary stimulus would lead to extremely high inflation. Instead, velocity of circulation of money dropped sharply and deflation was a much more serious risk.

While Bernanke was at the helm of the Federal Reserve Bank during the response to the global financial crisis, newly elected President Obama brought in another economist who studied the cause of, and recovery from, the Great Depression to help manage the administration's response to the crisis: Christina Romer became chair of the Council of Economic Advisors. Born in Illinois, Romer studied economics at the College of William and Mary and went on to obtain a PhD in economics from MIT in 1985. After a few years as an assistant professor at Princeton, Romer moved to the University of California, Berkeley, where she remains, and has an adjoining office with her husband and close collaborator, David Romer. Much like Schwartz, Christina Romer is deeply involved with the NBER, serving as the co-director of its Program in Monetary Economics and sitting on its Business Cycle Dating Committee.

Christina Romer was key to the US recovery from the financial crisis, attempting to put into practice the lessons from her own research into the Great Depression. Romer argued that the fiscal measures in President Roosevelt's New Deal package were insufficient, with recovery influenced more by devaluation of the dollar and attracting European capital to America, and proposed a stimulus package worth $1.8 trillion to help the economic recovery after the global financial crisis. Although it was reduced to $800 billion before it was sent to Congress, Romer and other policymakers drafting the administration's plan for how to bounce back from the recession are due credit for the US recovery from the recession, which was faster than that in Britain and other economies which instead pursued paths of austerity.

Bank Failures and Moral Hazard

Ben Bernanke said that the Fed would not make the same mistakes during the financial crisis as they did during the Great Depression, but Schwartz criticised the central bank for learning the wrong lessons – namely that the state must quickly come to the rescue of failed banks to stop contagion and a run on the banks.

One of the conclusions set out by Friedman and Schwartz in *A Monetary History* was that deposit insurance (the federal insurance system that protects savers in the event of a banking collapse) was one of the greatest successes of Roosevelt's New Deal after the Great Depression. Friedman and Schwartz felt it provided a degree of stability and confidence in the financial system and contributed to the sharp decline in bank failures in the aftermath of the Depression.

But it was a view that Schwartz revisited in the 1970s and 1980s when bank failures started to increase. Later Schwartz argued that the explanation for financial stability 'seems to be that a relatively stable world price level until the mid 1960s contributed to sound banking. Sound credit analysis depends on the assumption of price stability,' she reasoned, and 'unexpected price changes can invalidate the assumptions underlying bank lending and investing'.

Schwartz changed her opinion on financial regulation, emphasising not the role of regulation or federal insurance schemes in providing stability, but instead arguing that low and stable inflation is what is essential for financial stability. In a break from her previous work, Schwartz began to de-emphasise the impact of business failures on the real economy, arguing that they do not have major consequences for the economy if their effects are prevented from spreading through the financial system. Individual institutions, she argued, should be allowed to fail and ought not to be supported with taxpayers' money.

The Two Mothers of Monetarism

People tend to associate monetarism with Milton Friedman, but *A Monetary History of the United States*, the key textbook that first outlined the theory, was written by both Friedman and Schwartz – and was the first of three books that they jointly authored on the topic. As Friedman once observed, their relationship was 'an almost perfect collaboration': 'Anna did all of the work, and I got most of the recognition.' That 'recognition' included the 1976 Nobel Prize for Economics, which was awarded to Friedman with no reference to the contribution Schwartz made. It would be another thirty-three years after Anna Schwartz was snubbed by the Nobel

Committee (and of course after Joan Robinson also missed out the previous year for her work on economic growth) that the first woman would be awarded the Nobel Prize in Economics – Elinor Ostrom in 2009.

Schwartz was not the only woman with whom Milton Friedman worked. In stark contrast to the 'collaboration by mail' that characterised the Schwartz-Friedman partnership, Friedman's other woman co-author was his wife, Rose. Rose Friedman emigrated to the United States from what is now Ukraine as a baby. After graduating from the University of Chicago with a BPhil, she met Milton Friedman in 1932 when the pair were both graduate students in economics. Their marriage lasted sixty-eight years. Much like Anna Schwartz, Rose Friedman's path to a PhD was not as linear as her husband's. She completed all of the required work for the degree except a dissertation, and while she continued to work with her husband and remained an active researcher, she did not hold a doctorate until she was awarded an honorary LLD in December 1986 from Pepperdine University. Ultimately, she placed her own career as an economist on hold to further her husband's career.

Much of Rose Friedman's early economics research on consumer spending data is found inside her husband's early book *A Theory of the Consumption Function*. Milton Friedman's famed free-market manifesto, *Capitalism and Freedom*, was written in collaboration with Rose Friedman. The couple were co-authors of *Free to Choose* in 1980 which explained free-market theory and set out their case for less government economic intervention to a general audience. Their book *The Tyranny of the Status Quo* argued for the US Constitution to be amended to constrain the economic power of the US Government. Gary Becker, the Nobel Prize-winning economist and close friend of the Friedmans, remarked that the couple discussed ideas constantly and that 'her feelings about the importance of private markets, opposition to big government, were even stronger than his. Her lasting influence will be as a collaborator, but she was a major contributor to the collaboration, and that's a significant legacy.'

When President Reagan presented Milton Friedman with the Presidential Medal of Freedom, the US's highest civilian honour, he joked that Rose Friedman was known for being 'the only person to ever have won an argument against Milton'. Given the widespread respect for her, one might wonder whether Rose Friedman ever felt overshadowed by her husband – one of the most famous economic minds of the twentieth century. When asked, she always seemed triumphant about her own role in his success saying, 'I've always felt that I'm responsible for at least half of what he's gotten.' When the successes of Milton Friedman include both the Nobel Prize and the total reformation of how economists consider monetary policy, that is certainly a great deal of success to lay claim to.

Rose Friedman frequently collaborated with her husband, Milton. Neither she nor Anna Schwartz was mentioned in his Nobel Prize citation, though he did later acknowledge both their contributions.

Why Anna Schwartz Matters Today

Like Anna Schwartz, I strongly believe that price stability is important for a strong economy. It helps families manage their finances and plan for the future, and enables businesses to set prices and enter into contracts. It encourages investment and innovation because of the certainty it brings. But there are no short cuts. Inflation is not just a function of money in circulation, and with the concept of money now being even more difficult to grasp than ever with the sharp decline in cash transactions and the growing use of online banking and new forms of financial transactions such as the emergence of cryptocurrencies, it is not clear what a money target would even look like.

Experiments in monetarism have blighted industry and caused mass joblessness, and in the real world the relationship between money and prices is much more complicated and evolving than Schwartz thought. To control inflation I support inflation targeting – not through a simple formula but through the deliberations of a qualified committee looking at all of the available data and evidence, underpinned by central bank operational independence. It is this approach that can give confidence to markets, businesses and families, with expectations of inflation having the best chance of remaining anchored around a credible target.

You might say that attempts to control inflation have not worked too well with inflation recently at a forty-year high and still above target. But is the inflation we are experiencing being driven by an increase in money in circulation? I would argue that a far more important cause is the war in Ukraine, the restriction of gas supplies from Russia, the refusal of OPEC countries, those who control most of the world's oil, to increase the supply of oil and gas, and a failure to have invested in home-grown renewables – the cheapest forms of energy in history. That is alongside other factors including issues in supply chains as a result of the government's Brexit deal that makes trade harder and pushes costs up, and failures by successive Conservative-led governments since 2010 to maintain the security and resilience of the UK economy. The point is that one economic variable does not have all the answers. That has been proved in the real world.

It was twelve years of Tory economic mismanagement that led us to our current position, not an accounting identity. When Russia invaded Ukraine, the UK was hit hard not as a consequence of the money supply, as Schwartz's theory would suggest, but because of more than a decade of economic mismanagement and unpreparedness. In 2018, as Chair of the Business, Energy and Industrial Strategy Select Committee, long before the Covid pandemic and the invasion of Ukraine, I launched an inquiry into our energy supply chains and our preparedness in the event they should be disrupted. The government had closed gas storage facilities in the UK, leaving our supply chains vulnerable, undiversified and reliant on foreign imports. I saw then the risk of shortages and – as we now know all too well – price increases with an inflationary spike. Labour called on the government to secure the supply chains by storing reserves of gas, but they failed to act. The impact of the inflation we see now could have been mitigated – not by manipulating the money supply as Schwartz might suggest – but by having a government with an eye to the future, shoring up and diversifying our supply chains, willing to take action to secure the finances of British families.

My second disagreement with Schwartz is on financial regulation. In their analysis of the Great Depression, Friedman and Schwartz argued that the Fed's failure to recognise the contagion caused by bank failures was part of the reason why the recession became a depression. They argued that Roosevelt's bank deposit insurance that followed as part of the New Deal was a reason for banking stability in the years since. But then Schwartz's views hardened. She argued that price stability, not deposit insurance, was the reason for financial stability and then argued against the bailouts of financial services firms that surely stopped the 2008 recession becoming a depression and could have stopped the 1930s being a period of depression too. Perhaps most concerningly, Schwartz argues for less regulation in financial services, when surely the lesson of the financial crisis is that financial stability is essential for wider economic stability, and so regulation to keep banks and other financial institutions stable is essential to stop contagion extending from the financial sector to the real economy.

Friedman and Schwartz's blind belief in their theory, even when the relationship between money and prices broke down, and even when it is clear that 'short-run' increases in unemployment can have permanent scarring effects on people and communities, is, I think, the worst of economics. Economics has the potential to improve the quality of people's lives by helping policymakers create policies to contain inflation, maximise growth, alleviate poverty, stimulate investment and innovation, help ensure the sustainability of our environment and natural resources, and so much more. That is what is exciting about economics and what drives me as an economist. For economics to achieve its full potential we have to understand how economic models work in the real world and the consequences of policies on people's lives. Economics is more than lines on a graph or clever models to guess the behaviour of 'rational agents'. Trying to shoehorn models onto real people without recognising the impact on their lives when things don't go according to the model can end up destroying confidence in economic policy – and livelihoods too. At its most extreme, that is what the monetarist experiment did.

Schwartz was a great economic theorist but she took her theory too far. Monetarism is an example of how economic theory, when applied to a real world not consistent with its abstract models, can have terrible, unintended consequences.

7

Elinor Ostrom and the
Political Economy of the Environment

Economics is often thought of as the discipline that finds the right value or price of a service or commodity, but what if the things we value the most are hard to put a price on? That is the big challenge of environmental economics – too often neglected as a discipline and seen as someone else's problem to fix. Increasingly, however, and some might say far too late, environmental economics has risen up the agenda at both a national and global level. In my first speech as Labour's shadow chancellor to our party's conference I pledged to be the country's first green Chancellor of the Exchequer. Working closely with Keir Starmer and Ed Miliband, Shadow Secretary of State for Climate Change and Net Zero, we have put together a programme for economic renewal that puts tackling the climate emergency at its core. This focus reflects a moral conviction as well as an economic necessity. I feel a profound responsibility to hand on to future generations a planet that is inhabitable and even in better condition than the one we inherited from our parents and grandparents. But the transition to net zero also offers a huge opportunity for economic renewal with good jobs in sustainable energy, new ways of building and travelling, and new methods in farming, recycling, packaging and how we live our lives. If we can do this, we can create great new jobs paying decent wages, re-industrialising communities in a sustainable energy revolution and preserving our green spaces, rivers, lakes and oceans from pollution and destruction.

I remember in 2009, as the global economy was battling against the impact of the financial crisis, the Nobel Prize that year going not to an economist of finance or macroeconomics, but to a little-known polit-ical scientist, who from lots of different case studies formulated big-ger theories about how to manage shared resources – from rivers and water sources to forests and grazing land for cattle. Economists failed to predict the Global Financial Crisis, but Elinor Ostrom's work has huge significance for an even more existential question. The climate crisis was ignored by economists for far too long – but not any longer.

The conventional economic models of the respective roles of states and markets, and of human behaviour, completely miss out a sphere too often neglected by economists: voluntary and cooperative col-laboration between citizens. It is for this reason that Elinor Ostrom, the first woman to be awarded the Nobel Prize for Economics, is so important. Her research, often involving painstaking fieldwork looking at water management, fishing, forestries and clean air, rejects the idea that common land will be degraded and overused without either property rights in a privatised model or state controls and penalties in a public one. Her analysis about what happens in the real world, where people with a stake in a common resource come together and organise cooperative systems, was groundbreaking and supplies an economic framework by which to explore how resources can be managed for the common good, and how these systems often outperform government-managed or privatised models, because they build in more trust and give power to the people most directly impacted with a vested interest in their success.

Economics too often fails to value cooperation and places excessive weight on economic models which assume 'rational self-interest' – a term in economics that assumes a person will always act in ways that reduce costs and increase benefits for themselves and place this above all else. Such concepts often break down in the real world where other (and better!) motivations exist and often take precedence. At a national level, Ostrom's work also suggests that policy solutions are often better when they are developed in consultation with the people most directly involved, and con-tains important lessons for policymakers in questions relating to devolution, citizens' forums, contracting services and ensuring user-participation at a local level. Ostrom's work says we should pay more attention to these systems, which I see working every day on a local level as a constituency MP in Leeds. In Leeds we have what we call 'neighbourhood networks', focused on helping older people across the city stay independent for longer. These schemes are funded by a combination of city council and NHS contracts, but they are distinctly local and at arm's length from the state. They rely on a small army of volunteers, often retired themselves, to organise projects from shopping to fitness classes, memory groups and much more. They are trusted by the community because they are from the community – run by and for them. There is no reason why they couldn't be run by the council, or indeed by a private provider, but I am certain they would be much less successful if they were.

Early Years and Career

When Elinor Ostrom won the Nobel Prize for Economics in 2009 (the first woman to receive the award, after Joan Robinson was overlooked more than a quarter of a century earlier) many people hadn't heard of this political scientist from the University of Indiana. Even if they had heard of her, there were many mainstream economists who didn't regard her as a 'proper' economist. But Ostrom's work on how to manage shared resources, and her debunking of the famous 'tragedy of the commons', were key to her getting the prize. Ostrom's whole approach to economic analysis and problem solving was not without its sceptics because it was radical and new – pioneering a model where academics from different disciplines came together through workshops and co-working spaces, as well as in the community – to find solutions to real-world economic problems.

Ostrom's start in life would not have predicted her future successes. Elinor Claire Awan was born in Los Angeles, California, in 1933, the only child of musician Leah Hopkins and set designer Adrian Awan. The couple separated when Elinor was still a young child and she seems to have been shunted back and forth between the two, though mainly living with her mother. Growing up during the Depression had a lasting impact on Elinor, and she spoke about how her formative experiences – helping her family grow food in a large communal garden, for example – sparked her interest in cooperative institutions and people working together to address shared problems. Living opposite Beverly Hills High School was also, she felt, a stroke of good luck as she got to attend a school which had an established track record of getting its students into college. She was a natural debater and joined the school debate team, something she credited for her success in public policy – developing and critiquing an argument and recognising that there are always two sides.

Ostrom did well at high school, but her mother could not understand why she wanted to go to college and would not support her, so Ostrom worked three jobs to support herself, receiving a BA in political science in 1954. She met her first husband, Charles Scott, at university and moved with him to Massachusetts after graduation so he could attend Harvard Law School. Despite her degree, Elinor struggled to find a job without typing or shorthand skills – most jobs available to women at that time being as teachers or secretaries. She did learn shorthand, which she used throughout her career for interview notes on research projects, and eventually she got a job as a clerk for an electronics exporting company that had only ever hired women as secretaries before.

She was not satisfied, however, with her job or her life in Massachusetts. Elinor wanted to continue to study and pursue an academic career, but her family did not understand her interest in an academic life, and her husband tried to dissuade her. The marriage ended just a few years after it began, and Elinor returned to Los Angeles where she studied for and received an MA in political science from UCLA in 1962 and a PhD three years later. Ironically, her application to study economics was turned down as she hadn't done enough maths at high school. Her PhD, also in public policy, focused on the management of fresh water in Los Angeles, laying the groundwork for her life's work studying the management of shared resources.

While studying back in California, Elinor met Vincent Ostrom – a UCLA professor who led the research seminar she attended for graduate students studying an area of water management in Southern California. They married in 1963 and two years later moved to Bloomington, where Vincent had been offered a professorship at the University of Indiana, Elinor taking up a teaching role. Unlike her first husband, Vincent Ostrom had no intention of holding back Elinor's career and theirs was a great personal and political partnership which lasted fifty years. In her most famous book, Elinor Ostrom's dedication is to her husband – to the love and willingness to debate that she found in him.

The Workshop

It wasn't just Ostrom's work that was groundbreaking; her approach to work was, too. The Ostroms established the Workshop in Political Theory and Policy Analysis at Indiana University in 1973. Unlike a standard institute at a university, it came to resemble one of the local, community-led institutions that she sought to better understand through her research: self-organised and focused on problem solving. The students who attended didn't call themselves students or researchers, but 'workshoppers' and in her later years they called Elinor Ostrom 'Grandma'.

The premise of the workshop was simple. Vincent and Elinor Ostrom thought that the boundaries between academic disciplines were arbitrary and unhelpful. As Marco Janssen, a mathematician at Arizona State University who worked with them, said, 'A lot of important questions are on the narrow borders between disciplines, but it is difficult to find a home for that kind of work.' That being so, they simply created one in Indiana. The Workshop attracted like-minded academics from a range of disciplines, from computer science and political philosophy to ecology and sociology. It was the cross-section and cross-fertilisation that the workshop facilitated that led to some of its best research and ideas. The so-called 'Bloomington School' approach was based on what the Ostroms called 'polycentric governance', a concept that Vincent Ostrom had been promoting for several years that essentially proposed that resource management could happen at multiple levels. The Workshop was apparently modelled on a craft or artisan workshop, where artisans (in this case, academics) would work alongside each other – from tenured academics (masters) to new graduates (apprentices), allowing the transfer of knowledge and ideas – an example of Mary Paley Marshall's 'clusters' operating within academia.

Mainstream economists were not always welcoming to Ostrom and her approach. As Professor Nancy Folbre, from the University of Massachusetts, puts it: 'In economics every successive cohort of economists is trained to put greater emphasis on the arsenal of mathematical and econometric expertise.' This approach was a world apart from Ostrom's, who thought fieldwork, done in the community, was a more useful way of studying decision making in economics than relying on mathematical models. Nevertheless, George Akerlof, who won the Nobel Prize in 2001 for his own work on asymmetric information in markets and is the husband of US Treasury Secretary Janet Yellen, featured in Chapter 9, describes Ostrom's work, and how it was conducted, as 'utterly central' to the study of economic activity that is not reflected in markets. In a 2011 article in the journal *Finance and Development* Akerlof writes:

> Ostrom is interested in how social norms form and how they are enforced ... these norms are the 'missing matter' in economics. You may be very close to an equilibrium in which everybody co-operates, but then you need something additional that gets people to cooperate. And what gets people to cooperate are the norms.

In other words, the values and shared conventions that motivate people. Ostrom's former student, Professor Paul Dragoş Aligică, agrees that 'going beyond the dichotomy of market and state is one of the most revolutionary paradigms', and in the year after the Global Financial Crisis – which mainstream economists failed to predict – the prize was a fitting tribute to an economist who was not bound by the assumptions and limitations around what economics should be about. Reflecting her growing stature, in 2012 Ostrom was named one of *Time* magazine's 100 Most Influential People in the World.

The Tragedy of the Commons

Shortly after arriving in Indiana, having completed her PhD on how shared resources can be managed in common, Ostrom heard a lecture by Garrett Hardin, an ecologist who had recently written an essay in the journal *Science*, entitled 'The Tragedy of the Commons'. Hardin's essay drew on ideas first outlined in 1833 by the little-known British economist William Forster Lloyd. Lloyd used the example of herders grazing their cattle on common land in English villages to argue that for each additional animal that a herder brought to graze, an individual herder could receive additional benefits, yet the whole group suffered from the resulting damage to the common land. If all herders made this individually rational economic decision to increase their cattle, the common would be depleted or even destroyed, to the detriment of all. It was Hardin, however, who popularised the idea over a century later. His 1968 article draws the moral:

> Therein is the tragedy. Each man is locked into a system that compels him to increase his herd without limit – in a world that is limited. Ruin is the destination toward which all men rush, each pursuing his own best interest in a society that believes in the freedom of the commons.

If one accepts this view, then the solution to avoid such a tragedy is either government rules and oversight or the privatisation of the common resource whereby instead of sharing the resource in common, small portions of land are parcelled off to individuals who would have a greater stake in protecting their portion than they would in protecting the common land.

Ostrom, however, disputed the notion that tragedy was the inevitable outcome of shared resources, and challenged the underlying assumption that we are all rational, selfish individuals. Although open-access resource systems may sometimes collapse due to overuse, she countered, many examples have existed, and still do exist, where members of a community with regulated access to a common resource cooperate to exploit those resources prudently without collapse, or even create 'perfect order' where the resource is not depleted. Elinor Ostrom knew she had seen examples of resource management that worked and therefore the theory of the tragedy of the commons had to be flawed. It is from this insight we derive Ostrom's law: 'A resource arrangement that works in practice can work in theory.'

In Southern California, for example, Ostrom had become interested in the situation in the rapidly growing Los Angeles area. The West Basin aquifer could no longer keep up with the demand from the surrounding communities: too much water was being pumped out of the groundwater basin and ocean salt water began seeping in. The problem was that no single community had the incentive to reduce the amount of water it withdrew for as long as the others continued at their usual rate, and all the while the problem of the salt water continued. This problem came to form the subject of Ostrom's PhD dissertation.

But, instead of being destroyed through overuse, as Hardin would have predicted, the communities came together to solve the problem and manage the common resource for the benefit of all. This example was not unique. Many local communities were managing shared resources well – and although some free-riding by selfish

Elinor Ostrom was a pioneer of the use of fieldwork in economics, and the results of her research often challenged long-held economic assumptions.

people acting in their narrow self-interest was occurring, in many real-world scenarios it was not the rule. Ostrom knew this because, despite Hardin's theory and its apparent logic, she had seen and studied cases that disproved it in rural communities around the world. From fisheries in Turkey to farmers in Switzerland, she catalogued more than a thousand case studies of the management of common-pool resources around the world. She developed design principles to explain how the resources were managed, and noted that these techniques usually came from the bottom up rather than needing to be imposed or explained to participants. Most importantly perhaps, Ostrom's observations and experiments through simulated exercises in her workshops showed that communication between the people sharing the resource, and the opportunities to come together to negotiate and discuss, were incredibly important for the successful management of common-pool resources. The principles needed for success on the ground also included effective monitoring; graduated sanctions for those who break rules; and cheap access to conflict-resolution mechanisms. Seeing good management of shared resources, Ostrom concluded that 'there is no reason to believe that bureaucrats and politicians, no matter how well meaning, are better at solving problems than the people on the spot, who have the strongest incentive to get the solution right'.

It was these studies, and her belief in the power of cooperation and collaboration within communities, that culminated in Ostrom's book *Governing the Commons: The Evolution of Institutions for Collective Action*, published in 1990.

In the book Ostrom described how communities around the world were managing their common-pool resources effectively and, based on these examples, she developed what became known as the Institutional Analysis and Development Framework, which outlined a set of concepts to help in the understanding of common resources. Ostrom explored which institutional structures best support handling those resource stocks in a sustainable way, balancing individuals' use with the interest of a wider public. This theoretical framework was devised as an attempt to explain and predict outcomes by formally exploring and documenting the governance structures, the participants' objectives, and the informal and formal rules devised for individuals to extract resources from the common resource.

Thanks to Ostrom's work, this field of study is now considered to be a distinct area in its own right, and it was on the basis of her detailed analysis of real-life management of communal assets, and the analytical framework that went with it, that Ostrom, along with Oliver Williamson of the University of California, Berkeley, was awarded the Nobel Prize in 2009. The commendation noted that her work 'teaches us novel lessons about the deep mechanisms that sustain cooperation in human societies'. The Associated Press noted that her research 'brought this topic from the fringe to the fore-front of scientific attention ... by showing how common resources – forests, fisheries, oil fields or grazing lands – can be managed successfully by the people who use them rather than by governments or private companies'.

'I never would have won the Nobel but for being a part of that enterprise,' said Ostrom of the workshop, with a large degree of modesty. In a later interview she told Fran Korten, who had once worked with her, that when she received the Nobel she felt a sense of vindication that her work was finally being recognised as important. And it meant that much more because she had been 'doing a bunch of research through the years that many people thought was very radical and people didn't like'. It was a validation and acknowledgement from the broader academic community that going against the grain and challenging widely held assumptions about how human beings behave in an economic context was a worthwhile and important pursuit.

The Ultimate Tragedy of the Commons

Ostrom is often credited with disproving the tragedy of the commons. But that is not quite right. What Ostrom says is that 'Hardin's assertion that common property will *always* be degraded is wrong'. In situations where a community has the ability and opportunity to organise itself, human beings are perfectly capable of governing shared resources. As Ostrom is reported to have said, 'Organising is a process; an organisation is the result of that process.' It is this process of collaboration and organising that can avert tragedy – in this case the destruction of natural resources. Ostrom saw plenty of examples where common-pool resources were well governed – but as we know, that is not always the case. Ostrom said that there were 'no panaceas' to real-world problems; managing resources in common is not easy. Her principal argument is that in these situations it does not simply have to be a choice between privatisation or state control – community governance can also be a viable alternative.

Not everyone agrees, of course. Oxford professor Sir Dieter Helm has argued that these examples are context specific and that the tragedy of the commons 'is not generally solved this way. If it were, the destruction of nature would not have occurred.' While it may be true that cooperative, community-based action is not always possible, it perhaps shows that we have to work even harder to create the structures and organisations that can be used to protect the environment effectively.

Much of Ostrom's later work was on what academics began to call 'the ultimate tragedy of the commons': climate change. In a posthumously published 2014 article in *Annals of Economics and Finance*, Ostrom argues for 'a polycentric approach for coping with climate change' (also the title of the essay), and that the solutions for averting catastrophe exist on a number of levels, including most importantly, the local.

In economic terms, the key issue with addressing climate change is that while averting a climate catastrophe is a public good, there is a free-rider problem in getting there. We all benefit from reduced greenhouse gas emissions, whether or not we pay any of the costs. The analogy with the tragedy of the commons is clear: while herders all have access to the commons to graze their cattle, the best outcome for all is if no one over-grazes. But, as an individual the temptation is to put another animal on the common land to increase your own benefit – in economic language, it is in your own rational self-interest to do so, therefore the assumption is you will. Yet, if everyone does this, the commons are destroyed for all. Similarly, it is in all our interests that everyone reduces their carbon emissions. Yet, if one person (or country) does not take action, they still benefit if everyone else does – they can free-ride on the actions of others. But, if everyone knows this, who will comply? The only 'equilibrium' in the jargon is the worst one – where no one complies and Hardin's prediction comes true. Carbon emissions rise instead of fall and the ultimate tragedy – climate catastrophe – becomes reality.

But drawing on her own research and case-studies, Ostrom is more optimistic about the ability of people to cooperate in order to deliver lasting change, even in relation to global warming. As Nobel Prize laureate George Akerlof says, 'her theories apply not just to irrigation systems but to entities as large as countries or as large as the whole world, such as global warming'. Ostrom argues that while climate change is a global phenomenon, it is local action that is more likely to achieve the changes needed to protect the planet. 'Must we wait for a global solution?' Ostrom challenges us. If we wait for governments and international organisations to agree a course of action it may be too late, but it may also not be the best way to secure lasting change. Global 'solutions' are by their very nature imposed from above and do not build up the sense of trust, agency and engagement necessary to avoid the free-rider problem. Local experimentation on the other hand can give us an opportunity to work out what will or won't work and then scale up to a national or global level.

Ostrom promoted the maxim 'Think global, act local'. She argues that the decisions of families to better insulate their homes, use a car-pool, walk or cycle, or at a collective level invest in a community energy scheme – whether it be solar panels, car-charging points or district heating schemes – are better for the planet and also can improve individual quality of life, health and reduce costs for families, as well as bringing collective benefits in terms of reduced carbon emissions. Ostrom criticises mainstream economists for discounting the possibility of self-organised groups achieving anything at scale, and says that actions on a multitude of levels are necessary for tackling climate change (the polycentric approach). She also notes that 'a surprisingly large number of individuals facing collective action problems do cooperate', because while people recognise the short-run costs, they see longer-term benefits and believe – and observe – that others are taking action (and not free-riding). In Ostrom's view, 'reliance on a single solution (global agreements and action) may be more of a problem than a solution'.

Kate Raworth and Doughnut Economics

The idea of fostering local solutions for global problems in the economics of sustainability didn't end with Elinor Ostrom. Rather, she sparked a movement which has been taken forward by twenty-first-century climate economists like Kate Raworth. Raworth's 'Doughnut Economics Action Lab' exists with the mission of supporting communities across the world to turn the principle of a world living below our ecological ceiling, but with a population above the social floor, into a reality through smaller unique programmes in communities across the world. Helping humanity learn to live within its ecological limit, while guaranteeing a decent standard of living for all, is Raworth's aim, and her method is the polycentric action Elinor Ostrom devoted her entire career to.

In 2020, *Forbes* magazine did a feature on five economists 'changing everything'. They were all women and one of them was Kate Raworth. In a Twitter exchange on the article Raworth said that if you haven't heard of Elinor Ostrom then 'you're hanging out with the wrong kind of economists', adding that, were she still alive, Ostrom 'would top [her] list'. Both Ostrom and Raworth might be described as 'renegade' economists – challenging the status quo.

Raworth graduated from Oxford in PPE and went on to study an MSc in Development Economics. Between 1997 and 2001, she was the co-author of the United Nations Development Programme's Human Development Report. From 2002 to 2013 she was a Senior Researcher at Oxfam, and in 2021 was appointed to the World Health Organization's Council on the Economics of Health for All, chaired by fellow economist Mariana Mazzucato.

Like Ostrom, Raworth combines an interest in addressing global issues with local answers. Her most significant contribution to economic thought and development is her 2017 best-selling book, *Doughnut Economics: Seven Ways to Think Like a 21st-Century Economist*, in which she argues that economics must balance essential human needs with the limitations of the planet. She describes the economy using the analogy of a doughnut. The inner ring or edge of the doughnut is her 'social foundation' – the point above which we must strive for all humanity to be. Below this circular ring is the hole in her metaphorical doughnut, inside which we cannot allow populations to fall. Living above this ring is quantified by traditional economic indicators like income, housing, food and water, but also social indicators like gender equality, social equity and political voice. All people deserve access to these rights and when they do they are considered to be above the social foundation, out of the hole of the doughnut.

Raworth dubs the outer ring of the doughnut the 'ecological ceiling'. Everything beyond this point is unsustainable, depleting our natural resources and damaging our environment beyond repair. Climate change is one factor that puts us beyond this outer doughnut ring, and Raworth enumerates the specific ways in which we are living beyond our ecological means, including everything from ocean acidification to land conversion, air pollution and biodiversity loss.

The area in between this social foundation and ecological ceiling is what Raworth names 'the safe and just space for humanity'. This 'Goldilocks Zone', where we can meet humanity's basic needs whilst not using resources at a rate beyond which our Earth can sustain, is how Raworth defines her ideal landing point for the global economy. It's on the basis of this that she rejects economic growth, arguing for a reshaped global economy that fits inside her 'doughnut model' rather than a larger, expanded global economy.

Much like Ostrom, the focus of this is often on common-pool resources and how to ensure we govern the commons effectively – not just so that we don't ruin our shared assets, as Hardin warned and Ostrom feared, but so that everyone can live a meaningful life without destroying the planet that hosts us.

Kate Raworth is Professor of Practice at Amsterdam University of

Applied Sciences, and works with the Doughnut Economics Action Lab: a network through which students, lecturers and researchers, in collaboration with communities, develop tailored ideas for local places to combat global warming and ecological damage – not dissimilar to Elinor Ostrom's Workshop in Indiana. Ostrom asked whether we can wait for government action; Raworth says that we haven't got time to wait. What Raworth's Action Lab is trying to do is apply the frameworks Ostrom developed for the governance of the commons and use them to address the challenge we face in the global commons such as climate change. It helps communities ask how they can rise to the challenge of ensuring that in the place that they live, no one is below the floor of what is needed for human flourishing while at the same time the ceiling of sustainability is not reached. The analysis is done with the communities and the solutions found within them. In this way Raworth is very much taking Ostrom's analysis and applying it to the most important of pooled resources: the planet. Raworth explicitly states that,

> given the speed, scale and uncertainty of environmental and social change that we face in coming years – and the diversity of contexts from Beijing to Birmingham to Bamako – it would be foolhardy to attempt to prescribe now all of the policies and institutions that will be fit for the future. The coming generation of thinkers and doers will be far better placed to experiment and discover what works as the context continually changes.

In this framework, rules for governing common-pool resources should fit local circumstances, participatory decision-making is vital, and commons work best when nested within larger networks.

Controversially, and certainly in contention with – for example – Paley Marshall and Robinson, Raworth explicitly rejects the notion that economic growth is a useful measure for economic health and wellbeing. This idea is growing in support on the left, especially on the green-left. Raworth argues that 'what we need are economies that make us thrive, whether or not they grow', even rejecting the idea of green growth, saying she rejects the paradigm of growth altogether. Raworth contends that GDP is a false goal waiting to be ousted and that while it may have been useful when measurement techniques were developed in the 1930s, in the twenty-first century we need to get more specific about our goals – something she calls shifting 'from endless growth to thriving in balance'.

I disagree with Raworth on this point, and have set out how one of the key missions of a Labour government will be to increase the UK's rate of GDP growth so we lead our peers. But Labour's aim for high growth does not need to be in conflict with our ecological ambitions: quite the opposite. Achieving a higher rate of growth will make it easier for society to thrive and achieve the green transition our climate so desperately needs through new technology. A growing economy will also raise living standards and, if it is the sort of growth that I am aiming for, it will lift people out of poverty. Growth also delivers the revenues to invest in schools, hospitals, transport and all the other public services neglected after thirteen years of Conservative government. I won't give up on growth or the benefits it can bring. This is why our mission is to achieve broadly shared growth, with good jobs and productivity in every part of the country, so that we can make everyone better off, rather than just a few.

Why Elinor Ostrom Matters Today

The most inspiring thing about Ostrom's work is how refreshingly different her approach is. The field studies and her willingness to listen to people in order to understand and explain how they take ownership of their local communities and economies is a world apart from the economic modelling and top-down theoretical approach that has come to dominate mainstream economics. Ostrom's maxim that if it works in reality, it can work in theory is the right way round. As a constituency MP, I am often struck by the capacity of communities to self-organise. When a local public swimming baths in Leeds West, Bramley Baths, was threatened with closure as austerity struck in 2011, the community organised to save it. The pool is now more successful than ever – not as a public pool or a privatised business either. It is run as a cooperative for the benefit of the community by local people for the whole neighbourhood. As Joni Mitchell sang, 'You don't know what you've got / till it's gone.' Well, the baths didn't go but they nearly did, and people have never valued them more than since that happened. The day the pool reopened after the pandemic lockdown there were queues down the street and they reopened before either the public or private pools in Leeds too.

Another great example I have seen where people have been brought together to tackle a big problem was citizens' forums on climate action. Judith Blake and I separately took forward this idea when she was leader of the city council in Leeds where she convened citizens' forums across the city, and as Chair of the Business, Energy and Industrial Strategy Select Committee between 2017 and 2020, I also helped convene a UK-wide citizens' forum on climate change. The members of the forum were chosen from a cross-section of the country and were from different backgrounds, experiences and prior views. When they came together to take evidence, challenge and ask questions they were able to start developing practical and realistic solutions to huge problems. I like to think of this bottom-up action as an attempt to use the community-centric governance thesis of Elinor Ostrom as a framework to tackle climate change – the greatest threat to our global commons – from all angles.

Cambridge economics professor Diane Coyle has argued that Elinor Ostrom's theory on the governance of common resources may be applicable to data and the digital world. While data doesn't deplete like grazing grass for cows or fish in a lake, it does involve situations where people need to agree rules of access to a shared resource, and often requires some people to sacrifice personal gain for a common good. In Ostrom's work, it's a farmer upstream who, while he could benefit from not sharing water for irrigation with those downstream, chooses to engage collectively to enable higher crop yields for all. In the age of big data, individuals may sacrifice some privacy by sharing their data, but this can unlock much larger benefits for society as a whole. For example, in healthcare, people might allow their X-rays to be used to help Artificial Intelligence learn how to diagnose patients with greater accuracy – providing they are confident that the necessary checks and balances are in place to ensure their privacy is protected.

The space between the state and the market is often overlooked in economics, but not by Ostrom or Raworth. That is one of their most important insights and one that is essential for the design of effective public policy and services.

As well as her approach to working on the ground, I also find Ostrom's multidisciplinary work in finding solutions to complex problems groundbreaking and surely the right way to tackle difficult issues. Most people don't think about the economy as separate to other parts of their lives. How much is the food in the shops? Does their work pay well enough to live a decent life? Is the local park looked after? Is the water clean and well-managed? These are everyday concerns and it takes more than economics to make these things right. Public policy, economics, ecology, town-planning, conflict management should all be considered alongside each other if they are going to be relevant to everyday lives. In my 2018 pamphlet *The Everyday Economy*, I try to get economics back to what matters – work, family, place. Economists don't concentrate on these things enough. But Ostrom does focus on the local and the lived experiences of people in the economy and society. At the Bank of England I often worried that we spent too much time on abstract quantitative economics and not enough trying to understand how people and businesses were making decisions and how the decisions of policy-makers affected them. It is fitting that Ostrom got her Nobel Prize

In 2009 Elinor Ostrom made history by becoming the
first woman to be awarded the Nobel Prize, for her
work on economic governance.

in the aftermath of the financial crisis. By separating economics
too much from other academic disciplines and from the real world,
economists missed warning signs. The silos of the past can and must
be challenged. Ostrom and Raworth do this.

It is interesting how many women economists are challenging the
status quo and study the economics of everyday life – whether that be
Beatrice Webb in the early years of the last century when she wrote
the Minority Report to the Poor Law; Esther Duflo as she assesses
the impact of poverty eradication measures in some of the poorest
countries of the world; Elinor Ostrom as she looked at water management and the performance of local police districts; or Kate Raworth in
her own version of Ostrom's Workshop looking at how sustainability

and human needs can co-exist at a local and global level. All these women challenged the status quo, refusing to accept the limitations of what an economist is and what she analyses. I think this approach, grounded in the real world, is much more likely to help solve difficult economic problems compared to the best econometric models and data sets in the world. As chancellor I would want to learn from this sort of experimentation – whether it is the Welsh Government's work on supporting the foundational economy, Leeds's neighbourhood networks, Preston's community wealth building, or Kirklees's programme of retrofitting homes to reduce energy bills and tackle climate change. There is so much happening at the local level that is streets ahead of the national and motivates people to take action.

But local answers aren't the full answer. The most significant challenge to Ostrom's work, as noted earlier, comes from Dieter Helm, who questions whether the successes Ostrom records in some cases rely on specific contexts which tend not to exist more generally. I think this is especially important when you try to scale up her work to the global commons. It is surely good that people act locally – walk more and drive less, recycle and reuse, turn unnecessary lights off and unplug electrical appliances. But the scale of the changes we need to save the planet will not be achieved by these actions alone. Ostrom is right to say that a problem like climate change will benefit from polycentric policy responses – but averting a climate catastrophe is going to demand an awful lot more from political leaders than urging local solutions, and I worry that Ostrom understates the importance of global agreements and their enforcement. A cynicism about the possibility of global solutions does not make them any less urgent.

The commons Kate Raworth is concerned with are global in nature – how we can live within the ecological boundaries that the planet demands while also satisfying people's basic needs. But her repudiation of economic growth is misplaced.

Economic growth and growing the economy are not important just because they help political parties win elections or governments claim the top spot on the G7 leader board. They matter because they are essential ingredients in the recipe for improving living standards, reducing poverty and tackling the biggest issues of our time, including climate change.

It's no coincidence that world GDP increased sixfold between 1950 and 1998, and that this period is marked by decades of prosperity which enabled reform that lifted billions out of poverty and transformed the role of women across society from homemaker to boundary breaker. Despite the many obstacles they faced as women in economics, many of the twentieth-century economists described in these pages benefited from the reforms enabled by this period of immense growth.

Growth isn't an end in itself, but it is the economic mechanism which enables us to have the resources to fund a meaningful welfare state and make strides in the fight against climate change. Just because economic growth is an abstract concept doesn't mean that as we move into becoming 'twenty-first-century economists', like Raworth asks, we can forget about it. The fact that growth is a 'hard sell' or 'difficult to explain' is not a reason to dismiss it, although we are right to support broad-based growth – sustainable, inclusive, equitable – above growth based on trickle-down economics from the few at the top. Ultimately, however, expanding the productive capacity of our economy is what will give us the resources to tackle the most pressing issues of our time. On this important question I part company with Kate Raworth.

Labour have committed to go for growth in government. That does not need to be at odds with our environmental ambitions. Our Green Prosperity Plan will power the green transition and spur on economic growth by investing in the industries of the future. For the last thirteen years the UK economy has barely grown at all. As a result we have tens of billions less in tax revenue to invest in public services than if the economy had grown at a rate similar to that achieved under the last Labour government. The average working person earns £11,000 less today than they would if wage growth had continued at the rate achieved by that government. And most alarmingly, more and more people in poverty are also in work, relying on food banks and limited welfare payments to top up insufficient and insecure wages. Too many people are clearly not having their basic needs met and there is much suffering. But it also matters on a societal level when, for more and more people, work simply does not pay enough to live on. That is why a Labour government would for the first time ask the Low Pay Commission, the body that sets the minimum wage, to consider the cost of living when recommending a level of the minimum wage, alongside the state of the economy and median wages.

And despite anaemic growth, our carbon emissions have not fallen enough and we are not in the doughnut of human flourishing. Innovation, government leadership and money are needed to tackle climate change, and in doing so we can ensure that good jobs are created in more parts of the country – but it is very hard to progress towards net zero in an economy that is not growing and is unable to fund the necessary investment – both public and private – that is needed to get us there.

Raworth is right to say that economic growth is not a good thing in and of itself, but I reject the idea that we can help people live meaningful lives without more of it. And I reject the idea that growth at some point runs out or destroys the planet. In fact, more innovation, industry and entrepreneurial spirit can help us find solutions to climate change, whether that is through better non-meat alternatives or sustainable ways to travel – including sustainable aviation fuel, and innovations to make heat pumps and electric vehicles cheaper and more reliable.

I welcome Ostrom's idea of polycentric models. But we shouldn't fetishise the local over the national or global either. They all have their place. And despite the limitations of state and market, they too have important roles to play in tackling climate change, loss of biodiversity and over-consumption of limited resources while also helping people meet their basic needs. People want control over their own lives and want to have a voice in decisions that impact them and their communities – Ostrom popularised this and changed the idea of what economics is about. Kate Raworth is a worthy successor, looking at how economics can be applied locally for the public good. But people also want a well-functioning government and market-based economy – properly regulated but able to innovate and help grow the size of the economic pie too. I want to be, and have committed to being, Britain's first green chancellor, and the idea of living sustainably while meeting people's basic needs is appealing. But I am not willing to give up on growth – or government – just yet.

8

Esther Duflo and the Challenges of Development Economics

Ahead of Christmas 1984 I went with my dad to the record shop on Sydenham High Street in South East London to buy the Band Aid single 'Do They Know It's Christmas?' for my mum. I was only five, but I remember vividly the images from the television of famine in Ethiopia and feeling an overwhelming sense of sadness and incomprehension that people could be left like this without even enough food. My son is eight now and I wonder for how many years he will remember the scenes from Kyiv that he sees today.

A few years later, in a Year 9 geography class we learned about what was then called 'Third World' debt (well before I knew what 'economics' was). As Year 9s, it was explained to us that the money the poorest countries had borrowed from international economic institutions and banks in the richest countries – very much encouraged by Western governments – had very quickly become a crippling burden on the world's poor, taking much-needed money out of basic health and education provision.

In university I would later learn about the economics of development and how for decades flawed economic thinking had viewed developing countries through a developed country's lens, imposing inappropriate policies and creating the immense debt problems we observe in developing countries today. But also that good intentions and even lots of money are not enough to lift people and nations out of poverty. While for many years the Washington Consensus has governed how aid is spent – and the conditions that come with that aid – the story of development economics goes beyond this flawed

consensus that became the economic mantra for our global institutions. Development economics attempts to understand how we
can use aid to improve not only the GDP figures of nations, but the
everyday lives of real people living in them.

Around the world today over 700 million people live in extreme
poverty, at least 364 million of them women; 132 million girls are
not at school; 295,000 women die needlessly every year in childbirth. Poverty – of medicine, food, income and opportunity – is still
prevalent across huge swathes of the world, most of all in Africa,
but in South Asia and elsewhere too. Women are disproportionately
affected by poverty.

Since 1960, around $3.5 trillion of development assistance has
been distributed in aid, and the Millennium Development Goals of
more than twenty years ago prioritised reducing maternal mortality,
achieving universal primary education and promoting gender equality. There is a lot of evidence of policies and programmes that have
made a difference. The focus on technology and education in the
South East Asian 'tiger' economies resulted in rapid growth, opening up markets, boosting savings and delivering a sharp increase in
exports that has seen the Chinese economy grow by roughly 8 per
cent a year for around the last thirty years. But aid too has made
a difference, supplementing the recipient countries' own efforts to
create political and economic stability, better infrastructure, healthcare and life expectancy.

The United Nations goal of spending 0.7 per cent of gross national income on overseas development assistance is met by only seven
countries globally. Despite achieving this target previously, in 2021
the UK Government reduced its target to 0.5 per cent, below that
set by the United Nations, a decision that has directly resulted in the
cancellation of projects such as Concern Worldwide UK's healthcare programme in Bangladesh that would have reached over 2.6
million people and included specialist care in reproductive, maternal, newborn and child health, and has seen other projects starved of
the funding needed. While the government argued for an approach

that in their mind 'put British people first' in the wake of the Covid pandemic, in the House of Commons on 13 July 2021 I argued – as I summed up the debate that legislated for the 30 per cent cut in development spending – that this decision was devastating for some of the poorest people in the world, and especially women and girls. But also, it made bad sense for Britain's own national self-interest. To cut British overseas aid is to cut British influence on the world stage. This decision damaged Britain's position as a global leader: through the aid we give we show the world how we wish to be viewed as a country. The idea of 'Global Britain' that ministers speak of means nothing without the leadership that is needed on the global stage, and that includes leadership in reducing global inequalities and playing our part in an international effort. Outside the EU, facing into challenges of climate change, immigration and global terrorist networks, abandoning the world's poorest is precisely the wrong approach at the wrong time. But, like all economic debate, this view is hotly contested. Labour would return to the 0.7 per cent target for spending on overseas development as soon as the public finances allow.

Perhaps because development economics is an area that so clearly impacts people's lives on a global and local scale, it has attracted a significant number of influential women economists, and this chapter focuses on three women who have shaped the recent history of the subject and pioneered new thinking: Esther Duflo, Dambisa Moyo and Sakiko Fukuda-Parr.

Their very different approaches reflect the fact that development economics is not a discipline remote and separate from mainstream economic debate, and aid spending has been influenced by the economic theories of the times. In the 1950s, capital and technological advances were identified as the catalysts of economic growth, and international development aid was considered indispensable for financing investment in some of the poorest parts of the world. Over the span of the next two decades, Keynesianism became increasingly influential. The

British economist John Maynard Keynes popularised the idea that aggregate demand – defined as the total spending by households, businesses and the government – is the main driving force in an economy. Keynesianism shaped development economics in the 1960s and 1970s – public investments were viewed as the 'secret ingredient' for fostering economic prosperity. The 1980s, on the other hand, were marked by a rejection of these strategies and a reorientation towards free-market mechanisms for boosting the economies of the poorest countries.

While there has been a broad agreement until recently about the importance of development assistance (with some significant exceptions we will discuss later) the key question has been what type of intervention makes the most difference? In that context, perhaps the most interesting contribution to the debate around how to help lift the poorest people in the world out of poverty has come from the French economist Esther Duflo. Instead of asking how much should be spent and whether it's worth it, Duflo's approach is empirical and experimental.

Esther Duflo: A Pragmatic Optimist

Esther Duflo is a French-American economist who was born in Paris in 1972. During Duflo's childhood, her mother, a paediatrician, would regularly spend weeks away at a time aiding children who were victims of war. This upbringing in a home devoted to service entrenched in the young Esther Duflo a sense of responsibility, and as she grew up she knew that fighting poverty was a goal she would pursue, but imagined it would be through something like volunteering for an NGO. A trip to Russia radically changed her plans.

In an attempt to 'get some exposure to the world', she became the research assistant of well-known development economist Jeffrey Sachs, who at the time was advisor to Yegor Gaidar, the architect of the 'shock therapy' reforms aiming to trigger the transition from communism to capitalism in Russia. Duflo found her visit to Russia transformative: although initially convinced that economics was useless, ideological and – basically – boring, the visit to Russia made her declare, 'Wow, [being an economist] is the best job in the world.' She was drawn to the ability of economists to influence policy: 'They had the luxury to think about things and then to be heard by policymakers when they had something to say.' She realised that, unlike her other early career ideas, as an economist she could not just help ameliorate the effects of poverty, but could actively tackle it at its roots.

Beginning her PhD at MIT in 1995, she was determined to make her voice heard. Nevertheless, when that actually started happening, Duflo was quite surprised:

You arrive from France where you are used to being completely ignored. You come here and people are so . . . non-hierarchical. Here it doesn't matter that you are a student, that you just came from France yesterday. If you have something to say, if you have an idea, people listen.

And listen they did. Duflo was one of the youngest ever professors to secure tenure at MIT in 2002 at the age of twenty-nine, and won pretty much every prize for promising young economists before winning the best known prize of all, the Nobel Prize in Economic Sciences, in 2019 with her husband Abhijit V. Banerjee and her collaborator Michael Kremer at the age of forty-six – the youngest person and the second woman (after Elinor Ostrom) to win the award.

Esther Duflo is an economist who sees beyond theory. 'I don't have any answer on whether aid works, I don't have any answer on whether all countries should be like China. Because to me the questions are not even very well defined,' she says. As Professor of Poverty Alleviation and Development Economics at MIT, Duflo is considered one of the most influential 'economic thinkers' in the world. Together with Banerjee and Sendhil Mullainathan, she founded MIT's Abdul Latif Jameel Poverty Action Lab, where they work to change the way that economic analysis is done in exciting ways – not solely based on running abstract quantitative analysis, but, like Elinor Ostrom, by working on the ground.

Instead of having a theoretical view on development aid, arguing that it is either indispensable or useless, she is described as 'a student of detail'. Her method as a development economist is different because instead of looking at the economic impact of large-scale aid on a country as a whole, Duflo questions how that aid should be spent, down to the specifics of individual programmes.

Esther Duflo and Abhijit Banerjee, her husband and co-founder
(with Sendhil Mullainathan) of the Poverty Action Lab.

Duflo's innovative approach focuses on testing specific initiatives that could help the poor out of poverty and evaluates their effectiveness. For example, she asks questions such as:

Is it better to give people mosquito nets or make them pay? What is the best method of getting children into schools, and ensuring that they learn? Should you encourage immunisation by dispatching clinics to villages or reward parents with bags of rice? Or both? Or neither?

Only once she has established these very well-defined questions can she set up an experiment – a process quite similar to the testing of medical drugs.

In her 2011 book *Poor Economics* co-authored with Banerjee, which won the 2011 *Financial Times* and Goldman Sachs Business Book of the Year Award, she elaborated on this 'radical rethinking of the way to fight global poverty'. Rejecting the broad generalisation tendencies prevalent in development economics, Duflo offers a third viable alternative to the traditional free-market solutions, on the one hand, and expansive aid plans, on the other. The method consists of amplifying the voices of the poor, meaning an effort is made to understand the decision-making process of those in poverty on issues such as savings, business, healthcare and others. The randomised controlled testing ensures the scientific accuracy of their findings. Overall, it emphasises that minor changes and targeted support can be more impactful than grand attempts to solve global poverty doled out on a large scale without focus. Perhaps her most important message is that it is not about the amount of money spent on aid but how it is spent that has a bearing on the development of a nation and its ability to lift people out of poverty.

Using this empirical approach, Duflo identifies numerous strategies for eradicating poverty. Just to name a few: her work shows that financial incentives are not as effective as anticipated at motivating people ('People seem to be pretty inelastic to receiving money'). She shows that training and coaching sessions should accompany any cash transfers to empower people living in poverty to make decisions about how to use additional resources, giving them confidence, and teaching the technical skills necessary for taking care of their goods. One example of how she has altered thinking in development economics concerns microcredit schemes, which provide small loans to individuals who otherwise lack resources but need financing to help them start and grow businesses. For decades such schemes were thought to be extremely successful at alleviating poverty, but studies including those undertaken by Duflo have more recently questioned the success of microcredit schemes. Given their established credibility and controversy surrounding their effects, she only published the study 'when seven evaluations in different countries and contexts showed similar results'. The key findings of Duflo's work have now been adopted and incorporated into their policies by many aid distributors, and Duflo says that one of the most rewarding aspects of being a Nobel Prize laureate is the legitimacy awarded to her work: 'This [Nobel Prize] will help . . . in terms of opening doors and . . . reassuring various governments [that] this is legitimate and not a strange undertaking by some crazy people.'

Duflo's methods and apparent simplicity is quite disarming: 'You think hard about the problems and you can solve them,' she says. But there are a few voices that argue that we in the rich world cannot and should not be attempting to solve them. The most prominent of which is Dambisa Moyo's.

Dambisa Moyo: Aid is Dead

Born in Lusaka, Zambia in 1969, Moyo studied chemistry at the University of Zambia. After spending part of her childhood in the United States, where her father was studying, she decided to follow in his footsteps and pursued further study in the US at the American University in Washington before studying for an MBA. She then worked for two years at the World Bank before completing a Master of Public Administration at Harvard Kennedy School in 1997 and a PhD in economics at Oxford University. She worked at Goldman Sachs from 2001 to 2008, during which time she worked on developing markets and was head of research and strategy for sub-Saharan Africa. Since then she has been on the board of a number of multinational companies, as well as multinational organisations such as the World Economic Forum, and has become a well-known public speaker and columnist. In 2022 she received a life peerage from the UK Government and now sits in the House of Lords as Baroness Moyo of Knightsbridge.

Moyo is best known for her book *Dead Aid: Why Aid is Not Working and How There is a Better Way for Africa*, which she wrote while still working at Goldman Sachs. Some of her views build on the 'Washington Consensus' approach to development of the 1980s and 1990s and even go a step further. In *Dead Aid* she argues that development aid is worse than useless and indeed harmful because, with the exception of emergency assistance, governments can come to depend on regular aid and use it as an alternative to developing their own solutions. Worse than that, Moyo points out that a great deal of aid money given has been diverted from the people it is intended to help by corrupt governments.

Moyo attributes this catastrophe to pity, which makes donors 'turn the blind eye to corruption' and creates a 'continent-wide addiction' to aid. With an economy based primarily on development assistance, African governments – Moyo argues – lost the ability to plan for the future, and the confidence to act for and believe in themselves.

So, what should be done instead? First, Moyo recommends the replacement of loans and grants with bonds: the capital market does not have low interest rates for risky investments and is unforgiving of corruption, so the fear of messing up and losing the money or not being able to pay interest would be a great stimulant for growth and innovation. In Moyo's view this cheap money or free money with few consequences if it is lost or disappears, is the problem.

Second, and even more controversially, Moyo argues that, 'In the last sixty years, no country has made as big an impact on the political, economic and social fabric of Africa as China has since

Dambisa Moyo is known for being one of the few economists to
challenge the Western consensus on government development aid.

the turn of the millenium', because the Chinese Government treats
African policymakers as equals and does not pity or condescend.
Instead, the growing demand for both soft commodities such as
food and harder commodities (oil and metals) in China means that
the Chinese Government sees Africa as a potential long-term business partner that can supply the resources they need to sustain their
own growth and development. Given the large proportion of young
people in Africa, Moyo believes that sustainable economic growth
starts with the creation of jobs and this can be facilitated by dealings
with China. She does recognise that there are real worries associated with these business deals. Without a doubt, 'China is in Africa
for China,' says Moyo, which means that Chinese officials are ready
to ignore human rights abuses and might prefer importing their
own labour for their infrastructure projects, thus undercutting local

industry. However, Moyo suggests that such stories are 'exaggerated by the Western media', due to an 'ill-feeling about the fact that the Western development model hasn't delivered for Africa and the Chinese method so far is delivering'.

Third, Moyo recommends a shift in African governments' strategy, calling for a more efficient banking sector for savings and remittances by people working abroad to their relatives back home. Because savings are crucial for funding economic development, and remittances account for a major part of many developing countries' GDP, it is important for them to be properly administrated, says Moyo.

While many accept that these problems exist, Moyo's proposals and her solutions are highly contentious. Ultimately a free-marketeer (despite her compliments towards Chinese engagement in Africa), Dambisa Moyo pins her hopes on capitalism and the power of free markets (like Martineau before her) to lift people out of poverty and urges the end of overseas development assistance. As she writes in her book *Dead Aid*,

> The notion that aid can alleviate systemic poverty, and has done so, is a myth. Millions in Africa are poorer today because of aid; misery and poverty have not ended but have increased. Aid has been, and continues to be, an unmitigated political, economic, and humanitarian disaster for most parts of the developing world.

Sakiko Fukuda-Parr: Institutional Analysis

Sakiko Fukuda-Parr disagrees with both Moyo's analysis and prescription. The UN economist and academic has deep reservations regarding the neoliberal economic model endorsed by Moyo, warning that free-market capitalism is 'creating societies that are very troubling in their capacity to provide equitable opportunities for everybody'. Although aware of the shortcomings of aid highlighted by Moyo and others, Fukuda-Parr is convinced it would be a mistake to think markets can fix endemic poverty and economic stagnation, and fears they would create even more inequality.

Sakiko Fukuda-Parr was born in Japan in 1950 but as a child travelled around the world with her family because of her father's job for the Japanese Government. She has degrees from Cambridge University and Sussex University and a master's in law and development from the Fletcher School at Tufts University. After working at the World Bank, first as a loan officer and then as an advisor on the agricultural and rural development programmes, she worked for the UN Development Programme from 1979 to 2004, latterly as Head of the UN Development Reports. She returned to academia in 2004 which she has combined with serving on several boards, global committees and NGO networks advocating for human rights and inclusive development. She is currently Professor of International Affairs at the New School, New York, and director of the Collective for the Political Determinants of Health at the University of Oslo. Her co-authored book *Fulfilling Economic and Social Rights*, published in 2015, was awarded the Grawemeyer Award for Ideas Improving World Order.

Like many economists and practitioners, Fukuda-Parr shares some of Moyo's concerns about those sub-Saharan African countries whose 'entire capital investment budgets . . . are financed by external aid', listing the negative repercussions of aid dependence: 'It weakens states and the democratic accountability of states to their people; it makes coordination of economic management complex; and it leads to unpredictability of resource flows.' But instead of rejecting development assistance she instead suggests ways to improve 'aid effectiveness', such as greater focus on reporting on outcomes, not just money spent, and doing more to develop democratically accountable governments who are answerable to their own people for the use of donors' money.

Fukuda-Parr's knowledge of these issues is based on extensive experience in dealing with the practical issues of international development. As Director of the Human Development Report

Office at the United Nations Development Programme, she has tackled questions about how to improve development aid's effectiveness, working with countries to boost development spending in line with the 0.7 per cent of gross national income commitments made, and ensuring that that money is well spent.

In recent years Covid-19 has shut down economies and highlighted the inequalities of access to healthcare. In Africa, only 25.6 per cent of the population are fully vaccinated, but this number, when broken down, is even more worrying. In the Democratic Republic of Congo only 7.8 per cent are fully vaccinated, whereas Zambia and Botswana have vaccination rates of 48 per cent and 62 per cent respectively. While inequalities exist even within continents, the overall African vaccine rate compares with the 76 per cent in the UK and 68 per cent in the US. One of Fukuda-Parr's pleas is that the voices of the developing world are heard more loudly in debates around international policy. Largely forgotten is the struggle developing nations faced in procuring and administering the Covid vaccines. Even after donations through international programmes like Covax, many of the vaccines that were delivered were close to expiry, with a shelf life of four weeks by the time they arrived, in the case of one delivery to Nigeria. Fukuda-Parr's argument is that stories and experiences like these should not be forgotten in the aftermath of crises. In the context of the Covid-19 pandemic, she argued that we need more progressive debt relief for developing countries, urging the governments of creditor countries to take action. Fukuda-Parr emphasises the importance of 'international coordination and policy agreement' that would take 'this public emergency out of the logic of the market', since the priorities of the market do not coincide with those of public health. As we saw during the pandemic, the voices from 'resource-poor countries, low- and middle-income countries, the debtors as opposed to the creditors' are not given sufficient consideration in multinational institutions, which, Fukuda-Parr argues, is a matter that requires immediate rectification. With the voices of poor countries amplified and thus finally heard, the system of financing research in the health sector might be delinked from the institutions of the market. In this way, the health and wellbeing of people, regardless of their nationality or income level, will become the priority, instead of monetary interests.

As is clear, the debate in academic and practitioner circles is increasingly prevalent in politics. The question of whether development aid

For many years Sakiko Fukuda-Parr was the lead on the
UN Human Development Reports and is an expert on
health and global goal-setting.

makes a difference is an important one for policymakers and one that has become politically contentious again in a way that it hasn't been for two decades.

When Labour was elected in 1997, the amount of aid the UK gave as a proportion of our national income had halved over the preceding eighteen years and stood at just 0.26 per cent. By the end of Labour's time in office, in 2010, we were on our way to achieving the 0.7 per cent target. This was down to the political leadership of Tony Blair and Gordon Brown – and their first Secretary of State for International

Development from 1997 to 2002, Clare Short, who brought the lives of the world's poorest people into the heart of government.

And the determination that was shown in that period, in the UK and through the G7, was proof that politics can and does change things for the better: more babies born safely (and their mothers more likely to survive too); more children vaccinated (so they don't die of diseases that our children don't die of); and more children being able to attend school. This is so important, especially for girls, because we know how it opens a window on the world, improves life chances and boosts self-confidence and aspiration. It has been devastating to hear the stories of young Afghan women and girls and their crushed dreams of becoming doctors, engineers and teachers because of the brutal banning of women's education by the Taliban. It should be our mission as a global community to ensure any girl who wishes to be a doctor, teacher, engineer – or even an economist – has access to the education to do so, no matter where she is born.

Of course, money isn't everything. The right projects, governance and accountability matter too. As does empowering local people, not imposing solutions. But the political consensus, that saw David Cameron back the 0.7 per cent commitment under his leadership of the Conservative Party, and saw every major party at the last general election back that figure, has now been broken. In 2021 the Conservatives legislated to 'temporarily' override the 0.7 per cent commitment, resurrecting old divisions with development aid used again as a political football. As I said in the debate in parliament, development assistance had given more people access to clean water, had allowed girls to attend school, and helped invest in crucial infrastructure. It had also been an inspiring example of Britain's leadership in the world as we led the way and by example encouraged others to do more too.

Boris Johnson once described the Department of International Development (which he later abolished) as a 'giant cashpoint in the sky'. Even more depressingly, the Conservative government offers no alternative to the political consensus of the last twenty years or any practical suggestions as to how to lift people out of poverty and create a more just and more stable world, but instead promotes the feeling that it is all too expensive and not our responsibility.

The philosopher John Rawls asks us all to put ourselves behind a 'veil of ignorance', where we don't know our position in the world, our skills or talents. In that position what sort of political and economic system would you devise? How much redistribution would there be in the political economy you create? Would luck and hard work both be rewarded? I think that behind a veil of ignorance, not knowing whether you would be born into poverty in sub-Saharan Africa or prosperity in North America or Europe, then you would create a system which would alleviate the unnecessary suffering and the gross inequalities that exist today. I believe that we have a moral duty to help end maternal mortality, ensure that people have access to clean water wherever they live and supply a guarantee that children are at school, whichever country they are born in. That's why I was a supporter of Jubilee 2000, the campaign to cancel the debts of the poorest countries in the world, and of the Millennium Development Goals, spearheaded in the UK by Tony Blair and Gordon Brown and the G8 Make Poverty History summit in Gleneagles in 2005, which secured the writing-off of tens of billions of dollars of debt owed by the poorest and most indebted countries in the world.

So, while I respect the work of Dambisa Moyo, who is correct to point to waste and corruption, I refuse to accept her fatalism that there is nothing that the rich world can do, and that aid is misguided. Development assistance can and does make a difference. Sakiko Fukuda-Parr is not complacent or ignorant of the challenges in ensuring value for money with aid. By working with donors and international institutions, she has helped design and evaluate programmes that have made a material difference to people's lives, showing the difference that economics can make.

Why Duflo, Moyo and Fukuda-Parr Matter

An outspoken critic of development assistance, Dambisa Moyo calls attention to the limitations of aid. Sakiko Fukuda-Parr spearheaded and analysed international organisations' interventions to fight poverty and inequality. Esther Duflo, aware of the deficiencies of aid, is working towards eradicating the pervasive misconceptions about poverty and conducts experiments to identify the best methods for helping people out of poverty. Working out how to lift millions out of poverty is still a question that needs answering, because the truth is, despite good intentions, the poverty we saw on the TV in the 1980s, prompting the Live Aid concerts that stirred the consciousness of the West, still persists today. Although the prescriptions of these three economists differ, each of them has helped contribute to addressing this challenge – the right answer will save lives and change them too.

Giving her opinion on how to increase the number of women in economics, Esther Duflo recommended persuading more and more people that this field is not 'removed from any real person's life'. She thinks young students should be exposed to something beyond the 'Econ 101 course' and Phillips curves – they should come to see that economics is also about climate change, poverty and changing people's lives. Esther Duflo, Sakiko Fukuda-Parr and Dambisa Moyo have done exactly that – they changed the conventional wisdom regarding what an economist looks like, cares about, and where they come from.

These economists' fearlessness, courage and innovative spirit has helped open the door for a new, more diverse generation of economists. Their disagreements on methodology, on the other hand, are indicative of the dynamism of development economics – a large body of economic thought continuing to evolve and question itself.

I will continue to believe that we have the means and the obligation to help lift people out of poverty. When people say that politics doesn't make a difference, then the Millennium Development Goals, debt relief and achieving the 0.7 per cent target for aid spending by the UK show that it can and does. As Gordon Brown has said: 'Let no one say aid and debt relief don't make a difference and politics never works – what doesn't work is doing nothing.' Based on the evidence and well-designed programmes, such spending can save lives, boost school attendance, especially for girls, and contribute to the sustainable economic development of some of the poorest people and places on the planet. While aid of course is key to global development, its impact goes far beyond the economic.

Using the insights of economists like Esther Duflo, a Labour government will not only get back to our aid target when the fiscal situation allows, but we will get more from what we spend on aid. Through aid, the last Labour government helped lift three million people per year out of poverty, and it is my hope that the next one will also have a transformative impact on eradicating poverty. The Conservatives are projected to spend £3 billion of the development budget in Britain to cover the costs of incoming refugees – billions of pounds of our already reduced foreign aid budget will never leave Britain. A Labour government will get serious about our global responsibilities and get the most out of what Britain gives in aid by investing in tested, proven ways to bring us closer to stamping out global poverty.

9

Janet Yellen and the Role of Central Banks and Treasury Departments

My first memory of a Chancellor of the Exchequer was in the October half-term holiday when I was ten years old. We were visiting my grandparents in Kettering, Northamptonshire, but my sister and I were having tea up the road at the house of a great-aunt. On the television that evening it was announced that Nigel Lawson, Thatcher's second chancellor, had resigned because of disagreements with her about Britain's place in the European Exchange Rate Mechanism. I knew that my dad didn't like Thatcher or Lawson and so wanted to be the first to tell him the good news. I ran back to my grandparents' house (much to their surprise, as I wasn't really allowed to go running up and down the road on my own), and told my dad. He, to my surprise, didn't share my excitement. 'It will only be another Tory,' he said. It was a quick lesson in politics and democracy, but a disappointment that my good news was not what it first appeared. For of course the next chancellor was indeed another Tory – in fact it was John Major, who served for two years before he became prime minister. It wasn't until eight years after Lawson resigned that we were to have the Labour chancellor that my dad and I both wanted, and that of course was Gordon Brown. While we go through chancellors slightly faster these days (last year alone I faced four across the despatch box), one thing that hasn't changed is that they have all been men.

In the UK we haven't yet had a woman heading up the Treasury – as either chancellor or Permanent Secretary – or a female Governor of the Bank of England. In looking for women to take inspiration from I have had to look a bit further afield. Luckily, around the world, women are rising to those top jobs – three leap out: Janet Yellen, Christine Lagarde and Sri Mulyani Indrawati. Politically, I am closest to Janet Yellen, a Keynesian economist and professor of the labour market and macroeconomics. Her modern supply-side economics is transforming the US economy today, increasing investment, wages and employment – an example of the inclusive growth that I hope to emulate in Britain as chancellor. But Lagarde and Sri Mulyani have also provided economic and political leadership while championing women's economic participation too. While many of the women whose stories are chronicled in this book have redefined how we think about economics, these three women stand out for having redefined economies, rather than economics, and for taking theories and applying them to make real change.

In the US, at the time of writing, Janet Yellen is Treasury Secretary, appointed by President Biden in 2021. Before that she served as chair of the US Federal Reserve Bank in Washington, and before that as chair of President Clinton's Council of Economic Advisors. In Europe, Christine Lagarde was appointed as chair of the European Central Bank in 2019. Before that she was Head of the International Monetary Fund (IMF) between 2011 and 2019, and previous to that served as finance minister in France, even though her original training was as a lawyer. In Indonesia, Sri Mulyani Indrawati, known as Indonesia's Iron Lady for her unrelenting approach to reform, has served two stints as finance minister, first between 2005 and 2010, and then from 2016 onwards. In between she was at the World Bank in Washington.

These three women have steered three very different economies through turbulent economic times, including the Global Financial Crisis, the Covid pandemic and now the war in Ukraine. Each has faced unique challenges ranging from reducing inequality while dealing with a hyperpolarised politics to tackling relative decline and economic inflexibility and dealing with endemic corruption, and this chapter tells the stories of these three remarkable women and how they have navigated both the economics and politics of their roles and what we can learn from them.

Janet Yellen

Yellen was born in 1946, the second of two children, and raised in Brooklyn, New York City. Her father's family emigrated to the US from a small town in Poland, from where nearly all of the population, including many of her relatives, were deported or murdered during the Holocaust. Her mother Anna was a primary school teacher, and her father Julius was a doctor who worked from the ground floor of their house. She attended Fort Hamilton High School, where she was editor of *The Pilot*, the school newspaper. She was an outstanding student, graduating as class valedictorian, and in line with the school tradition that the editor of *The Pilot* interview the valedictorian, she conducted an interview with herself in the third person!

Enrolling at Brown University after High School, Yellen initially intended to study philosophy, but switched to economics. After graduating, she studied at Yale University where she earned her PhD in 1971, the only woman among the two dozen economists awarded doctorates from Yale that year. Her professors at Yale included the Nobel laureates James Tobin and Joseph Stiglitz. Stiglitz has called Yellen one of his brightest and most memorable students.

After completing her PhD, Yellen taught economics at Harvard, one of only two women in the faculty, the other being Rachel McCulloch, and the two struck up a close friendship, going on to write several academic papers together. After Harvard, Yellen began working for the US central bank, the Federal Reserve. It was while working there that she met her husband, George Akerlof, in the cafeteria. They got married in 1978, less than a year after meeting, and moved to the UK where they spent two years at the London School of Economics before returning to the US and the University of California, Berkeley, where Akerlof had been offered a full professorship and Yellen a position at the Haas business school. Their son Robert (now an economics professor at the University of Warwick in England) was born in 1981.

Yellen had always been interested in policy and in 1994 she received her first public appointment when President Bill Clinton nominated her as a member of the Federal Reserve Board of Governors. She was only the fourth woman to serve as a governor, serving alongside Susan M. Phillips, the first time that two women have served on the Board simultaneously. Phillips was herself a distinguished academic and policy economist, who had previously served as chair of the Commodity Futures Trading Commission, a role she took on in 1983, making her the first woman to lead a US regulatory agency. This was the era in which women economists in the United States were beginning to shatter the highest, hardest glass ceilings of public policy economics.

In monetary policy terms Yellen is regarded as a 'dove' – more concerned about employment rates than inflation. In July 1996, with Yellen on the Board, the Federal Reserve, under chairman Alan Greenspan, resisted pressure to raise interest rates as unemployment declined, a stance Yellen endorsed. She also presented academic research to dissuade Greenspan from committing to a zero inflation policy, arguing that central banks should seek to moderate inflation rather than eliminate it. The study showed that a little inflation, around the 2 per cent range, was a better basis to minimise unemployment and increase economic growth than the proposed goal of zero. This is now mainstream economic thinking, especially after the experience of the difficulty of Japan escaping from deflation, and has its roots in the work of Janet Yellen. The UK Government's inflation target is set to 2 per cent and the policy of moderating inflation in the UK has existed under successive Labour and Conservative governments – a testament to the influence of Janet Yellen's work.

In 1996, two years after starting at the Fed, Yellen became chair of President Clinton's Council of Economic Advisors (CEA), replacing her old Yale tutor, Joseph Stiglitz. Yellen was the second woman to hold the job, following Laura Tyson (who suggested Yellen for the post at the Fed in 1994). Tyson's own work has focused on trade and entrepreneurship with a particular focus on the economic empowerment of women. She is one of two co-authors of the UN's 'Leave No One Behind: A Call to Action for Gender Equality and Women's Economic Empowerment' report which calls for inclusive growth as a vehicle to empower women and take strides towards gender equality.

When Tyson was appointed by President Clinton, she broke boundaries for women in public policy economics. Her recommending of Yellen for the post at the Federal Reserve shows a woman in economics who not only shatters glass ceilings but throws down a ladder to help other talented women get the roles they deserve, drawing us closer to gender equity in the profession.

During Yellen's term as chair of the Council of Economic Advisors, she oversaw a landmark report, 'Explaining Trends in the Gender Wage Gap', concluding that discrimination, not productivity or job choice, was the main reason for women's lower pay compared with their male counterparts. After the CEA Yellen returned to Berkeley to her academic post but in 2004 took on the role as chair of the San Francisco Federal Reserve Bank. She reflected in a podcast with Marketplace in 2019, nearly ten years after the event, that this was an interesting vantage point from which to watch the seeds of the Global Financial Crisis being sown. The West Coast of America – particularly the Bay Area of San Francisco, but right across to Phoenix, Arizona, and Las Vegas, Nevada – saw a huge construction of new homes coupled with an increase in land prices that fuelled the bubble that would so spectacularly burst with the difficulties at the mortgage loan companies Fannie Mae and Freddie Mac and precipitate the financial crisis which left devastation in its wake. Yellen saw much of this at first hand as chair of her regional Federal Reserve, meeting businesses, developers, banks and investors to understand what was happening.

Nearly a decade after leaving Washington for the West Coast,

Janet Yellen speaking at her nomination ceremony as chair
of the Federal Reserve in October 2013.

Yellen returned during President Obama's second term in office,
first as vice chair and then chair of the Federal Reserve from 2014
to 2018, the first woman to take the top spot in the hundred-year
history of the US central bank. Her role at the San Francisco Fed
was taken by Mary Daly, a mentee of Yellen's who is equally as fascinating. Daly dropped out of high school when she was just fifteen
and by sixteen was living alone and working multiple jobs to make
ends meet. She is now a respected authority in the fields of macroeconomics and labour economics, has published extensive influential
work on income inequality and was the first openly gay woman to
lead a regional Federal Reserve bank.

Yellen was the first Democratic nominee to run the Federal
Reserve since Paul Volcker in 1979. As Fed chair, Yellen found herself in charge at a time of economic recovery but with a huge deficit

on the balance sheet built up in response to the financial crisis and the quantitative easing programme that followed. Yellen's approach during these years was to tighten monetary policy only very cautiously, resulting in a strongly growing economy with record employment. As she described in an interview with Sam Fleming from the *Financial Times* in 2018 after her time at the Fed had come to an end: 'I really thought we needed to pull every rabbit out of the hat' (as the economy continued its recovery from the Global Financial Crisis). Her approach was also a very collegiate one: having been a Fed staffer at the beginning of her career, Yellen was at home working with the large research staff and understood the cogs and wheels of the economy. It was also while chair of the Federal Reserve Bank that Yellen ended up at the receiving end of then presidential candidate Donald Trump's attacks when he accused Yellen of keeping interest rates artificially low to help President Obama. As president, Trump refused Yellen a second term as Fed chair. Later asked whether she thought that Trump understood macroeconomics she replied simply: 'No. I don't.'

After three years away from the political and economic spotlight during the Trump presidency, Yellen was appointed Secretary of the Treasury by President Biden in January 2021, and was, once again, the first woman to take up that position. She is also the first person in American history to have led the White House Council of Economic Advisors, the Federal Reserve and the Treasury. There has simply never been an economist with as much experience of managing the policy levers that oil the machine of the US economy as Janet Yellen.

Yellen says her husband, George Akerlof, has been her biggest intellectual influence, and the couple have been an economic powerhouse, supporting each other as they moved between the West and East Coasts of the US, as well as a stint in England, sometimes his and sometimes her career coming first. They have achieved a huge amount together and individually. Akerlof was awarded the 2001 Nobel Prize in Economics, jointly with Michael Spence and Joseph

Stiglitz, 'for their analyses of markets with asymmetric information', and is perhaps most well known to economic undergraduates for 'Akerlof's lemons', from his 1970 paper 'The Market for "Lemons": Quality Uncertainty and the Market Mechanism', which examines how the quality of goods traded in a market (think second-hand cars) can fall in the presence of information asymmetry between buyers and sellers, leaving only 'lemons' (or dud cars) behind. Yellen also describes her Yale professors James Tobin and William Brainard as 'lifelong mentors', who provided the main intellectual foundation for her views on the economy.

Another close friend, contemporary and collaborator of Yellen's, Rachel McCulloch, whom she met at Harvard, went on to become an economics professor at Brandeis University, where she worked until her death in 2016. She was a leading figure in the field of international trade, and served as a consultant to the World Bank and Asian Development Bank. McCulloch was the 2013 winner of the Carolyn Shaw Bell Award from the Committee on the Status of Women in the Economics Profession.

Today, there are other powerful women rising up through economic policymaking in the US, not least Lael Brainard, current head of President Biden's National Economic Council and former deputy chair of the Federal Reserve Bank. Brainard is tipped by many as the next chair of the US Federal Reserve. Meanwhile, Celia Rouse is chair of President Biden's Council of Economic Advisors, whose members include Heather Boushey, an economist specialising in inequality and economic growth.

Economic Thinking

Yellen's academic career largely focused on unemployment and labour markets, monetary and fiscal policies, and international trade, often collaborating with her husband. Since the 1980s, Yellen and Akerlof have worked on what is called 'efficiency wage theory': the idea that paying people more than the market wage increases their productivity. While Joan Robinson argued that workers did not receive the full value of their labour in their pay packets because of the lack of bargaining power, Yellen makes an argument based on the interests of the employers themselves in paying higher wages – as higher wages generate loyalty and motivation, encouraging the workers to put in extra effort which increases their productivity and output.

As Yellen described in an interview in 1995 with the Minneapolis Federal Reserve Bank when she was first appointed as a Federal Reserve Bank governor, her work 'takes seriously the ideas that firms' wage policies impact the productivity and morale of workers and that firms constantly take those impacts into account in setting and changing wages'. In their 1990 paper 'The Fair-Wage Effort Hypothesis and Unemployment', Yellen and Akerlof also explain why wages don't tend to fall or rise quickly with changes in the economic circumstances as businesses also use wages to motivate their workers and not just to pay what the market dictates. Yellen and Akerlof also introduced the argument that workers who receive less than what they perceive to be a fair wage will purposely work less hard as a way to take revenge on their employer.

Yellen has been described as a 'Keynesian to her fingertips'. During the Great Recession, and while head of the San Francisco Federal Reserve Bank, she 'warned against an over-hasty removal of stimulus', instead insisting that the government 'pay as much attention to unemployment as to inflation'. She believes the state has a 'duty to tackle poverty and inequality'. When her appointment as Treasury Secretary was announced in December 2020, Yellen was viewed by Wall Street as a 'Treasury Secretary who will push hard for expansionary policies aimed at boosting growth, profits and share prices'.

Since being appointed by Biden to the Treasury she has worked in partnership with him on policies to improve the supply-side capacity of the economy, with policies to boost US manufacturing and industry, and to improve the quality of the labour force and the number of people available for work through better childcare and support for older and disabled workers. She has also worked to develop a raft of policies to invest in renewable energy and electric vehicles, identifying them as industries of the future, by which America, with government support, can develop a comparative advantage, securing well paid, unionised and skilled jobs for the American people. While criticised domestically for stoking inflation in the US, and internationally for favouring US production, President Biden is hoping that this stimulus and the well-paid jobs it is creating in regions desperately in need of them will help him secure a second term against whoever stands for the Republican Party in 2024.

In his appointment of Janet Yellen, President Biden chose one of the best economists in the world to run his economics department. It was a wise choice, and Yellen is delivering. The US economy has bounced back quicker than almost anywhere in the world from Covid – it is now 5 per cent bigger than before Covid; the UK economy is barely larger than it was in 2019.

And Yellen's policy programme is both bold and focused. Identifying the barriers to growth and putting in policies to tackle them, Yellen is helping grow the economy. Her focus on new industries is also instructive. Yellen is taking a bet on industries like electric vehicles that are growing, but need a kick-start from government, through subsidies or direct investment. Every country wants these jobs; Yellen is doing all in her power to get them in the US.

Much of my securonomics approach has its roots in Yellen's modern supply-side economics. The Inflation Reduction Act should be an inspiration to us in Britain, not a threat, as the current government paint it. Yellen's policies have identified insecure areas of the US economy and have invested in building national resilience – that's what I want to do in Britain. A Labour government will strengthen our economy in areas where we must become more resilient, rebuild the industrial foundations we have lost, leaving us exposed to global shocks, and make Britain a world leader in the industries and technologies that will determine our future economic success. Our overarching goal will be the building of financial security in each and every household in Britain, just as Janet Yellen has set out to do in the United States.

By focusing too on social outcomes – that growth is properly broadly based – wages for the working and middle classes are rising, not just the profits for those at the top. The focus on good jobs as well as growth is key here. Economic prosperity and social justice go hand in hand – Yellen's policy programme shows that. It's a philosophy that I will take to the UK Treasury if I get that chance.

Christine Lagarde

While Yellen has been a lifelong Democrat, on the centre left of politics, Lagarde is a French Republican, on the centre right.

Christine Lallouette was born in Paris into a family of professors and teachers but she and her three younger brothers spent their childhood in Le Havre, where she attended the school where her father, who died when she was just seventeen, taught. As a teenager, she was a member of the French national synchronised swimming team and remains a keen swimmer. Unlike the majority of the women in this book, Lagarde did not study economics but instead studied English, labour law and social law. But this lack of formal training in economics hasn't stopped her rising to the very top of the economics profession.

Lagarde joined the international law firm Baker & McKenzie in Paris in 1981, specialising in anti-trust and labour law, and became the first female member of the executive committee and chair in 1999, moving to Chicago to take up the role.

Lagarde returned from Chicago to France in 2005 to join Prime Minister Dominique de Villepin's government as trade minister, encouraging foreign investment in France and the opening of new markets for French products, with a particular interest in the technology sector. In June 2007, Lagarde was designated finance minister by newly elected President Nicolas Sarkozy. She was the first woman in any of the G7 countries to hold this position, and during her tenure oversaw the government response to the late 2000s Global Financial Crisis, for which the *Financial Times* ranked her the best finance minister in the Eurozone. Her initial appointment reflected the end of a political leadership in France dominated by anti-globalisation and the beginning of an acceptance of the measures needed to revitalise France's increasingly uncompetitive and flagging economy. In contrast to her predecessors, Lagarde held the controversial view in France that the country's thirty-five-hour work week was a symbol of laziness. She advocated for labour law liberalisation and a stronger work ethic, a sentiment mirrored and respected by the French business community.

Four years after starting as finance minister in France, Lagarde succeeded Dominique Strauss-Kahn as head of the IMF, following his arrest for sexual assault. Lagarde was the first woman to hold the post. Her appointment came amid the intensification of the European sovereign debt crisis, especially in Greece, with fears looming of loan defaults. The United States in particular supported her speedy appointment in light of the fragility of Europe's economic situation.

During her tenure at the IMF, Lagarde consistently rejected suggestions of her candidacy for any other senior positions in Europe, including those of President of the European Commission and President of the European Central Bank. 'I have a very important job here that I want to do,' she said in 2018, 'and I'm not going to leave that beautiful vessel when there might be rough waters out there.' But in 2019, Lagarde was persuaded to return to Europe and was appointed to succeed Mario Draghi as President of the European Central Bank, another first for a woman.

Christine Lagarde in her most recent role as President of the European Central Bank. Throughout her career she has promoted equality for women.

Economic Thinking

Economically and politically, Lagarde is committed to a liberal market-based economy, arguing for reforms to make economies, especially the French economy, more competitive. Asked to describe her economic philosophy by the fashion magazine *Vogue* in 2011, Lagarde aligned herself 'with Adam Smith – that is, liberal'. Certainly, when she was in government, Lagarde implemented liberal economic reforms: in the labour market; lowering taxes to stimulate economic activity; and through implementing an austerity plan for public services.

Two speeches best encapsulate her economic thinking. The first at the World Economic Forum in Davos in 2013 focused on the importance of economic growth, arguing for greater openness, stronger inclusion, and better accountability to achieve the aim of a growing economy. The second, five years later, was in Hong Kong, where Lagarde argued firmly against protectionism in all its forms, saying:

> History shows that import restrictions hurt everyone, especially poorer consumers. Not only do they lead to more expensive products and more limited choices, but they also prevent trade from playing its essential role in boosting productivity and spreading new technologies. Even protected industries eventually suffer as they become less dynamic than their foreign competitors.

Lagarde argued that free trade and openness have transformed our world over the past generation. In her view, expanded global trade is responsible for helping halve the proportion of the world's population living in extreme poverty, reducing the cost of living and creating millions of new jobs with higher wages. This reverence for interconnectedness is probably the strongest and most consistent theme in Lagarde's economics – a belief that the global economy is more interconnected than ever; that this is a good thing for living standards, innovation and productivity; that such interconnectedness requires greater cooperation between nations; and that further integration of our economies should be a policy objective: 'Solidarity is self-interest,' Lagarde argued in a speech in Washington in 2018.

Despite such enthusiasm, the truth is that the impetus towards economic integration has faded and Lagarde acknowledges that 'public worries related to globalisation, like inequality and equitable integration, have arisen in recent years'. One of her primary concerns is that rising inequality could generate what she described in a speech to the US Library of Congress as an 'age of anger', where the gap between 'aspirations and realities' could 'feed anger and bitterness'. The solutions Lagarde argues for centre around a more equitable distribution of the rewards of globalisation, so that the benefits of economic integration are felt by all in society. She calls this a 'new multilateralism' – where practical policies could include reducing barriers to trade; tax cooperation, especially so that global multinationals pay their fair share; and tackling the dangerous effects of climate change, including in some of the poorest parts of the world.

Although she feels equivocal about it, Lagarde is clearly correct in identifying the key emerging trend in global political economy as deglobalisation, and the increasing importance of the nation state. Whether it is Brexit, 'Make America Great Again', or reshaping and building stronger supply chains, the impetus for ever increasing globalisation has faded and a more assertive economics of the nation state is emerging. The risk is higher prices, as cheap imports are replaced by domestically produced goods, and a slowing of global poverty alleviation as trade slows. But Covid, the war in Ukraine, and the resultant energy and food crises show too the limits of globalisation. Britain and Europe have been too reliant on Russia, and other states that don't share our values, for gas and our essential energy needs. Ukraine, the breadbasket of the world, is under siege, impacting not just Europe but much of Africa with a real risk of widespread famine. This failure of supply to meet demand for essential goods shows how interconnected we are but also the risks that poses.

I agree with Lagarde that the near future will see a retrenchment of trade integration as countries seek to be more resilient. Unlike her, I think this rebalancing is due, and that we should think about our domestic security through an economic lens – using an approach that I call securonomics and upon which my policies to buy, make and do more in Britain are all based. And because this is a global trend, we cannot afford to be naive in Britain. The US's 'Buy America' programme, and Europe's single market – which we have left – mean we must try to build up British industry, and support production, research and science in Britain, because no one else will look after our national interest, while we also need to strengthen our ties with our closest trading partners.

Sri Mulyani Indrawati

Sri Mulyani Indrawati was born in 1962 in Sumatra, Indonesia. The seventh of nine children, her parents were both university lecturers, and she obtained her first degree in economics from the University of Indonesia in 1986, then continued her studies in the US, earning her PhD in economics in 1992. Like Yellen and many other women in this book, Sri Mulyani is married to a fellow economist, Tony Sumartono.

After graduating, she returned as an economics lecturer to Indonesia, where she witnessed the Asian Financial Crisis of 1997 and the end of the thirty-year authoritarian rule of President Suharto. These formative experiences confirmed for Sri Mulyani the importance of a careful, fact-based approach to economic policy, or as she put it, a frustration with 'the wrong policy, the wrong approach' in Indonesia. In 2001 Sri Mulyani moved back to the US, to serve as a consultant with the US Agency for International Development (USAID) for programmes to strengthen Indonesia's autonomy. As a specialist of monetary economics and banking, as well as labour economics, she was chosen to be the Executive Director at the IMF representing twelve countries in South East Asia, including Indonesia.

Not long after, in 2004, she received her first cabinet appointment as Indonesia's Minister of Development Planning, leading the Indonesian National Development Planning Agency, during which time she coordinated the reconstruction effort following the 2004 Boxing Day tsunami.

A year later, she began her first stint as Minister of Finance. One of her first acts was to fire corrupt tax and custom officers, successfully tackling corruption and initiating reforms in Indonesia's tax and customs office – developing a reputation for both ruthlessness and integrity. *World Finance* magazine, in a profile of Sri Mulyani in

2020, argued that her hostility to corruption comes from spending her formative years as a child under 'one of the most dishonest autocrats of all time, President Suharto'. Sri Mulyani herself recalls being at university with President Suharto's daughter, and told Bloomberg in 2017 that 'if you're not a friend of those people, then your career path is going to be very different'.

Sri Mulyani is credited with stabilising the economy during her time in office, and is known for her prudent fiscal policy, decreasing the cost of loans and managing the country's debt, while building trust with investors – securing a huge increase in foreign direct investment into Indonesia. She was known as a tough reformist, and successfully steered South East Asia's largest economy through the 2007–10 Global Financial Crisis. She was crowned as the best Minister of Finance in Asia at the World Bank and IMF's Annual Session in Singapore in 2006, and the best Minister of Finance for 2006 by *Euromoney* magazine. Her time in office saw Indonesia record 6.6 per cent economic growth in 2007, its highest rate for a decade, and the following year she became the Coordinating Minister for the Economy in Indonesia.

In 2010, however, after four years as a minister, Sri Mulyani returned to the World Bank to become one of three managing directors there. Her resignation and escape to Washington was thought to have been largely motivated by the fact that she had made powerful enemies in her attempts to clean up politics and finance in Indonesia, and a controversial bank bailout during the Global Financial Crisis gave her opponents a reason to attack her, which they did with some success. Such was her reputation, and the trust the markets placed in her leadership, that her resignation disturbed markets in Indonesia, the *Jakarta Globe* describing her departure as 'Indonesia's loss, and the world's gain'. After another successful stint in Washington, six years later, in 2016, Sri Mulyani returned to Indonesia to take up her old job at the Finance Ministry. In 2018, the World Government summit in Dubai named her the 'Best Minister in the World'.

What stands out in Sri Mulyani's career is her focus on fundamental economic principles: a belief in a stable currency, a determination to tackle corruption, and a conviction that Indonesia can and should be a hub for global investment – an opportunity that Sri Mulyani is keen to seize today as the West falls out of love with China. These beliefs did not always win her friends but they did win her respect from economists and financial markets around the world. Such respect was crucial in turning around the Indonesian economy. Sri Mulyani could have stayed at the World Bank where she was already number two, but she wanted to return to Indonesia, answering the call of public service. This too is to be admired and respected: through her decision, she has been able to provide some stability and investment to the country that is her home.

Why Janet Yellen, Christine Lagarde and Sri Mulyani Indrawati Matter Today

Yellen, Lagarde and Sri Mulyani come from very different political traditions and have been responsible for dealing with very different economic challenges. But all three have shown leadership and a rare ability to prioritise key issues – such as climate change, women's empowerment and inclusive growth – that I can both relate to and learn from. Labour's economic policy development draws especially heavily on Biden and Yellen's economic programme in the US, and its focus on the green economy, and on what Yellen calls 'modern supply-side economics' to boost the underlying growth capacity of the economy. In these areas, these three women have made transformative contributions in their own right.

The Climate Crisis

Across the world, climate change is finally being recognised not only as an existential threat but also as posing a major economic challenge. The UK's Office for Budget Responsibility has said that delaying the target of getting to net zero by a decade will double the costs, while Lord Stern's landmark study, known as the Stern Review, showed clearly in 2006 that the costs of inaction are much higher than the costs of taking action. It estimated that if we don't act on climate change, the overall costs and risks will be equivalent to losing at least 5 per cent of global GDP every single year. If a wider range of risks and impacts is taken into account, the cost of the damage could rise to 20 per cent of GDP or even more. In contrast, the costs of action if carried out efficiently can be limited to around 1 per cent of global GDP each year. The former Governor of the Bank of England, Mark Carney, is now focusing on these issues in his role as the United Nations Special Envoy on Climate Action and Finance. Yellen and Lagarde have also taken up the cause.

Yellen was a founding member of the Climate Leadership Council, and as chair of the Group of Thirty Working Group on Climate Change and Finance, she addressed climate risks, supporting a phased-in carbon price to accelerate a shift to net-zero carbon emissions. One of the Biden administration's flagship policies has been the Inflation Reduction Act, which aims to reduce inflation through a range of strategies, including huge subsidies and tax breaks to encourage the development of climate-change-combatting technology and domestic energy production. While controversial, the legislation is attracting huge investment in the US and is being emulated elsewhere, showing that with concerted effort, it is possible to work alongside business to stimulate investment in green industries.

Catalysing investment in the industries of the future to support growth while decarbonising our economy will be central to the mission of a Labour government. Through our national wealth fund and the creation of a publicly funded sustainable energy company – GB Energy – we will aim to partner with business in investing in the industries of the future. We will secure jobs and bring investment to the former industrial heartlands of Britain, that have been hollowed out over the last forty years. The Inflation Reduction Act is a prime if controversial example of how countries are trying to boost their own resilience, by diversifying and securing supply chains because of global upheavals from the Covid pandemic to the war in Ukraine. It also demonstrates the difference that concerted direction setting by government can make: by providing a clear signal to business about government's policy priorities, and how investments will be supported by that policy, we can drive inclusive, green growth. Labour's commitment to buy, make and do more in Britain reflects our goal to boost the resilience of the UK economy in the face of global shocks and adversaries, and ensure we are less exposed to complicated supply chains. We also wish to ensure that in future the UK economy is not held hostage by the whims of authoritarian regimes who do not share our values.

At Davos in 2013 Lagarde said that the issue of climate change is by far the greatest economic challenge of the twenty-first century. 'Make no mistake,' she asserted. 'Without concerted action, the very future of our planet is in peril.' Lagarde set out how this informed her vision of green growth – economic growth that respects environmental sustainability. Lagarde summed this view up as the idea that 'good ecology is good economics'. In the same speech she argued that this was why getting carbon pricing right and removing fossil-fuel subsidies should be one of our top global economic priorities. In 2018, while at the IMF, talking about the necessary transition to a low-carbon economy, Lagarde underscored the importance of ensuring that policy measures to accelerate economic recovery are 'not only consistent with but further the objectives of the EU Green Deal'. Lagarde has consistently reaffirmed the need for the climate crisis to be at the forefront of the minds of economic policymakers.

The war in Ukraine has shone a powerful light on the long-existing crisis of Western democracies relying on Russia for gas imports. Lagarde argues it has highlighted the need to significantly accelerate our transition to renewable energy away from fossil fuels. And, while a firm believer in free trade and the benefits of globalisation, Lagarde now argues that we need a 'neo-globalisation' based on principles other than being 'ever cheaper and ever faster'.

In a 2022 interview she reaffirmed her conviction that 'the rationale of being ever more secure and ever nearer will prevail', and that 'Europe has a very strong position indeed': a similar position to that of Yellen and the US Administration, who see energy transition and global insecurity as both a reason and an opportunity to reshore and build up domestic resilience and secure supply chains.

The truth is that globalisation has its limits. Globalisation without sufficient regard to those who lost out fostered resentment and increased inequality, while a wave of outsourcing and offshoring left countries exposed to supply shortages in moments of crisis – including pandemics and wars. Being agnostic about where essential goods and services (from energy supplies to food to computer chips) come from has left us all vulnerable. A reassessment of the costs and benefits of globalisation was well overdue, and now, through force of circumstance, policymakers are finally responding and recognising that, in an age of insecurity, resilience and security are more important than further global economic integration.

Equality for Women

Despite their differing political perspectives, both Yellen and Lagarde have used their roles to argue for the empowerment of women, and have shone a spotlight on the structural barriers and discrimination women face.

At the IMF Lagarde argued in 2013 that 'when women do better, the economy does better', going on to say that empowering women was key to growth and the reduction of poverty. Later at the ECB, Lagarde argued that we should challenge the view that economics is 'for boys only' and that we had to challenge 'perceptions of what we think an economist should be and how they should behave'. As this book has shown, these perceptions are incorrect. Throughout history, and indeed today, there have been great economic thinkers and policymakers who prove economics has never been 'for boys only'.

And while the majority of professional economists have not tended to look like Yellen, Lagarde or Sri Mulyani, that is starting to change.

Lagarde has also said that, given two equally qualified candidates, for the moment she would hire the woman. 'We want to hear women's voices properly positioned,' she told *Vogue* in an interview in 2011 upon taking charge of the IMF. Lagarde goes further in a 2022 interview with the magazine *Madame Figaro*, arguing that, whether 'by chance or out of necessity, women are often called on when there's a crisis', and quoting with approval Eleanor Roosevelt's remark that 'a woman is like a teabag; you can't tell how strong she is until you put her in hot water'. 'There's some truth in that,' she added.

Indeed, as her career has progressed, so has Lagarde's outspokenness on issues relating to the role of women in the economy and society, including a profile in 2018 entitled 'Christine Lagarde on Why Women Will Save the Economy'. In it Lagarde tells her interviewer, 'If it had been Lehman Sisters rather than Lehman Brothers, the world might well look a lot different today': a clear attack on the 'hairy-chested' testosterone culture that dominated much of the world of finance and significantly contributed to the Global Financial Crisis of 2008. At her confirmation hearing with the European Parliament for the role of ECB President, Lagarde said that as well as 'all my work on monetary policy', she would also address the topic of climate change and women's issues. It is fair to say she has done both.

Yellen too has used her economic research to explicitly look at the gender pay gap. While she was heading up the Council of Economic Advisors, she analysed data spanning three decades to determine the causes that led to women earning substantially less than men. By observing trends attributable to such issues as occupation or industry, as well as familial status, the study was able to establish that while the Equal Pay Act of 1963 was a step forward, there was no explanation as to why there was a 25 per cent difference between average pay for women and men – although it was an improvement from the 40 per cent gap two decades earlier. It concluded that this gap had no correlation with differences in productivity and, as such, was the result of discrimination within the workforce.

Earlier on in her career, Yellen was asked in a 1995 interview about feminist author Betty Friedan's comments that 'economics is the basis for women's progress towards equality'. Yellen agreed. Noting that she hadn't felt any discrimination in her own life, Yellen nonetheless expressed her worry that it will take a 'long time to change' the dominance of men in so many parts of the economy. The right education and training, Yellen says, and help for women juggling work and childcare, are the key for helping women realise their economic potential. Years later, however, Yellen reflected again on discrimination in economics. In a 2018 interview she admitted that twenty years earlier she would probably have argued that being a woman had done nothing to slow her career progress. But, the interviewer notes, 'Today her take is darker.' A lot of work in academic economics is done jointly, she said, and it was very difficult for women to break into the male-dominated social and professional circles in which ideas were shared and projects hatched. She went on to note the existence of 'extremely aggressive and hostile' attitudes by some men towards women – including in economic seminars. Reflecting the slow progress, she adds that 'there is not much of a pipeline of women in the field'. In a 2019 podcast she reflects again that 'there are too few women in the profession, and there are some aspects of the way the profession works that I think hold women back and are hostile'.

As Treasury Secretary, Yellen is able to help break down some of these barriers, both personally and for other women. Crucially, Yellen's modern supply-side economics includes big policy innovations to improve childcare, specifically to help more women into work. But any woman, at whatever level of seniority, in economics today knows that the problems of inequality in the field have far from disappeared.

Closing the gender pay gap will be a top priority for a Labour government. It is why I have asked my friend Frances O'Grady, the former TUC general secretary, to review this issue working with me and my colleagues Anneliese Dodds and Angela Rayner. Progress in closing the pay gap has been made but it has been too slow. At the current pace I will be nearly eighty before we close it entirely. We literally cannot afford to wait that long.

Shared Prosperity and Inclusive Growth

Despite being a committed liberal and free-marketeer, Lagarde repeatedly emphasises the importance of inclusive economic growth. Inclusion, Lagarde says, relates to growth 'at its core', stating the need for all people to share in rising prosperity – and, by the same token, to share fairly in any economic adjustment needed to achieve or restore prosperity. Quoting Franklin Roosevelt, Lagarde asserted in a 2013 speech that 'the test of our progress is not whether we add more to the abundance of those who have much; it is whether we provide enough for those who have too little.'

The problem is that too few people feel that this growing abundance is working for them. When the use of food banks has increased 50 per cent since 2019 and 6.8 million people in the UK live in fuel poverty, that is an economic model gone wrong. We need economic growth, but how that growth is generated and who it benefits matters too – we must build a more inclusive model.

Making an economic (not just a moral) argument, Lagarde went on to say that 'excessive inequality is corrosive to growth; it is corrosive to society.' The economic participation of women is also essential to Lagarde's vision of inclusive growth: 'All studies point to the economic benefits of full female participation in the labour force, in the economy, in society.' A contemporary study estimated that by simply raising women's employment rates to the level of men, GDP would jump significantly – by 5 per cent in the United States, 9 per cent in Japan, 10 per cent in South Africa, 27 per cent in India and 34 per cent in Egypt.

Sri Mulyani described in detail in the *Guardian* in 2012 the bitterness that arises from inequality. She argued that politicians must focus on 'making sure that not only a few people can enjoy so excessively while the majority feel they have to work so hard'. It's a lesson on the dangers of inequality that's reflected in Lagarde's fear of an 'age of anger'.

Janet Yellen has perhaps made some of the most powerful and impactful interventions on a different, new kind of growth and an agenda to achieve it through her 'modern supply-side economics'. In a speech at the World Economic Forum in Davos in 2021, she argues that while 'it is, unquestionably, important to properly implement regulation and maintain a pro-growth tax code, they are not sufficient and can often be overdone. Modern supply-side economics, in contrast, prioritises labour supply, human capital, public infrastructure, R&D, and investments in a sustainable environment.' Yellen goes on to argue that, 'essentially, we aren't just focused on achieving a high top line growth number that is unsustainable – we are instead aiming for growth that is inclusive and green'.

The policies being pursued by Yellen include efforts to boost labour supply, for example by helping mums get back to work by expanding childcare provision and making it more affordable. While US growth has still outpaced the UK in recent years, it is still below its long-term average. In terms of productivity, Yellen's priority is boosting skills – not just in schools, but also in college and later life, with a constant emphasis on investing in the skills of the working classes whose wages have fallen behind those of white-collar workers.

On infrastructure, Yellen places particular emphasis on energy infrastructure, tackling climate change and promoting R&D to steal a march on the industries of the future. And in terms of tax, she is critical of tax incentives for business, and the shift of the burden of taxation towards workers rather than capital. Instead, Yellen has been the key proponent on the world stage for a global minimum rate of corporation tax to ensure businesses pay their fair share of tax and so that we can reduce inequality both domestically and internationally. She is confident that 'these policies' (and this novel approach) 'will promote a modern supply-side expansion that boosts long-term sustainable growth, protects the environment, and distributes expanding national income more equally'.

We have had many chancellors during the last thirteen years or so under Conservative governments – many more than we might have expected – but what we've never had before is a female chancellor. I hope – like Yellen, Lagarde and Sri Mulyani – to smash that glass ceiling here in Britain, and I would also like to see the first female Governor of the Bank of England.

The remarkable thing about the three women discussed in this chapter is that as well as providing outstanding leadership within Treasury departments, central banks and global economic organisations, they have also championed issues that have been neglected, or approached new issues in interesting ways.

Sri Mulyani has provided the authority and resilience to tackle corruption and by doing so has attracted much needed private investment in Indonesia. Lagarde has consciously and conspicuously

Indonesian Minister of Finance Sri Mulyani Indrawati with
Janet Yellen, at the G20 meeting in Indonesia in 2022.

championed women's rights, and has called out the fact that decisions made without the voices of women are always worse decisions. And Yellen is today approaching economic growth and the policies needed to get there in exciting new ways – more inclusive, environmentally sustainable, and involving the contributions of women and minorities. Under Yellen's leadership, growth matters – but so too does the question of who benefits from that growth and how it is created.

There are plenty of ideas from these three leaders that I want to take into government. The UK economy has not been delivering for working people for some time. Prices have gone through the roof, growth and productivity have stalled, nothing in Britain – from trains to hospitals – seems to be working very well, and living standards have taken a hammering. Drawing inspiration from these women, a disciplined and responsible management of the public finances, a modern growth plan, and a relentless focus on the lives of ordinary working people would guide me as chancellor.

10

The Women Managing the Global Economy

In 2002 I was seconded from the Bank of England to the British Embassy in Washington. I had never been to Washington before, so it was all incredibly exciting. But it was also a very challenging time. The attack on the World Trade Center and Pentagon had happened just six months earlier, and part of the reason for my posting was that the Treasury secondee to the embassy, Dermot Finch, had been in the building next to the World Trade Center when the planes hit. He escaped, running north of Ground Zero. More capacity was needed at the embassy because of the increased workload and pressure on the team. As well as the military response they prompted, the terrorist attacks on 9/11 brought with them a huge economic impact. So I joined the embassy as the Second Economic Secretary on secondment from the Bank of England.

My boss in Washington was Sue Owen, a UK Treasury official who would go on to become Permanent Secretary at the Department for Culture, Media and Sport. Her boss was Tom Scholar, who during his time in Washington was the UK's Executive Director to the IMF and World Bank, and would later go on to become Permanent Secretary at the Treasury. Working for Tom at the IMF was Nick Joicey, seconded from the Treasury to support the work of the UK at these two global economic institutions. In my first couple of weeks at the embassy, I was invited for lunch at the IMF canteen on 1900 Pennsylvania Avenue with the UK team, and it was there that I first met Nick – my future husband. So my time in Washington was special in lots of ways, and I spent quite a bit of time at the IMF and with IMF staff during my year and a half in Washington.

The Fund and the World Bank have employed some of the most interesting and innovative women economists of the last fifty years. From Anne Krueger to Christine Lagarde, Kristalina Georgieva, Gita Gopinath, Carmen Reinhart and Ngozi Okonjo-Iweala, a hugely diverse set of women from around the world have coalesced in Washington, all working on development economics, financial stability and growth policies. Many are distinguished academic economists who devoted many years to public service at these global institutions – often before or after time spent in finance ministries or economic administration. This chapter tells some of their stories and the lessons I have learned from their leadership.

Anne Krueger

First among these women striking out at the IMF and World Bank was Anne Krueger. Krueger was born in 1934, in Endicott, New York. Her father was a physician and her uncles include the Australian politician Sir Reginald Wright and the physiologist Sir Roy Wright. Krueger's interest in economics was sparked by the change that came with the creation of the IMF and World Bank at the Bretton Woods Conference. These new global institutions were tasked with promoting economic stability and development in the aftermath of the Second World War. That early interest led her to study economics at Oberlin College, gaining her undergraduate degree in 1953. She was awarded her MA and PhD in economics from the University of Wisconsin in 1956 and 1958. 'I was always interested,' Krueger (then aged eighty-one) told the *Financial Times* in a 2015 interview. 'Economics is a function of understanding the world. If you understand it you can say, "Here is what's not working." It's about understanding behaviour.' Her early interest sparked a lifetime of research and leadership in economic thinking.

Krueger's academic career focused on international trade and development – specifically, how free trade and 'light touch' regulation stimulate growth and development. Krueger's article 'The Political Economy of the Rent-Seeking Society' was published in 1974. Rent-seeking (a concept popularised by Krueger but first identified by Adam Smith) occurs when interest groups lobby for government favours in the form of tariffs, patents, subsidies, import quotas and other market regulations. Rent-seeking behaviour is inefficient because it manipulates the existing market, rather than creating new wealth – the 'rent-seeker' contributes nothing to productivity in return for the favour. Krueger argues that rent-seeking behaviour in the form of restricting imports means consumers carry the 'welfare costs' of tariffs – they pay the price for the rent-seekers' behaviour. Krueger also argues that rent-seeking behaviour breeds further rent-seeking behaviour by creating an economic environment where rent-seeking is the only way to successfully enter the market. In markets dominated by rent-seeking, new firms must dedicate their resources to lobbying for advantages. In 2011, Krueger's article was named, by the American Economic Association, one of the twenty best articles in the first hundred years of the *American Economic Review*.

It was on the back of a successful academic career that Krueger became the World Bank's Chief Economist (and Vice President of Economics and Research) from 1982 to 1986, becoming the first woman Chief Economist at either the World Bank or IMF. Her appointment coincided with a time when the World Bank had begun to give out structural adjustment loans to reduce the medium-term deficits of borrowing countries and help fund 'adjustment programmes'. These loans came with conditions intended to help the borrower adjust its economy (by reducing inflation or tax reform) so it would be easier for them to pay back their creditors and develop economically. Their effectiveness has been widely debated, but during Krueger's time at the World Bank, they were new and seen as a long-term solution to economic crises.

The conditions that came with these loans would later be

formalised by English economist John Williamson into a set of ten economic policy priorities which came to be known as the 'Washington Consensus'. It covered reform policies promoted by the IMF and World Bank for countries in economic crisis, ranging from privatisation of public services to tax reform, trade liberalisation, deregulation and increased openness to foreign direct investment. The Consensus also promoted legal protection of property rights, fiscal responsibility and the redirection of spending towards services like health and education. Despite the term 'consensus', the policies were never without their critics, and economists like Nobel laureate Joseph Stiglitz argued that their use in Latin America and sub-Saharan Africa not only failed to boost productivity and growth but had the opposite effect to that intended and often boosted inequality and weakened existing social networks.

After the World Bank Krueger returned to academia, and in 1996 was President of the American Economic Association. In her 'Presidential Address' Krueger argued that successful trade policy resulted in stronger and more lasting development for the economies that need it most. Trade liberalisation, she argues, is 'even more important for developing countries than it is for the industrial economies. Developing countries impose much higher tariff barriers on each other than those imposed by the rich countries on poor ones. It is developing countries that will be the principal beneficiaries'.

In 2001 Krueger returned to Washington, nominated by President George W. Bush to serve as First Deputy Managing Director of the IMF (second in command at the Fund), remaining in the role until 2006. During her tenure she served as Acting Managing Director in 2004, following the resignation of Horst Köhler. Until the appointment of Christine Lagarde in 2011, she was the only female to have filled the top role at the IMF.

Former IMF colleagues note the challenges that Krueger encountered at the IMF as a woman. 'You have a woman [Lagarde] at the head of the IMF now, but don't imagine life for a female staff member was plain sailing. In those days it was a boys' club,' said former

Fed staffer Peter Doyle. Others claim it was her politics rather than her gender that alienated colleagues. 'She's smart and very energetic, but she loves the idea of markets and not the participants,' was the view of one (unnamed) former colleague quoted in a *Financial Times* profile. It seems likely that in such a male-dominated environment Krueger was neither the first nor the last woman forced to stare down resentment and misogyny.

Economic Thinking

In her 2012 book, *Struggling with Success: Challenges Facing the International Economy*, Krueger takes a robust stance on globalisation and the role it has played in improving the world and people's lives. She argues that 'globalisation has proceeded at a rapid pace since about 1800 and the degree of interdependence has greatly increased'. For Krueger, globalisation has ushered in an era of higher living standards and the alleviation of poverty.

Krueger is in favour of a free-market approach and argues that regulation negatively impacts the country that imposes it and can bring 'spillover effects' to countries that trade with the nation implementing regulation. As an example, she takes the United States' interest equalisation tax and how it caused financial capital to be moved from New York to London, how US anti-dumping duties caused the move of computer assembly firms abroad and how the Sarbanes-Oxley Act of the early 2000s (which tightened rules on US corporate governance) saw corporate headquarters move out of the United States. Krueger believes unprecedented economic growth observed in open trade regimes has led to a further appreciation of supply-side economics (growth by lowering taxes and lessening regulation) and the liberalisation of rules, regulations and tariffs to the benefit of growth and prosperity. Although these arguments have become increasingly tested by those on the left, and indeed the populist right, the basic premise that the opening up of the global economy has resulted in growth and poverty alleviation has held true. That said, questions about standards of employment in poorer countries, the security of supply chains and the environmental consequences of unfettered free trade are also valid and have rightly received more attention, challenging the more orthodox free-market approach.

A more left-field idea of Krueger's is that countries should be able to declare themselves bankrupt. So, instead of bailouts, austerity and budget cuts, a country should be able to 'wipe the slate clean and start again'. While there have been instances where debts to international institutions have been wiped out and partial relief has been applied, Krueger's idea goes further. It's not one that has taken off, but with some countries today still struggling to bounce back from the financial crisis followed by the economic havoc of the pandemic, with rising interest rates adding to already unsustainable debt burdens, the question of how to manage sovereign debt crises has become more prominent again.

Whether one agrees with her economic views, there is no doubt that Krueger's successful career at the World Bank and IMF opened opportunities for the next generation of women economists. Before women were being promoted in Treasury departments or central banks in great numbers, women in economics were making successful careers in Washington at the institutions that provide the global economic architecture for the international economy and trading system.

Carmen Reinhart

Carmen Reinhart also follows in the mainstream of what would typically be thought of as the Washington Consensus, and like the other women who have made successful careers in Washington, she is a first-rate economist, with a reputation for diving deep into data and meticulous analysis.

Born Carmen Castellanos in Havana in 1955, she arrived in the United States at the age of ten with her mother, father and just three suitcases for the whole family. They initially settled in Pasadena, California, before moving to South Florida where she spent her late teens. When the family moved to Miami, Reinhart started a two-year programme at Miami Dade College. A course on fashion merchandising introduced her to economics, and she transferred to Florida International University, where she received a BA in economics in 1978. From Florida she went to Columbia University, where she received her master's degree in 1981 and her PhD in 1988. She met her husband, Vincent Reinhart, when they were classmates at Columbia in the late 1970s.

Carmen Reinhart's first significant job was as an economist at the investment bank Bear Stearns, which she joined in 1982. From investment banking she moved to the IMF and then academia, spending fourteen years at the University of Maryland before moving to the Harvard Kennedy School where she serves today as a Professor of International Finance. For just over two years – from 2020 to 2022 – she was on public service leave from this role, to take up the position as Chief Economist of the World Bank and then promoted to Senior Vice President. With Reinhart as Chief Economist, the bank became a leader in the support of developing countries through the greatest challenges of the pandemic with emergency operations rolled out to over a hundred countries and $12 billion to finance the purchase and distribution of Covid-19 vaccines, tests and treatments.

Reinhart describes her approach as combining analysis of data and historical events to come to a conclusion based on them, rather than preconceived theories. She summed up her reverence for data in a 2013 interview:

Data is good. It is central to me. In the end, it is about solving puzzles, about solving mysteries. And the way I go about solving mysteries is [by] delving into data and looking for empirical regularities, for recurrences of patterns . . . You know, when Sherlock Holmes says, 'The game is afoot.'

Collaboration and Financial Crises

Like many of the women in this book, including Yellen, Webb and Paley Marshall, Reinhart has collaborated with her husband on several academic papers and projects. Vincent Reinhart held several positions in the Federal Reserve Bank of New York before going on to work as an economist at a number of global investment banks. Her most important academic collaboration, however, has been with fellow economist, and chess grandmaster, Kenneth Rogoff. At the age of sixteen, Rogoff dropped out of school to concentrate on chess. He won the United States Junior Championship in 1969 and spent time living in Europe and playing in tournaments. However, at eighteen he made the decision to go to college and pursue a career in economics rather than become a professional player. Like Rogoff, I was a keen chess player at school, winning the British Girls' Chess Championships when I was fourteen, but I was not at a standard to give up the day job! Rogoff, whom I've met through both chess and economics, went on to become a Harvard professor and Chief Economist at the IMF. His work with Reinhart focuses on growth, as well as recessions and financial crises. During the 2010 UK general election, Rogoff contributed to an open letter to *The Sunday Times* endorsing the Conservative Party and then shadow chancellor George Osborne's demands for greater austerity during the European debt crisis – a policy that, when enacted in government, would prove disastrous for our public services, including our NHS.

Reinhart's most notable work, co-authored with Rogoff, was *This Time is Different: Eight Centuries of Financial Folly*, studying the striking similarities of the recurring booms and busts that have characterised financial history. The book analyses hundreds of economic crises – debt, banking, currency and inflation – in sixty-six countries, going as far back as the Middle Ages. Reinhart and Rogoff's research (half the book is data, much of it assembled from painstaking searches of obscure sources) shows the vast similarities in how economic crises build and how they unfold despite in many cases being centuries apart. Despite such similarities, the authors argue, economists and policymakers during the build-up to such crashes are often too keen to explain away the signs. Reinhart and Rogoff called it the 'This Time is Different' syndrome, which they said was

> rooted in the firmly held belief that financial crises are things that happen to other people in other countries at other times; crises do not happen to us, here and now. We are doing things better, we are smarter, we have learned from past mistakes. The old rules of valuation no longer apply.

Invariably, Reinhart and Rogoff conclude, things are not different, and, as the book's title suggests, it is folly to think otherwise.

As well as their work on financial crises, Reinhart and Rogoff have also written extensively on the link between government debt and economic growth – a hotly contested terrain in both politics and economics. Their 2010 paper 'Growth in a Time of Debt' argues that when gross external debt reaches 60 per cent of GDP, a country's annual growth declines by 2 per cent, and 'for levels of external debt in excess of 90 per cent GDP growth was roughly cut in half'. The paper appeared in the aftermath of the financial crisis of 2007–8 and made governments around the world sit up. Many had intervened to stop recession turning into depression – pushing up their debt. The evidence for the 90 per cent debt threshold hypothesis was used as a justification for pro-austerity policies globally – including in the UK under David Cameron and George Osborne.

But Reinhart and Rogoff found themselves in the spotlight after researchers discovered that their data-crunching contained errors. Economists found problems with both the data and their conclusion regarding the negative correlation between debt and growth – countering that growth does not collapse when debt increases above 90 per cent, as the pair had contended. A separate and previous criticism is that the negative link between debt and growth is nothing more than a correlation – not causal. Rogoff and Reinhart claimed that their fundamental conclusions were accurate, despite the errors.

Further papers by Rogoff and Reinhart, and the IMF – which were not found to contain the errors – reached conclusions similar to the initial paper, though with a much lower impact on GDP growth than the slash in half first predicted. The threshold hypothesis retains adherents as well as critics, who suggest that the thresholds in the relation between public debt and economic growth lack robustness.

This work neglects another issue that in my view is a key point: what is the alternative? The increase in debt and deficit finance in the wake of the Global Financial Crisis was because financial markets were in turmoil, unemployment was rising and businesses folding. Without government spending and temporary tax cuts the recession could have become a depression with disastrous consequences for living standards, economic stability, working people and the longer-term public finances.

Despite the contested nature of the conclusions, however, the paper was influential. Former UK chancellor George Osborne relied on it to portray excess debt as the universal cause of financial crises: 'As Rogoff and Reinhart demonstrate convincingly, all financial crises ultimately have their origins in one thing [i.e. debt],' Osborne argued, to great effect, in the 2010 general election campaign in Britain.

Princeton economist Paul Krugman argues that the problem with Rogoff and Reinhart's article and its impact is that a 'disputed hypothesis' was treated as an 'unquestioned fact' when there was division among economists from the day of its publication – long before its inconsistencies were brought to light. The impact of governments like that of Cameron and Osborne in retrenching government spending so quickly will be long felt. When they won the general election of 2010, Cameron and Osborne launched an austerity-driven policy programme that left our public services on their knees and those working in them with wages down in real terms by about 20 per cent since the financial crisis – all while cuts to welfare spending drove up poverty and inequality across the country. Despite all this pain, growth, investment and productivity have fallen and our national debt has doubled.

Ngozi Okonjo-Iweala

Another woman who has broken boundaries, is at the forefront of managing our global economy, and also an alumna of the World Bank, is Ngozi Okonjo-Iweala. A former finance minister in her home country, Nigeria, and now the first woman, and the first African, appointed to the position of Director General of the World Trade Organization, Okonjo-Iweala was born in 1954 in Delta State, Nigeria. She came from an important Nigerian family: her father, Professor Chukwuka Okonjo, was the Obi, or King, of the Obahai

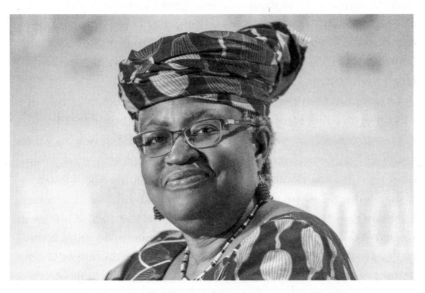

Ngozi Okonjo-Iweala is the first woman and the first African to serve as Director General of the World Trade Organization, and also the first woman Finance Minister of Nigeria.

royal family of Ogwashi-Ukwu in the Nigerian chieftaincy system. Okonjo-Iweala was educated in Nigeria before moving to the US to attend Harvard University. She earned both a master's degree and PhD in regional economics and development from the Massachusetts Institute of Technology, completing her studies in 1981.

After her studies, Okonjo-Iweala moved to Washington, DC, where she had a twenty-five-year career at the World Bank as a development economist, rising to the number two position of Managing Director for Operations – a position she held between 2007 and 2011. As managing director, she had responsibility for the World Bank's $81 billion operational portfolio in Africa, South Asia, Europe and Central Asia, and led the World Bank's programmes to assist low-income countries during the 2008–9 food crises and the financial crisis. In 2010, she drove the World Bank's initiative to raise $49.3 billion in grants and low-interest credit to assist with poverty alleviation and economic development for the poorest countries in the world.

Having built a successful career in the US, Okonjo-Iweala served her country as finance minister on two occasions, the first between 2003 and 2006, and the second between 2011 and 2015. She also briefly acted as foreign minister for two months in 2006 – the first woman to hold both positions.

During her first term, in the administration of President Olusegun Obasanjo, she led negotiations with the Paris Club which wiped out US$30 billion of Nigeria's debt. In 2003, she led efforts to improve Nigeria's macroeconomic management, including the implementation of an oil-price-based fiscal rule: revenues above a reference benchmark oil price were saved in a special account. This meant greater stability for Nigeria because unexpected profits from high oil prices were kept in a separate account and the nation's budget was not at the mercy of the fluctuating price of oil. She also started publishing much more detailed numbers on the public finances, helping Nigeria obtain its first ever sovereign credit rating in 2006 – thus improving the prospects for foreign investment. Three years in government were followed by five years back in Washington as the government in Nigeria changed hands. In 2011 Okonjo-Iweala was appointed again as Minister of Finance by President Goodluck Jonathan, and in this second term she was responsible for leading reform that enhanced transparency of government accounts and strengthened institutions against corruption.

The focus on securing the public finances and encouraging investment improved the economic performance of Nigeria's economy:
under her leadership Nigeria had the largest economy in Africa. It
was also an economy where growth started to increasingly benefit
women and the young, both issues which Okonjo-Iweala paid great
attention to during her time in office.

Nigeria undoubtedly benefited from Okonjo-Iweala's experience
at the World Bank – her rigour in economic policymaking, experience of best practice in development economics and a contact book
that helped with debt reduction efforts and encouraging investment. The same is also true of Sri Mulyani Indrawati, an executive
director at the World Bank and managing director at the IMF, who
served as Indonesia's Minister of Finance on two occasions, and
who, like Okonjo-Iweala, focused during her time as finance minister on tackling corruption, and establishing fiscal stability and
transparency with data and economic policymaking. Like Okonjo-
Iweala and Sri Mulyani, I am concerned about the state of public finances, including here in Britain, where a failure to grow the
economy, along with a series of crises, has resulted in our debt to
GDP ratio reaching 100 per cent. At the same time there is not enough
rigour when it comes to public spending, including in the pandemic
when public contracts were beset with cronyism and where criminals
and other fraudsters were able to get their hands on huge quantities of
public money to which they had no right. I have announced a strong
set of fiscal rules that an incoming Labour government would stick to,
as well as a commitment to recover every penny I possibly can from
the dodgy loans and contracts given out during the pandemic when
Rishi Sunak was Chancellor of the Exchequer.

In 2012, Okonjo-Iweala was a candidate for President of the World
Bank, losing out to physician, anthropologist and former Dartmouth
College President Jim Yong Kim. Had she been successful, she would
have become the organisation's first female president. The World
Bank has still not had a woman at its helm. Eight years later, however,
another opportunity arose. Okonjo-Iweala was appointed as Director

General of the World Trade Organization in March 2021, and is the first woman and first African to lead that organisation.

As a development economist and finance minister, Okonjo-Iweala steered through reforms that changed the macroeconomics of Nigeria, opened it up to trade, promoted fiscal stability, and made strides in women's empowerment. At the centre of her economic thinking is a belief in the power of trade to lift developing countries out of poverty while achieving economic growth and sustainable development. As finance minister, Okonjo-Iweala was involved in trade negotiations with other West African countries and contributed to the overhaul of Nigeria's trade policy, giving it the power to enhance its competitiveness. This approach is one she has taken with her to the WTO.

Okonjo-Iweala argues that the best way forward for Nigeria's economy is to pursue job-creating foreign investment so that higher levels of employment in this emerging young workforce can create a stable environment for Nigeria's economy to achieve sustainable growth.

Perhaps most importantly, Okonjo-Iweala was successful in wiping out billions of dollars of Nigeria's external debt as finance minister – reducing the costs of servicing the debt and freeing up resources for investing at home to benefit the lives of everyday Nigerians. Reflecting a critique of the colonial history of much of Africa, Okonjo-Iweala has said that Africa 'shouldn't be on the defensive' when countries like the UK and US try to give back. She poignantly notes 'the UK and the US could not have been built today if it weren't for Africa's aid. It is all the resources that were taken from Africa, including human, that built those countries today.' Under Okonjo-Iweala's leadership of her country's Treasury, public finances improved and investment and growth increased: a set of circumstances that can act as a catalyst for opportunity for the young people of Nigeria. In the first chapter of this book I reflected on the contribution of the nineteenth-century economist and writer Harriet Martineau. In her short story *Demerara*, Martineau railed against slavery and the exploitation perpetuated by slave owners and all those who benefited and profited from it. Today, economists like Okonjo-Iweala use their positions and influence to seek remedies for those grave injustices committed on the continent of Africa and beyond, as they seek to strengthen and grow their economies and reduce global inequality.

Kristalina Georgieva

Kristalina Georgieva took over as Managing Director of the IMF in 2019 from Christine Lagarde. Georgieva was born into a family of bureaucrats in Sofia, Bulgaria, in 1953, and was brought up during the communist era. Her upbringing was privileged for the time because of her father's job as a civil engineer. His grandfather was the famed nineteenth-century revolutionary Ivan Karshovski, a lawyer and journalist prominent at the time of building the Bulgarian state after independence from the Ottoman Empire. During her childhood, however, her father fell ill, plunging the family into financial trouble – an experience she credits with teaching her never to panic in the midst of a crisis, financial or otherwise.

After graduating from the prestigious Karl Marx Higher Institute of Economics in 1976, Georgieva went on to complete a PhD thesis in 1986 in environmental policy and economic growth in the US – a brave choice for a researcher in Eastern Europe before the fall of the Iron Curtain. In 1987, she came to the UK to study natural resource economics and environmental policy at the LSE as a British Council scholar. At the age of thirty-four, in London, she opened her first ever bank account, depositing her £361 grant and the £21 she had brought from Bulgaria.

In 1993 she started work at the World Bank in Washington as an environmental economist, rising to become Vice President in 2008, and was then appointed director of the Environment Department leading on environmental policies, strategy and lending.

In 2010, Georgieva returned to Europe and, with Bulgaria a member of the EU since 2007, she took a series of key roles within the

European Commission. She began as European Commissioner for Humanitarian Aid and Crisis Management, then Commissioner for International Cooperation and Development and Commission Vice President for the Budget and Human Resources. After Brussels, she returned to the World Bank, first as CEO and then Acting President – climbing to the top level of the organisation she had joined as an economist in 1993. But her big break came later in 2019 when she was appointed to lead the IMF.

Two themes stand out during Georgieva's tenure at the IMF so far: a focus on women's empowerment and a commitment to bolstering environmental policy – Georgieva's passion ever since her PhD days. In both areas Georgieva has moved the dial on what is

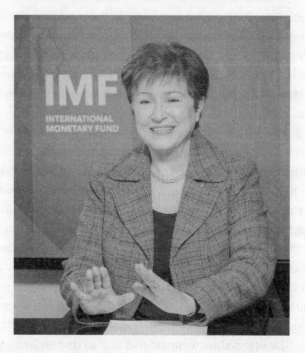

During her time as Managing Director of the International Monetary Fund, Kristalina Georgieva has reformed its focus, with a new emphasis on women's rights and environmental action.

regarded as good economic policy deserving the IMF's praise – and money. A sea change from the liberal, free-market reputation of the IMF under Krueger.

Gita Gopinath

The woman who has served as a key deputy at the IMF to both Lagarde and Georgieva is Gita Gopinath. Appointed by Lagarde as Chief Economist, Georgieva has since promoted her to be the second in command at the Fund.

Gopinath was born in 1971 in West Bengal, India. Her father headed a farmers' collective and she worked on his farm. The family are related to A. K. Gopalan, the Indian communist politician. Gopinath loved athletics as a child but surprised her family when she quit sports to focus on her studies. Her father recounts how she told him: 'Sports is a tricky affair. Unless you are number one in India, you are a nobody! But if you come first or second in university, you could be somebody big.' Her exam grades soared. Gopinath received her first degree from the University of Delhi in 1992 and a master's from Delhi School of Economics – where she met her husband, Iqbal Singh Dhaliwal – in 1994. She then completed a further master's degree at the University of Washington in 1996 and was awarded a PhD in economics from Princeton University in 2001 under the supervision of former Fed chairman Ben Bernanke, former IMF Chief Economist Kenneth Rogoff and the current IMF Chief Economist Pierre-Olivier Gourinchas.

Joining the University of Chicago in 2001 as an assistant professor, Gopinath then moved to the economics department at Harvard, where she worked for seventeen years, becoming a full professor in 2010. She is the third woman and the second Indian after Nobel laureate Amartya Sen to be made a permanent member of the economics department at Harvard.

In 2018 Gopinath was appointed Chief Economist of the IMF. As part of her many significant initiatives in this role, she co-authored the 'Pandemic Paper'. The paper set globally endorsed targets for vaccinating the world and led to the creation of the Multilateral Task Force, including the IMF, World Bank, WTO and WHO. Its goal was to help end the pandemic and establish a working group with vaccine manufacturers to identify trade barriers and bottlenecks in supply to accelerate the delivery of vaccines to low- and lower-middle-income countries. She also helped set up a Climate Change team inside the IMF (central to the priorities of her boss, Georgieva) to analyse and devise, among other things, optimal climate mitigation policies. 'Gopinath made history as the first female Chief Economist at the Fund,' Georgieva has said, 'and we benefited immensely from her sharp intellect and deep knowledge of international finance and macroeconomics as we navigate through the worst economic crisis since the Great Depression.'

The central focus of Gopinath's research is international finance and macroeconomics. She is known in her academic work for always being willing to follow the empirical evidence wherever it leads – even if it may be at odds with her preconceived beliefs. This is thought to be one of the main reasons she was taken on by the IMF: her ability to recommend practical and evidence-based solutions at a time when the free-market principles that have been promoted by the IMF for decades were under attack.

Gopinath has said that she uses the 'broadest lens possible' in search of solutions, and that a rethink of globalisation is 'pressing'. Any such rethink, she believes, should address the distribution of benefits as well as the impact of new technologies. Like her boss, Kristalina Georgieva, Gopinath is radically changing the focus and priorities of the IMF in ways that are more centred on the real-life impacts of economic policy and the sustainability of economic growth, particularly on the environment and climate. As someone committed to sustainable growth, I am delighted by the change ushered in by Georgieva and Gopinath at the IMF.

A brilliant macroeconomist, Gita Gopinath, the First Deputy
Manager of the International Monetary Fund, represents the
next generation of women shaping the global economy.

Issues Championed

All of the women in this chapter are impactful and successful
economists in their own right, but together they have helped shape
and reshape the World Bank, IMF and now the WTO, changing the
face of our global economic architecture in the last fifty years. While
getting on with their substantial day jobs they have also championed
a number of economic causes. From the environment to aid and
development to trade and globalisation, debt and financial stability
and women's empowerment, these women have focused on the issues
which are central to how we think about the modern economy.

Trade and Development

For many years developing countries were encouraged to borrow from Western governments and financial institutions while embarking on reform at home: opening up markets to trade and bringing in the private sector to run services. The success of the model has been marked – globally, the number of people living in poverty has fallen sharply; the number of children and mothers dying in childbirth and from preventable diseases has been cut; the number of children at school has increased. Trade has given developing countries access to new markets, while inward investment has created the jobs needed to lift people out of poverty while also bringing in capital and technology.

It has not all been a success, however. Lending to developing countries resulted in unmanageable debt; trade, while opening up new markets, can be exploitative; and the benefits of foreign investment may be enjoyed by the owners of capital rather than the host country. The privatisation of state assets has also often resulted in profits going straight to investors who are free to set the price of essential goods and services, and as a result the benefits never reach those in need. These outcomes have called into question the role of trade and aid, and the role of the private sector in poor countries in stimulating growth. The breakdown in the Washington Consensus has led to a more nuanced debate about how to lift developing countries and poor people out of poverty, and how to use trade and aid as a force for good.

Anne Krueger in many ways represented the economic orthodoxy at a time when the Washington Consensus prevailed, and her academic work and time at the IMF focused on free markets and trade in the pursuit of economic development. Much of what she proposed was correct – her famous paper on rent-seeking is an example of the corruption of free markets by firms seeking protections from competition and trade, creating the imperfect competition Joan Robinson had written about forty years earlier.

Okonjo-Iweala's work – at the World Bank, as Nigerian Finance Minister and now at the WTO – shows how to stimulate growth in developing economies. The force of market and fiscal disciplines, aid used well and the promotion of trade and foreign direct investment are all important tools for developing countries to grow their economies and populations out of poverty.

Lagarde, during her time at the IMF, was also a classic free-marketeer – promoting the virtues of markets and free trade in stimulating growth and reducing poverty. And there are plenty of examples where such approaches have been effective. However, there is an increasing focus now on sustainable growth and tackling climate change. We have shifted to an economic landscape that values bottom-up rather than trickle-down economics. We now, at last, recognise the role of women and marginalised groups and how they participate in and benefit from growth and investment. There is also a renewed focus on the role of public services – particularly health and education in promoting growth and wellbeing. The modern face of the IMF – under the leadership of Georgieva and Gopinath – has increasingly prioritised issues of sustainable and inclusive growth rather than the unfaltering free-market principles of the past.

Environmental Policy

The IMF and World Bank have not traditionally been seen as champions of the environment or warriors in the climate crisis. But the global economic consensus is changing, and with it our global economic architecture. Today, it is impossible to think about economic growth and development without considering sustainability.

It is particularly notable that the current IMF chief, Kristalina Georgieva, has brought her own background as an environmental economist to the IMF. In a powerful article in the journal *Finance and Development* in 2021, Georgieva starts by saying that changing climate, biodiversity loss and environmental degradation all 'threaten the health and wellbeing of the future our children will inherit'. She argues that all fossil fuel subsidies most go and that we need to scale up green investments across and within countries. Georgieva contends this could boost global GDP by 2 per cent this decade and, with that boost, create millions of new jobs that bring us closer to the just transition to a low-carbon economy. 'Knowing is not enough; we must apply,' she says, channelling Leonardo da Vinci. 'Being willing is not enough; we must do.' I could not agree more. The change at the centre of the IMF is encouraging sustainable growth while respecting the limits of markets in how prices are set – without writing off the private sector's role in delivering the finance for the just transition.

In 2020, Georgieva urged EU leaders to introduce a higher carbon price to reflect its true cost, and added that 'just as we must price carbon, so we must learn to price climate risk. That means financial institutions need to disclose climate-related risks, and price these risks accordingly' – a sentiment also echoed by the former Governor of the Bank of England and current UN representative on climate finance, Mark Carney. Recognising that tackling the climate emergency requires united action from the public and private sectors, Georgieva says that 'the role of markets and the private sector is critical to mobilising and efficiently allocating resources, while putting a price on climate risks'.

Along with Georgieva, Gita Gopinath as her second in command has also put a focus on the environment, setting up a team inside the IMF to specifically focus on tackling climate change and the destruction it is already leaving in its wake. In a lecture at the Jackson Hole Economic Symposium for central bankers in 2022, Gopinath delivered a presentation entitled 'How Will the Pandemic and War Shape Future Monetary Policy?' In it she argued that the world must come together to tackle climate change as it did to tackle Covid. IMF analysis, Gopinath argues, shows that 'delaying the [energy] transition even a couple of years will substantially increase the economic costs and heighten the risk of a disorderly transition . . . to limit the devastating effects of climate change'.

Minouche Shafik, now the first female President of Columbia University in New York, served for sixteen years at the World Bank between 1988 and 2004, rising to be vice president before going on to serve as Deputy Governor of the Bank of England and Permanent Secretary of the now obsolete UK Department for International Development. Shafik has spoken of her belief that World Bank officials need to change the way they approach the climate crisis, with an overhaul of funding for poorer countries. She argues that big carbon emitters and those countries with huge amounts of locked-up carbon – such as China and India – should be targeted with more support than the criteria allow at the moment. 'It won't only help them,' Shafik told the *Guardian*. 'It will benefit all of us.'

Women's Empowerment

During her tenure at the IMF, Christine Lagarde started a process that Kristalina Georgieva has taken up in earnest. Given that Lagarde's predecessor – Dominique Strauss-Kahn – had to leave the IMF in disgrace following his arrest for sexual assault, the focus of Lagarde and Georgieva on the empowerment of women across the world at the IMF is both welcome and overdue.

Okonjo-Iweala is also passionate about the economic inclusion and empowerment of women which she showed in her tenure at both the World Bank and as Nigeria's Finance Minister. In 2007, while serving in the number two role at the World Bank, she said that 'resources in the hands of African women are a powerful tool' and that 'transfers into the hands of women result in healthier children, more for the household, [and] more for the economy', citing a 2001 study from the World Bank as evidence. She has been a champion for women through the Growing Girls and Women in Nigeria Programme, a pro-women budgeting system that has also worked with young people to support entrepreneurship and business creation.

Minouche Shafik has also argued for a special focus on the role of women in the economy. Shafik believes that the changing role of women alongside technological innovation now represent the two driving forces of change in the world of work today. Society, Shafik argued in a recent *Guardian* interview, hasn't found a way to adjust to women's advancement in education and work, saying 'the cost of [women] not working is really high, so you want them to work. Yet we haven't found a way to adjust – a way to look after the young and old without women providing free labour.' Shafik points to the pandemic as something which has worsened this dynamic, 'heaping more care responsibilities on those already on the frontline'. While most countries have equalised educational opportunities for girls and boys, Shafik, in her 2021 book *What We Owe Each Other: A New Social Contract for a Better Society*, shows how women are still disadvantaged in the workplace because they do, on average, about two hours a day more unpaid household work than men. She argues that more generous parental leave, public funding to support families, and a fairer division of labour at home would make better use of female talent and allow more people to contribute to the common good.

Shafik's book, and her way of capturing both the importance of women's contribution to the economy and the barriers they find in participating, are important. I refer to the everyday economy as being the foundations on which the rest of our economy is built. The most high-tech and innovative parts of financial services or advanced manufacturing would not be able to function without the street cleaning, catering, security, adult and children's care that enable society, and the economy, to function. Yet these foundations are neglected. Women's economic participation, as Shafik highlights, would be an awful lot higher if we had a properly functioning, well trained and motivated workforce in adult and childcare. That's why Labour have been clear that if we form the next government our plans for productivity will rest as much on childcare as on roads and rail links.

Why These Women Matter

While women are still under-represented in much of economics – in Treasury departments, central banks, academia and global banking – some remarkable women have risen to senior roles at the World Bank and IMF, answering the call to global public service.

As a result of being promoted and recruited into top jobs, these women – Krueger, Lagarde, Georgieva, Reinhart, Shafik, Okonjo-Iweala and Gopinath – have shaped global institutions and their priorities. They have put the role of women in the global economy front and centre while reducing poverty and making economic policymaking more transparent, evidence based, and free from corruption.

Like many of the women in this chapter, I believe that trade can be a force for good, as can inward investment. But we mustn't be naive. Trade has not always brought the promised investment, privatising public services has certainly not always improved them, and borrowing from international markets to boost development can pose big risks. The Millennium Development Goals driven forward by the government of Tony Blair and Gordon Brown, with Clare Short as International Development Secretary, made a huge difference in improving life chances and quality of life for some of the poorest people in the world and paved the way for the UN's Sustainable Development Goals – today's framework for green, inclusive development. Over time the priorities and thinking of the IMF and World Bank have changed to put more focus on environmental protections, tackling climate change and empowering women and communities.

If I become chancellor, I want Britain to be actively engaged again in these institutions. As one of the countries with a permanent director on the board of the IMF and World Bank, Britain should help provide the global leadership and vision to reduce global inequalities, focusing on the lives of people in some of the places where poverty has become endemic. We should be leaders in the fight against the impact of climate change, building coalitions of nations to slow down the rise in global temperatures and support investment in green infrastructure and initiatives.

At home, there is also much to learn from finance ministers like Okonjo-Iweala, who fought against corruption and the misuse of public finances. In Britain during the pandemic, billions of pounds of taxpayers' money were spent on contracts that went to friends and donors of the Conservative Party. A VIP fast lane for contracts was established where ministers and MPs could refer people with no transparency as to how they got on the fast track or what checks had been done. As a result, £3.5 billion went to firms with links to the Conservative Party, £9 billion in contracts for unusable PPE have been written off without even attempting to get the money back, and fraudsters got their hands on loans that were supposed to go to businesses struggling to get back on their feet after the pandemic. I have committed to do all I can to get that money back for taxpayers as well as establish a new Office for Value for Money to get a better grip on waste, fraud and accountability in public spending. It is foolish to think that as a rich, developed economy we are immune to such corruption, and I am determined, along with Keir Starmer, to root this out so that trust in politics can be restored and taxpayers can have the confidence that their money is used wisely.

Finally, extreme climate events – from forest fires to floods, coastal erosion to rising sea levels – are happening everywhere, including in the UK. But it is the poorest countries in the world – from Bangladesh to Madagascar to Malawi – that suffer most from catastrophic climate change events and are least able to mitigate the impact of these changes. Given the UK is one of the biggest contributors not only to the UN, IMF and World Bank but also of bilateral aid, I want to see climate action and mitigation play a much bigger role in our development work and, among other things, work to protect carbon sinks, like the Amazon rainforest basin.

Next year is the eightieth anniversary of the creation of the IMF and World Bank: if they didn't exist today we would be trying to establish them. The crucial role they play in fostering sustainable growth, reducing poverty and sharing best practice in economic policymaking cannot be overstated. The next Labour government, like the last one, will help strengthen and support both these institutions. And I hope the next generation of female economists will be working with us from Washington.

Conclusion

Where Are All the Women?

Part II

We've heard the stories of the two women overlooked for the Nobel Prize in Economics in the 1970s – Joan Robinson and Anna Schwartz. It would be over thirty years until Elinor Ostrom became the first woman to be presented with the award. To this day, only two of the ninety-two Nobel Economics medals in the prize's history have been given to women – and never to a woman who didn't share it with a man. The stories in this book prove that even without recognition or reward, women have made modern economics what it is today.

Women are still vastly under-represented in every segment of professional economics. Today, in the Treasury, 38 per cent of economic staff are female and only 32 per cent of senior staff at the Bank of England are women. The picture is no brighter in the US Federal Reserve or the European Central Bank, where the figure is around a third. Overall just 9 per cent of central bank governors globally today are women. The imbalance is not unique to the public sector. In financial services women hold only 19 per cent of the most senior 'C-suite' roles, and only one in every twenty CEO jobs.

Gender inequity in economics isn't a problem that starts in the workforce. Women are certainly much better represented today than they were when Mary Paley Marshall became the first woman to study and then lecture in economics at Cambridge. But in nearly 150 years progress has been slow. As a recent report from Discover Economics, a charity campaigning to increase diversity in economics, shows, one in four boys from private schools study A-level Economics, while only one in twenty-five girls in state schools do. And the young women who go on to study economics at university are greeted by lecture halls in which they represent only one in four of the student body. According to a report published by the Royal Economic Society, in 2021, only 19 per cent of economics professors in the UK were female and they represented only 28 per cent of all academic economics staff.

The challenges for women in economics do not end with under-representation. The *New York Times* found 'evidence that female economists are less likely to have their economic research published by central banks, that they are less likely to be promoted, and that their careers are more likely than men's to suffer when they become parents'. As Christine Lagarde argued in 2018, this is bad not just for gender equality, but for decision making too. She contends that 'a higher share of women on the boards of banks and financial supervision agencies is associated with greater stability'. It's

Kristalina Georgieva, when CEO of the World Bank, in conversation with Christine Lagarde, then Managing Director of the International Monetary Fund, 2018.

exactly what I learned working at HBOS during the financial crisis: diversity at the top levels of decision making is not just good for creating a more equal society – it is good for business as well.

The narrative of historical economics omits women. But it is simply that: a narrative. It is not that women have been entirely absent from our economic story, but from its written record their names have been crossed out – be they Anna Schwartz's from Milton Friedman's Nobel Prize citation or Mary Paley Marshall's from the front cover of *The Principles of Economics*. My book shows that women have been behind ideas that have changed how we think about the economy – from Joan Robinson's monopsony to Esther Duflo's total reimagining of development economics. But still, even with this chain of great women economists, we have not done enough to hold open the doors unlocked by the women in these chapters for future generations.

The women in this book have all, in their own ways, helped make modern economics. And as I hope I will be Britain's first female Chancellor of the Exchequer, they inspire me in my journey to make a modern British economy that reaches its full potential – because we desperately need it. In the last thirteen years growth under the Conservatives in the UK has averaged just 1.4 per cent a year. That compares to an average of 2 per cent with Labour in the thirteen years before that. Under the Conservatives, we have seen inequality and the number of working people in poverty going up and up. Britain needs more growth – but it must be the type of growth that reaches hard-working, ordinary, people.

That is my ambition and, taking inspiration from economic ideas and leaders around the world, this is my plan. Central to Labour's growth mission is a Green Prosperity Plan – a programme of investment in the industries of the future that will tackle climate change and safeguard our planet's future. We know that growth and prosperity can only be built on the rock of economic and fiscal stability – and after thirteen years of Conservative mismanagement, our economy desperately needs stabilising. With fiscal responsibility

at the front of our minds, we will phase in our programme of transformative investment in these industries of the future. From green
hydrogen, and floating offshore wind farms, to battery storage and
tidal energy, we will work alongside business to secure investment
in industries that create well-paid jobs for a population in desperate
need of economic and energy security. We will breathe new economic life into parts of the country that the spoils of prosperity have
not reached in decades.

For centuries economic policy has under-represented and
under-served women. As chancellor, I want to continue the work
of fixing that. Some of the greatest economic work on the gender
pay gap has been done by women economists – starting with Mary
Paley Marshall and continuing until today. More women economists
would have meant we did not allow the gender pay gap to go totally
unchecked for as long as it did. But it has, and it's compounded by
the unsustainable cost of childcare in Britain. The burden of childcare has historically fallen on women, and in the twenty-first century,
we cannot expect working mothers to struggle so much to access
affordable childcare. I can't help but think that if more women had
been around the tables that craft and draft economic policy, successive governments might have been more responsive to the billions a
year our economy misses out on through hours women can't work
due to childcare constraints.

Since the Covid pandemic the number of workers who have
left the UK labour market now stands at about two million. Many
are workers who have taken early retirement, but some are part of
the seven million people on waiting lists for hospital operations.
Strengthening the public services that make up the modern version of Beatrice Webb's welfare state is essential for a secure, strong
economy. This is why I have vowed to close the 200-year-old tax
loophole that allows people who live here permanently, but whose
fathers weren't born here, to domicile themselves elsewhere for tax
purposes. I will use that money to invest in one of the biggest ever
expansions of the NHS workforce, making our most vital public

service function once again. This agenda will centre on combating the insecurity of the time we live in.

While the old 'Washington Consensus', from the time of the first female Chief Economist at the IMF, Anne Krueger, might have been swept away, a new economic consensus is emerging. At its heart is Janet Yellen's modern supply-side economics. A new era of multi-lateral partnership between nations who share values and interests is emerging and I want to bring Britain to its fore. In this age of insecurity, with the increased aggression of China, Putin's illegal invasion of Ukraine and existential threats like climate change and the growing power and potential of Artificial Intelligence, we need bold innovative leadership. The challenge, and my primary goal, is to secure not only our economy but the finances of families across the country. Never again should working people face a cost of living crisis on the scale they have under this government.

As chancellor, I want to boost our resilience with this vision for Britain. I call my approach securonomics. Securonomics is about securing our national economy and the finances of the families whose hard work makes it function. Caring about where things are made and who owns them is not a choice but increasingly an economic necessity, especially for energy and technology. Globalisation must have limits and, above all, work with us, not against the majority of working people and their families.

But to help British businesses succeed we need to help them export and trade, and for that we need a closer relationship with our nearest neighbours and trading partners. Trade boosts productivity. It can reduce prices and drive up the quality of goods and services. That's why, in order to help boost growth, we need to fix the patchwork Brexit deal the Conservatives negotiated. I would seek a new deal for fishing and farming that sees checks reduced to speed up trade; the mutual recognition of professional qualifications so that our service sector which represents more than 80 per cent of the economy can operate across borders; touring rights for our cultural industries to help them be able to perform across European countries; and the participation of the UK in schemes such as Horizon to help our fantastic universities and talented young people take up the opportunities for funding, collaboration and partnership across borders. We'll secure the interests of British businesses and families. We won't rejoin the Single Market or Customs Union or bring back freedom of movement, but ours are practical policies that I am confident we can deliver to boost and secure our economy.

My vision of securonomics draws much of its design from the modern supply-side approach of US Treasury Secretary Janet Yellen. The policies of Biden and Yellen are helping the US win the race for new, well-paid jobs. While they have turned the industrial heartlands of the Rust Belt into the 'electric vehicle belt', Britain under the Conservatives has allowed the Midlands and North of England, the home of the first industrial revolution, to flounder. Securonomics will invest alongside business in the industries of the future in the industrial heartlands of the past.

I don't want to just be the next Labour or the first woman chancellor, I want to be a transformative chancellor improving people's everyday lives. Under this government working families have suffered – be that through the worst cost of living crisis in a generation, the Tory mortgage bombshell Liz Truss left behind after her drive-by premiership, or the managed decline today under Sunak and Hunt. That is not the track record of an economy that's been working for working people. In the introduction to this book I told you about a family I met in Worthing. I think about them often. Two parents who work five jobs and still can't make ends meet. They've sacrificed family time and a decent work–life balance in the name of security. Full of entrepreneurial zeal and a desire to do right by their family, our economy still is not doing right by them. That cannot be allowed to continue. The test I will set myself as chancellor is whether their lives, and those of other families like them, have improved by the end of Labour's first term in government.

Many of the women economists in this book had and have a mission. It is their ideas and insights that help guide me as I work to steady our economy and tackle the challenges and opportunities of our time. From Elinor Ostrom and protecting our natural environment, to Mary Paley Marshall and her ideas around industrial economics, Beatrice Webb's ideas about how to make life better for working people in an age of huge inequality, or Esther Duflo and the fight to eradicate global poverty. Each has inspired me in different ways in my mission as chancellor to build a more secure British economy. Each of these women is, in their own way, a role model in the field of economics for young women. It is my hope that I too as chancellor will be a role model for these young women. Not only by being the first woman to stand outside Number 11 Downing Street, budget box in hand, but also on the basis of my actions as chancellor, to make the modern British economy work for working people again.

Acknowledgements

When I became shadow chancellor in May 2021, I started to think about the women in economics who I admired and took inspiration from. In the same way that my 2019 book, *Women of Westminster*, told the stories of brilliant women who changed politics, this book tells the stories and writes back into history some of the women who have shaped economics.

Speaking of amazing women, I would like to thank my editor Sarah Caro, whose knowledge of economics and what makes a good book helped me get to this point. And also Caroline Michel, my agent, a woman who has achieved so much in the world of books – and is the best-connected person I know!

Thanks for research assistance to Cormac Savage and Rebecca Lewis and to my team, especially Katie Martin and Gabriel Forcella-Burton, who have let me carve out a bit of time to write and think amidst everything else, and Spencer Thompson, Neil Foster and Neil Amin-Smith for spending weekends reading various drafts. Thank you to Lord John Eatwell, Murray Milgate and Michael Ward who commented on earlier versions of chapters and to Professor Diane Coyle who read and commented on the whole manuscript. Thanks must go to Professor Sarah Smith for providing statistics from her fantastic work on diversifying economics.

Thank you also to my old economics tutor at Oxford, Chris Allsopp, who thought I would make a decent economist and encouraged me to pursue that career.

ACKNOWLEDGEMENTS

The book has been written on trains and during recess. Thank you to my husband and children for tolerating me typing away in North Wales last summer, while they were off enjoying ice creams on the beach. Thanks too to my old boss and former Treasury civil servant Dame Sue Owen for helping to make that happen.

And, most of all, thank you to the women who have inspired me to write this book. Between you, you've shaped modern economics. I hope I get the chance to do that too as the first female Chancellor of the Exchequer.

250

Picture Credits

Alamy Stock Photo: Millicent Fawcett, Kristalina Georgieva, Kristalina Georgieva with Christine Lagarde, Gita Gopinath, Sri Mulyani Indrawati with Janet Yellen, Christine Lagarde, Harriet Martineau, Beatrice and Sidney Webb, Janet Yellen.

Sadie Tanner Mossell Alexander: Photo Afro American Newspapers/Gado/ Getty Images.

Esther Duflo with Abhijit Banerjee: Photo Jim Davis/The Boston Globe via Getty Images.

Milton and Rose Friedman: Photo Roger Ressmeyer/Corbis/VCG via Getty Images.

Sakiko Fukuda-Parr: Photo courtesy of The New School, New York.

Rosa Luxemburg: Photo Ullstein bild via Getty Images.

Mary Paley Marshall: Reproduced with the kind permission of the Marshall Librarian, Marshall Library Archive, Marshall Papers Box 10 (call number 10/4/28).

Eleanor Marx: Public domain.

Dambisa Moyo: Photo Takaaki Iwabu/Bloomberg via Getty Images.

Ngozi Okonjo-Iweala: Photo Fabrice Coffrini/AFP via Getty Images.

Elinor Ostrom: Photo courtesy of the Ostrom Workshop collection, Indiana University.

Eleanor Ostrom at Nobel Prize Awards Ceremony: Photo Pascal Le Segretain/Getty Images.

Joan Robinson: Photo Denver Post via Getty Images.

Anna Schwartz: Photo Teresa Zabala/The New York Times/Redux/eyevine.

Select Bibliography

Introduction: Where Are All the Women?
Part I

Carlin, Wendy, and David Soskice, *Macroeconomics and the Wage Bargain: A Modern Approach to Employment, Inflation and the Exchange Rate* (Oxford: Oxford University Press, 1990)

Criado-Perez, Caroline, *Invisible Women: Exposing Data Bias in a World Designed for Men* (London: Chatto & Windus, 2019)

Lagarde, Christine, 'Ten Years After Lehman – Lessons Learned and Challenges Ahead', IMF Blog, 5 September 2018, imf.org

Chapter 1: Harriet Martineau and
Popularising Economic Theory

Cicarelli, James, and Julianne Cicarelli, *Distinguished Women Economists* (Westport, CT: Greenwood Press, 2003)

DeLamotte, Eugenia C., Natalie Meeker and Jean F. O'Barr, *Women Imagine Change: a Global Anthology of Women's Resistance from 600 B.C.E. to Present* (New York: Routledge, 1997)

[Empson, William], '*Illustrations of Political Economy*: Miss Marcet–Miss Martineau', *Edinburgh Review*, vol. 57, no. 115 (April 1833), pp. 1–39

Hill, Michael R., and Susan Hoecker-Drysdale (eds), *Harriet Martineau: Theoretical and Methodological Perspectives* (New York: Routledge, 2001)

Hobart, Ann, 'Harriet Martineau's Political Economy of Everyday Life', *Victorian Studies*, vol. 37, no. 2 (Winter 1994), pp. 223–51

Hoecker-Drysdale, Susan, *Harriet Martineau: First Woman Sociologist* (New York: Berg, 1992)

Logan, Deborah Anna, *The Hour and the Woman: Harriet Martineau's 'Somewhat Remarkable' Life* (DeKalb, IL: Northern Illinois University Press, 2002)

Martineau, Harriet, *Demerara: A Tale* (London: Charles Fox, 1832)

——, *Life in the Wilds: A Tale* (Boston, MA: L. C. Bowles, 1832)

——, *A Manchester Strike: A Tale* (Boston, MA: L. C. Bowles, 1833)

——, *Berkeley the Banker: A Tale* (Boston, MA: L. C Bowles, 1833)

——, *Society in America* (New York: Saunders and Otley, 1837)

——, *History of the Peace: Pictorial History of England during the Thirty Years' Peace 1816–1846*, rev. ed. (London: W. and R. Chambers, 1858)

——, *Biographical Sketches* (New York: Leypoldt & Holt, 1869)

——, *Harriet Martineau's Autobiography* (London: Smith, Elder, 1877)

O'Donnell, Margaret G., 'Harriet Martineau: A Popular Early Economics Educator', *Journal of Economic Education*, vol. 14, no. 4 (Autumn 1983), pp. 59–64

Pichanik, Valerie Kossew, *Harriet Martineau: The Woman and Her Work, 1802–76* (Ann Arbor, MI: University of Michigan Press, 1980)

Chapter 3: Beatrice Webb, Social Research and the Emergence of Welfare Economics

Booth, Charles, *Life and Labour of the People in London: Volume 1: East, Central and South London* (London: Macmillan and Co., 1892)

Burnette, Joyce, 'An Investigation of the Female–Male Wage Gap During the Industrial Revolution, *Economic History Review*, vol. 50, no. 2 (May 1997), pp. 257–81

Caine, Barbara, 'Family History as Women's History: The Sisters of Beatrice Webb', *Feminist Studies*, vol. 12, no. 2 (Summer 1986), pp. 294–319

Churchill, Randolph S., *Winston S. Churchill* (Boston, MA: Houghton Mifflin, 1966)

Cicarelli, James., and Julianne Cicarelli, *Distinguished Women Economists* (Westport, CT: Greenwood Press, 2003)

Hamilton, Mary Agnes, *Sidney and Beatrice Webb: A Study in Contemporary Biography* (London: Sampson Low, Marston & Co. Ltd, 1933)

Harris, José, *William Beveridge: A Biography* (Oxford: Clarendon Press, 1977)

Harrison, Royden, 'Bertrand Russell and the Webbs: An Interview', *Russell: The Journal of Bertrand Russell Studies*, vol. 5, no. 1 (Summer 1985), pp. 44–9

Muggeridge, Kitty, and Ruth Adam, *Beatrice Webb: A Life, 1858–1943* (London: Secker & Warburg, 1967)

Nyland, Chris, 'Beatrice Webb as Feminist', *Labour and Industry*, vol. 6, no. 2 (1995), pp. 67–85

Pember Reeves, Maud, *Round About a Pound a Week* (London: G. Bell and Sons, 1913)

Ross, Ellen (ed.), *Slum Travellers: Ladies and London Poverty, 1860–1920* (Berkeley, CA: University of California Press, 2007)

Taylor, A. J. P., *English History 1914–1945* (Oxford: Oxford University Press, 1965)

Thompson, E. P., *The Making of the English Working Class* (London: Victor Gollancz, 1963)

Trade Union Congress, 'Child Poverty in Working Households Up By 1 Million Children Since 2010, Says TUC' (7 May 2018), tuc.org.uk

Tribe, Keith (ed.), *Economic Careers: Economics and Economists in Britain 1930–1970* (Abingdon: Routledge, 1997)

Ward, Michael, *Beatrice Webb: Her Quest for a Fairer Society: A Hundred Years of the Minority Report* (London: Smith Institute, 2011)

Webb, Beatrice, *My Apprenticeship* (London: Longmans, Green and Co., 1926)

——, *Our Partnership*, ed. Barbara Drake and Margaret I. Cole (London: Longmans, Green and Co., 1948)

——, *The Diary of Beatrice Webb: Volume One 1873–1892*, ed. Norman and Jean MacKenzie (London: Virago, 1982)

Webb, Sidney, 'The New Statesman', *Manchester Guardian*, 9 April 1913

——, and Beatrice Webb, *Industrial Democracy* (London: Longmans, Green and Co., 1902)

Chapter 3: Mary Paley Marshall, Industrial Economics and the Benefits of Clusters

Bowley, Arthur L., *Wages in the United Kingdom in the Nineteenth Century* (Cambridge: Cambridge University Press, 1900)

Chassonnery-Zaïgouche, Cléo, 'Is Equal Pay Worth It? Beatrice Potter Webb's, Millicent Garrett Fawcett's and Eleanor Rathbone's Changing Arguments', in Kirsten Madden and Robert W. Dimand (eds), *The Routledge Handbook of the History of Women's Economic Thought* (Abingdon: Routledge, 2019), pp. 129–49

Corry, Dan, Anna Valero and John Van Reenen, 'UK Economic Performance Since 1997: Growth, Productivity and Jobs', Special Paper No. 24 (London: London School of Economics and Political Science, December 2011)

Fawcett, Millicent Garrett, *Tales in Political Economy* (London: Macmillan and Co., 1874)

Groenewegen, Peter D., 'A Weird and Wonderful Partnership: Mary Paley and Alfred Marshall 1877–1924', *History of Economic Ideas*, vol. 1, no. 1 (1993), pp. 71–109

——, 'Keynes and Marshall: Methodology, Society, and Politics', *History of Political Economy* vol. 27 (Annual Supplement, 1995), ed. Allin Cottrell and Michael S. Lawlor, pp. 129–55

Keynes, John Maynard, *Essays in Biography* (London: Palgrave Macmillan, 2010)

——, and F. A. Hayek, 'Obituary: Mary Paley Marshall (1850–1944)', *The Economic Journal*, vol. 54, no. 214 (1944), pp. 268–86

Marshall, Alfred, *Principles of Economics* (London: Macmillan and Co, 1890)

——, and Mary Paley Marshall, *The Economics of Industry* (London: Macmillan and Co., 1879)

Office for National Statistics, 'International Comparisons of UK Productivity (ICP), Final Estimates: 2020' (January 2022), ons.gov.uk

Paley Marshall, Mary, *What I Remember* (Cambridge: Cambridge University Press, 1947)

Pande, Rohini, and Helena Roy, '"If You Compete with Us, We Shan't Marry You": The (Mary Paley and) Alfred Marshall Lecture', *Journal of the European Economic Association*, vol. 19, no. 6 (December 2021), pp. 2992–3024

Tribe, Keith (ed.), *Economic Careers: Economics and Economists in Britain 1930–1970* (London: Routledge, 1997)

Chapter 4: Rosa Luxemburg and Revolutionary Economics

Cicarelli, James, and Julianne Cicarelli, *Distinguished Women Economists* (Westport, CT: Greenwood Press, 2003)

Clark, Katerina, 'Rosa Luxemburg, "The Russian Revolution"', *Studies in East European Thought*, vol. 70, no. 2 (September 2018), pp. 153–65

Coburn, Elaine, 'Rosa Luxemburg's Political Economy: Contributions to Contemporary Political Theory and Practice', *Socialist Studies*, vol. 6, no. 2 (Fall 2010), pp. 38–42

Georg, Adler, Peter Hudis and Annelies Laschitza (eds), *The Letters of Rosa Luxemburg* (New York: Verso, 2011)

Holmes, Rachel, *Eleanor Marx: A Life* (London: Bloomsbury, 2014)

Lenin, V. I., *Lenin's Collected Works: Volume 33: August 1921–March 1923* (Moscow: Progress Publishers, 1965)

Luxemburg, Rosa, *The Junius Pamphlet: The Crisis in the German Social Democracy, February–April 1915* (London: Merlin Press, 1967)

——, *The Russian Revolution, and Leninism or Marxism?* (Ann Arbor, MI: University of Michigan Press, 1970)

——, *The Accumulation of Capital* (London: Routledge, 2003)

——, 'Order Prevails in Berlin', in *Socialism or Barbarism: Selected Writings*, ed. Helen C. Scott and Paul Le Blanc (London: Pluto Press, 2015)

——, *The Complete Works of Rosa Luxemburg, Volume III: Political Writings 1: On Revolution, 1897–1905*, ed. Peter Hudis and Paul Le Blanc (London: Verso, 2019)

Marx, Eleanor, 'How Should We Organise?', *Arbeiterinnenzeitung* [*Working-Women's Journal*], 5 February 1892

Milgate, Murray, 'The Complete Works of Rosa Luxemburg', *Contributions to Political Economy*, vol. 38, no. 1 (2019), pp. 105–8

——, 'Rosa Luxemburg', *Contributions to Political Economy*, vol. 40, no. 1 (2021), pp. 95–102

Mills, Dana, *Rosa Luxemburg* (London: Reaktion Books, 2020)

Shepardson, Donald E., *Rosa Luxemburg and the Noble Dream* (New York: Peter Lang, 1996)

Zetkin, Clara, *Selected Writings*, ed. Philip S. Foner (Chicago, IL: Haymarket Books, 2015)

Chapter 5: Joan Robinson and the Global Reach of Keynesian Economics

Arenson, Karen W., 'Prof. Joan Robinson Dies at 79; Cambridge University Economist', *New York Times*, 11 August 1983

Carter, Zachary D., 'The Woman Who Shattered the Myth of the Free Market', *New York Times*, 24 April 2021

Centre for Public Impact, 'Introducing a National Minimum Wage', 12 April 2016

Cicarelli, James, and Julianne Cicarelli, *Distinguished Women Economists* (Westport, CT: Greenwood Press, 2003)

Harcourt, Geoffrey, and Prue Kerr, *Joan Robinson* (Basingstoke: Palgrave Macmillan, 2009)

Keynes, John Maynard, *The General Theory of Employment, Interest and Money* (London: Macmillan and Co., 1936)

Living Wage Foundation, '4.8 Million Jobs in the UK Pay Below the Real Living Wage', 14 November 2021

Low Pay Commission, 'Low Pay Commission Welcomes Historic Introduction of National Minimum Wage', April 1999

Robinson, Joan, *The Economics of Imperfect Competition* (London: Macmillan and Co., 1933)

——, 'Disguised Unemployment', *The Economic Journal*, vol. 46, no. 182 (June 1936), pp. 225–37

——, *The Accumulation of Capital* (Homewood, IL: Richard D. Irwin, 1956)

——, *The Cultural Revolution in China* (Harmondsworth: Pelican, 1969)

Skidelsky, Robert, 'George Osborne's Cunning Plan: How the Chancellor's Austerity Narrative Has Harmed Recovery', *New Statesman*, 29 April 2015

——, 'Austerity: The Wrong Story', *The Economic and Labour Relations Review*, vol. 26, no. 3 (September 2015), pp. 377–83

Sraffa, Piero, 'The Laws of Returns Under Competitive Conditions', *The Economic Journal*, vol. 36, no. 144 (December 1926), pp. 535–50

Wittgenstein, Ludwig, *Philosophical Investigations: The English Text of the Third Edition*, trans. G. E. M. Anscombe (New York: Macmillan, 1968)

Chapter 6: Anna Schwartz and the Mixed Blessings of Monetary Economics

Cicarelli, James, and Julianne Cicarelli, *Distinguished Women Economists* (Westport, CT: Greenwood Press, 2003)

Fettig, David, 'Interview with Anna J. Schwartz', Federal Reserve Bank of Minneapolis, 1 September 1993, minneapolisfed.org

Friedman, Milton, and Anna J. Schwartz, *A Monetary History of the United States, 1867–1960* (Princeton, NJ: Princeton University Press, 1963)

Goldin, Claudia, 'Interview with Anna Jacobson Schwartz', NBER, 19 November 2001, nber.org

Nelson, Edward, 'An Interview With Anna J. Schwartz', *Macroeconomic Dynamics*, vol. 8, no. 3 (June 2004), pp. 395–417

Rockoff, Hugh, *Review: 'A Monetary History of the United States, 1867–1960'*, Economic History Association, EH.net (accessed 4 July 2023)

Sorman, Guy, 'Remembering Rose Friedman', *Forbes*, 19 August 2009, forbes.com

Schwartz, Anna Jacobson, 'Man Without a Plan', *New York Times*, 25 July 2009

Weber, Bruce, 'Rose Friedman, Economist and Collaborator, Dies at 98', *New York Times*, 18 August 2009

Chapter 7: Elinor Ostrom and the Political Economy of the Environment

Burke, Maureen 'The Master Artisan', *Finance & Development*, vol. 48, no. 3 (September 2011), imf.org

Fennell, Lee Anne, 'Ostrom's Law: Property Rights in the Commons', *International Journal of the Commons*, vol. 5, no. 1 (2011), pp. 9–27

Hardin, Garrett, 'The Tragedy of the Commons', *Science*, vol. 162, no. 3859 (13 December 1968), pp. 1243–8

Helm, Dieter, *Natural Capital: Valuing the Planet* (New Haven, CT: Yale University Press, 2015)

Korten, Fran, 'Elinor Ostrom Wins Nobel for Common(s) Sense', 27 February 2010, yesmagazine.org

Ostrom, Elinor, *Governing the Commons: The Evolution of Institutions for Collective Action* (New York: Cambridge University Press, 1990)

——, 'A Polycentric Approach for Coping with Climate Change', *Annals of Economics and Finance*, vol. 15, no. 1 (2014), pp. 97–134

Rampell, Catherine, 'Elinor Ostrom, Winner of Nobel in Economics, Dies at 78', *New York Times*, 12 June 2012

Raworth, Kate, *Doughnut Economics: Seven Ways to Think Like a 21st Century Economist* (White River Junction, VT: Chelsea Green Publishing, 2017)

Tarko, Vlad, *Elinor Ostrom: An Intellectual Biography* (New York: Rowman & Littlefield International, 2016)

Chapter 8: Esther Duflo and the Challenge of Development Economics

Banerjee, Abhijit V., and Esther Duflo, *Poor Economics: A Radical Rethinking of the Way to Fight Global Poverty* (New York: Public Affairs, 2011)

Cowen, Tyler, 'Esther Duflo on Management, Growth, and Research in Action', *Conversations with Tyler*, episode 84 (December 2019), conversationswithtyler.com

Edemariam, Aida, 'Interview: "Everyone Knows it Doesn't Work"', *Guardian*, 19 February 2009

Fukuda-Parr, Sakiko, 'Recapturing the Narrative of International Development', in *The Millennium Development Goals and Beyond: Global Development after 2015*, ed. Rorden Wilkinson and David Hulme (London: Routledge, 2012)

——, Terra Lawson-Remer, and Susan Randolph, *Fulfilling Social and Economic Rights* (New York: Oxford University Press, 2015)

——, 'COVID-19 and Global Inequality', *Development Policy and Multilateralism after COVID-19* (United Nations, July 2020), pp. 15–19

Gapper, John, 'Lunch with the FT: Esther Duflo', *Financial Times*, 17 March 2012

Holder Josh, 'Tracking Coronavirus Vaccinations Around the World', *New York Times*, 13 March 2023

Moyo, Dambisa, *Dead Aid: Why Aid Is Not Working and How There is a Better Way for Africa* (New York: Farrar, Straus and Giroux, 2009)

Pereira, Eva, 'Dambisa Moyo: An Economist with a Vision', *Forbes*, 19 April 2011, forbes.com

Strauss, Delphine, 'Nobel-winner Esther Duflo on What Mainstream Economics Got Wrong', *Financial Times*, 5 December 2019

Chapter 9: Janet Yellen and the Role of Central Banks and Treasury Departments

Chandra, Vikram, 'When Women Do Better Economies Do Better: IMF Chief Christine Lagarde', *NDTV*, 1 February 2013, ndtv.com

Curran, Enda, Yudith Ho and Karlis Salna, 'Indonesia's Fearless Finance Minister Is Ready for Her Next Fight', *Bloomberg*, 28 March 2017, bloomberg.com

Dowd, Maureen, 'Christine Lagarde on Why Women Will Save the Global Economy', *Town & Country*, 8 May 2019

Federal Reserve Bank of Minneapolis, 'Interview with Janet Yellen', 1 June 1995, minneapolisfed.org

Fleming, Sam, 'Janet Yellen on Trump, Fed Politics and Nurturing Recovery', *Financial Times*, 26 October 2018

International Monetary Fund, 'The Age of Womenomics: A Conversation on Women in Economics and Finance', 8 March 2021, imf.org

Johnson, Diane, 'Christine Lagarde: Changing of the Guard', *Vogue*, 22 August 2011

Lagarde, Christine, 'A New Global Economy for a New Generation', speech to World Economic Forum, 23 January 2013, imf.org

——, 'Fix the Roof While the Window of Opportunity is Open: Three Priorities for the Global Economy', speech at University of Hong Kong, 11 April 2018, imf.org

——, 'Age of Ingenuity: Reimagining 21st Century International Cooperation', Eighth Henry A. Kissinger Lecture, Library of Congress, 4 December 2018, imf.org

Miel, Morgane, 'Christine Lagarde: "Ma foi en l'homme est inébranlable"', *Madame Figaro*, 25 August 2022

Politi, James, and Sam Fleming, 'Lagarde Warns of US-China Trade War "Shock" to Emerging Markets', *Financial Times*, 11 September 2018

Stern, Nicholas, *The Economics of Climate Change: The Stern Review* (Cambridge: Cambridge University Press, 2007)

Stewart, Heather, 'Sri Mulyani Indrawati: "You Must Make Growth Inclusive – You Have To Protect The Poor"', *Guardian*, 12 February 2012

Walker, Garrett, 'Fighting Fires in the Engine Room: A Conversation with Christine Lagarde', *Harvard International Review*, 7 October 2020, hir.harvard.edu

Yellen, Janet, 'Remarks by Secretary of the Treasury Janet L. Yellen at the 2022 "Virtual Davos Agenda" Hosted by the World Economic Forum', home.treasury.gov, 21 January 2022

Chapter 10: The Women Managing the Global Economy

Georgieva, Kristalina, 'Managing Director Georgieva's Closing Remarks EU Environment Ministers Videoconference', International Monetary Fund, 13 July 2020, imf.org

——, 'No Time to Waste', Finance & Development, September 2021, imf.org

——, 'Managing Director Kristalina Georgieva's Opening Remarks at IMF Policy Dialogue: Climate-Related Financial Risks and Green Finance in Asia and the Pacific', International Monetary Fund, 1 June 2022, imf.org

Gopinath, Gita, 'How Will the Pandemic and War Shape Future Monetary Policy?', Presentation at the Jackson Hole Symposium, 26 August 2022, imf.org

Inman, Phillip, 'Minouche Shafik: "The idea that You Are Successful Because You Are Hardworking Is Pernicious"', *Guardian*, 22 January 2022

International Monetary Fund, 'IMF Chief Economist Gita Gopinath to Return to Harvard University' (Press Release No. 21/302), 19 October 2021, imf.org

Krueger, Anne O., 'The Political Economy of the Rent-Seeking Society', *The American Economic Review*, vol. 64, no. 3 (June 1974), pp. 291–303

——, 'Trade, Jobs and Growth: Why You Can't Have One Without the Others', Address to Reuters Trade, Globalisation and Outsourcing Conference, 15 June 2004, imf.org

——, *Struggling With Success: Challenges Facing the International Economy* (Singapore: World Scientific Publishing Company, 2012)

Krugman, Paul, 'The Excel Depression', *New York Times*, 18 April 2013

Mayeda, Andrew, 'Nothing's Taboo for Gita Gopinath, IMF's New Chief Economist & First Woman in Job', *The Print*, 22 January 2019, theprint.in

Moore, Elaine, 'Anne Krueger: The Economist in a Hurry', *Financial Times*, 7 August 2015

Nandakumar, Prathima, 'Gita Gopinath: From A Middle-Class Indian Girl To IMF's Chief Economist', *The Week*, 15 October 2018

Okonjo-Iweala, Ngozi, 'Ngozi Okonjo-Iweala on Aid Versus Trade', TEDTalk, June 2007

Reinhart, Carmen M., and Kenneth S. Rogoff, *This Time is Different: Eight Centuries of Fiscal Folly* (Princeton, NJ: Princeton University Press, 2009)

——, 'Growth in a Time of Debt', *American Economic Review*, vol. 100, no. 2 (May 2010), pp. 573–8

——, 'From Financial Crash to Debt Crisis', *American Economic Review*, vol. 101, no. 5 (August 2011), pp. 1676–706

Rowe, James L., 'Solving History's Puzzles', *Finance and Development*, vol. 50, no. 2 (June 2013), imf.org

Shafik, Minouche, *What We Owe Each Other: A New Social Contract for a Better Society* (Princeton, NJ: Princeton University Press, 2021)

Stiglitz, Joseph E, *Globalisation and its Discontents* (New York: W. W. Norton, 2002)

Conclusion: Where Are All the Women?
Part II

Bateman, Victoria, Danula Kankanam Gamage, Xianyue Liu and Erin Hengel, 'The Gender Imbalance in UK Economics: Royal Economic Society Women's Committee Silver Anniversary Report', 13 July 2021, res.org.uk

Deloitte, 'Advancing More Women Leaders in Financial Services: A Global Report', June 2022, www2.deloitte.com

European Central Bank, 'ECB Gender Targets: Interim Assessment' (Press Release, 31 March 2023), ecb.europa. eu

Ewing, Jack, 'Women Are Missing at Central Banks', *New York Times*, 22 October 2019

Keys, Roberta, 'Economics: Where Are All the Girls?', Assessment and Qualifications Insight, 17 February 2022, aqi.org.uk

Lagarde, Christine, 'Ten Years After Lehman – Lessons Learned and Challenges Ahead', IMF Blog, 5 September 2018, imf.org

Official Monetary and Financial Institutions Forum, 'Gender Balance Index 2019', omfif.org, 2019

Wolfers, Justin, 'Why Women's Voices Are Scarce in Economics', *New York Times*, 2 February 2018

World Bank, 'GDP growth (annual %): United Kingdom', data. worldbank.org, June 2023

Index